Writers of Italy

Italo Calvino

Writers of Italy

edited by
LINO PERTILE
and
PETER BRAND

Other titles in the series:

Zygmunt G. Barański and Lino Pertile (eds)
The New Italian Novel
ISBN 0 7486 0918 0

Joseph Farrell
Leonardo Sciascia
ISBN 0 7486 0620 3

Vivienne Hand
Zanzotto
ISBN 0 7486 0411 1

Italo Calvino

MARTIN McLAUGHLIN

EDINBURGH UNIVERSITY PRESS

Edinburgh University Press
22 George Square, Edinburgh

Typeset in Bembo by
Bibliocraft, Dundee,
and printed and bound in Great Britain
by The University Press, Cambridge

A CIP record for this book is available
from the British Library

ISBN 0 7486 0735 8 (hardback)
ISBN 0 7486 0917 2 (paperback)

Contents

Acknowledgements

Many people have helped me in writing this study. Calvino's widow, Esther Singer, was enormously generous with her time, her hospitality and her intelligent and witty answers to questions she must have heard many times before, as well as allowing me crucial access to the thesis on Conrad. My main intellectual debt is, like that of any Calvino scholar working in the 1990s, to those 'three musketeers of Calvinology', Mario Barenghi, Bruno Falcetto and Claudio Milanini, who not only edited the collected fiction and non-fiction, but who have also been generous with their company and scholarship. Luca Baranelli has also given me the benefit of his precious knowledge of Calviniana, and Lino Pertile offered invaluable editorial advice. Needless to say, I alone am responsible for any errors or misinterpretations.

I am grateful to the editors of *Italian Studies* for allowing me to republish, in a slightly modified form, an article which appeared in the journal in 1993, and which now constitutes Chapter 4 of this book, a chapter which owes much also to Maria Corti and the helpfulness of the staff at the Fondo Manoscritti di Autori Moderni e Contemporanei at the University of Pavia.

I would also like to thank my colleagues and students in Italian at Oxford who have offered helpful comments on these ideas at seminars and lectures. I am particularly grateful to Robert Gordon for his expert help with the Pasolini background to Chapter 9. I am indebted to the Faculty of Medieval and Modern Languages of the University of Oxford, and particularly to my college, Christ Church, for their generosity with sabbatical leave and research grants. Last, but certainly not least, I thank Cathy and Mairi for their patience during the writing of this book.

MARTIN McLAUGHLIN
Christ Church, Oxford

Abbreviations

All page references in this book to Calvino's fictional works are to the collected *Romanzi e racconti*, 3 vols, ed. Claudio Milanini, Bruno Falcetto and Mario Barenghi (Milan: Mondadori, 1991–4), given in parenthesis in the text with volume and page number.

References to the non-fictional works are, where possible, to the collected *Saggi*, 2 vols, ed. Mario Barenghi (Milan: Mondadori, 1995), with the abbreviation *S* followed by the page number.

References to Calvino's letters are to those contained in *I libri degli altri. Lettere 1947–1981*, ed. Giovanni Tesio (Turin: Einaudi, 1991), with the abbreviation ILDA, followed by the page number.

Other abbreviations used in the text include *DL* (*Difficult Loves*) and *LM* (*The Literature Machine*) – full bibliographic details of these English-language translations will be found in the Bibliography.

Introduction

> The written page is not a uniform surface like a piece of plastic; it is more like the cross-section of a piece of wood, in which you can see how the lines of the fibres run, where they form a knot, where a branch goes off. I believe that the duty of criticism is also – or perhaps is primarily – to observe these differences in the written text: to observe parts that are 'more written' and those that are 'less written'. (Calvino, 'Lettera a Mario Boselli', 106)

It may be difficult to justify yet another book on Italo Calvino, when there are already at least eleven monographs in English and over three times that number in Italian (see Bibliography), and publications on the author have increased exponentially in the last decade (see McLaughlin (1996b) for a survey of the years 1985–95). However, in the decade since the author's death in 1985 Mondadori has published the collected fiction (*Romanzi e racconti*, 3 vols, 1991–4) and most of the non-fiction (*Saggi*, 2 vols, 1995), as well as a collection of pivotal autobiographical writings and interviews (*Eremita a Parigi*, 1994). A selection of 308 of the 5,000 or so letters written when Calvino worked for the publisher Einaudi has also been crucial in providing evidence of the writer's evolving poetics and his relations with other writers, minor and major (*I libri degli altri* (*Other People's Books*)). Furthermore, the collected fiction includes all the unpublished narratives or unfinished book projects, thus placing critics writing after 1995 in a uniquely privileged position to gain for the first time a full overview of the output of Italy's greatest postwar prose-writer. This advantage alone is one justification for this study.

However, it is not just the superabundance, but also the nature of the Calvino material published since 1985 which prompts a particular, complementary critical approach. What the volumes of collected fiction and non-fiction reveal above all is the diachronic evolution of the texts, the manuscript and published variants in different printed editions, as well as the author's painstaking concern for the structure of every work: the crystalline style for which Calvino was famous was often the result of patient elimination of elements that detracted from the 'lightness', 'rapidity' or 'exactitude' of his writing. The literary tools that this material therefore demands are the established but still useful ones of chronology, philology and structure. These three areas represent a network of critical concerns that the author himself privileged, both with regard to his own texts and in his assessments of others. As for chronology, Calvino scrupulously noted the dates of composition of all his works, and up until 1963 appended these dates to each fiction; and even though he no longer made the dates of composition explicit in later works, for reasons which will be discussed in the appropriate chapters, he kept precise notes for himself and communicated these to critics when he thought it was significant. For this reason the Appendix provides a full list, in strict chronological order of composition, of Calvino's fictional output, a list which underlines his penchant for working on diametrically opposed literary projects at the same time, but which also contains important contextual information about the minor works which are contiguous with the better known texts.

Calvino was also interested in textual variants and in the rewriting of his own or other texts: apart from his fascination with the variants of the Italian folktales he collected, a substantial part of his major essay on one of his favourite authors, Robert Louis Stevenson, is devoted to the merits of the two redactions of *The Pavilion on the Links*, one in a journal and one in book form (*S*, 974–6), a duplicate textual format often encountered in Calvino's own works. Similarly, in *Six Memos for the Next Millennium*, the finale of his lecture on 'Visibility' is devoted to a comparative study of the different versions of Balzac's *Le Chef-d'oeuvre inconnu* (*S*, 711–14; *Six Memos*, 95–9); while on a microtextual level the conclusion to the lecture on 'Exactitude' offers a minute analysis of Leonardo's rewriting of the same sentence three times to convey the bulk of a sea-monster threshing amid the waves (*S*, 694–6; *Six Memos*, 77–80).

Calvino's obsession with structure is evident in many areas, not least in his meticulous organising of the major selection of over fifty tales in the *Racconti* of 1958 (*ILDA*, 262–4), and in his constant restructuring of the order of already written stories to produce divergent contextual effects, in other collections such as *Ultimo viene il corvo* (*The Crow Comes Last*) (between 1949 and 1969), *Gli amori difficili* (*Difficult Loves*) (between 1958 and 1970) and the cosmicomic tales (between 1968 and 1984). For Calvino structure was an integral part of the meaning of a literary text: as he said in the important interview with Maria Corti, 'I do not consider any literary operation concluded until I have given it a sense and a structure that I can consider definitive' (*S*, 2921). Consequently the quotation at the head of this introduction, which is one of the lesser known pronouncements of this eminently quotable author, I regard as his most significant statement about the critic's task, and it is both the inspiration and the justification for the critical approach adopted in this book.

In what follows, then, we shall be looking into the workshop of this great artisan, to use Milanini's metaphor (III, xxiii), or to stay with Calvino's imagery, we shall be examining the trunks of the trees in the thick vegetation of his works.

The critic's first job, in Calvino's own words, is to discern the different layers of writing beneath the uniform surface of the text, and to point out where the page has been more or less worked: this is the primary focus of this study. Naturally, it is not possible to observe in every text the different layers of writing without having access to every single manuscript draft and printed edition. But in a surprisingly high number of cases, we do have evidence of the rewriting of printed editions, particularly in the early short stories, the first novel, *La speculazione edilizia* (*A Plunge into Real Estate*), the cosmicomic tales, *Il castello dei destini incrociati* (*The Castle of Crossed Destinies*) and *Palomar*. The whole question of 'parti piú scritte (more heavily written parts)' and 'parti meno scritte (less heavily worked parts)' is dealt with in the final chapter on style, which also deals with questions of rewriting in other works such as the trilogy and *Gli amori difficili* (*Difficult Loves*).

This volume adopts a strictly chronological approach, covering the earliest short stories (Chapter 1), the first novel (Chapter 2), the fantasy trilogy (Chapter 3), the most problematic realist text (Chapter 4) and then a chapter (Chapter 5) devoted to a survey of Calvino's thematic interests in the first twenty years of writing from 1943 to 1963 and acting as a link to the second half of this study. The last five chapters follow a symmetrical pattern to the first five: four studies of the major texts – the cosmicomic tales (Chapter 6), the experimental works, *Le città invisibili* (*Invisible Cities*) and *Il castello dei destini incrociati* (Chapter 7), the hypernovel *Se una notte d'inverno un viaggiatore* (*If on a Winter's Night a Traveller*) (Chapter 8) and *Palomar* (Chapter 9) – followed by a more wide-ranging chapter (Chapter 10), this time not on thematics but on stylistic questions.

This is the first study to exploit the textual apparatus of the collected fiction and non-fiction as well as the author's university thesis on Joseph Conrad, and the first in English to devote major attention to Calvino's style and his intertextual sources. I concentrate primarily on the fiction, since the author's fame resides primarily in his creative rather than in his theoretical works; but the non-fiction will be considered for the light it throws on Calvino's narratives and his evolving poetics, particularly when the barriers between narrative and essays are consciously dismantled in the 1980s (see especially Chapter 9). Use will also be made of the uniquely high number of authorial prefaces and introductions, those 'autocommenti' and paratexts which accompany so many of his works and are now usefully gathered in the volumes of collected works, though Calvino himself always warns against seeking too close a correspondence between the creative and theoretical works (*S*, 7).

BIOGRAPHICAL NOTICE

Italo Calvino (1923–85) died on 19 September 1985. In terms of international reputation Calvino was at the time of his death the best-known and most-translated contemporary Italian writer. He was lionised particularly in the

Anglo-American world: indeed the work he was engaged upon when he succumbed to a cerebral haemorrhage was the result of an invitation to deliver the Charles Eliot Norton lectures at Harvard University, later published as *Lezioni americane. Sei proposte per il prossimo millennio* (*Six Memos for the Next Millennium*). Had he lived, Calvino would probably have become (after Montale) Italy's second winner of the Nobel Prize for Literature in the second half of the twentieth century.

Calvino was born on 15 October 1923 at Santiago de las Vegas, near Havana in Cuba, where his father taught agriculture and floriculture. Soon afterwards, in 1925, the family returned to Italy, to his father's home town of San Remo, where Mario Calvino continued his researches into *agronomia*, achieving the distinction of an entry in the *Dizionario biografico degli italiani* as being responsible for the introduction into Europe of then exotic fruits such as grapefruit and avocado: the luxuriant flora to be found especially in Calvino's early fiction derives from this paternal legacy. As his mother and many other relations also had scientific careers, the young Calvino felt himself to be something of 'a black sheep' on account of his literary interests and initial rejection of the sciences; but if the flora dominated the early works, the sciences were to reappear with particular emphasis in his later fiction. Other genetic legacies include the parents' anticlerical, masonic republicanism and occasional anarchic socialism. Life was spent largely in the spacious Villa Meridiana in San Remo with its extensive grounds covered in exotic plants, and the ancestral land further up the valley to the north of the town in San Giovanni, both constituting a world which Calvino himself described as 'il mondo della natura'.

His first school was the English nursery school, St George's College, followed by attendance at another private school, run by Waldensians, which consolidated his unconventional early education. For secondary schooling he attended the Liceo Gian Domenico Cassini where his exemption from religious instruction forced him to explain and defend this anticonformist stance: this experience of justifying a non-conformist viewpoint was a salutary one for the young Calvino (*S*, 2736–7), and its echoes resound through the early works. His first excitement in literature was reading Kipling's jungle stories, and also enjoying American comics and films. His first literary exploits were comic scenes for the stage (III, 1258), drawing cartoons (some published in *Album Calvino*), writing short stories, *apologhi* or fables, and even some poetry, inspired by his fellow-Ligurian, Eugenio Montale. In 1941–42 he enrolled in the Faculty of Agriculture at the University of Turin, passing four exams in his first year, but becoming aware through his reading of Montale, Vittorini and others of the potential for a more pronounced antifascist stance. In 1943 he transferred to the University of Florence where he passed three more exams in agriculture, but at the end of that year, refusing to be a conscript for the Fascist puppet Republic of Salò, he was forced into hiding. In spring 1944 he joined the Garibaldi partisans in the

Alpi Marittime: as a result of his refusal to sign up for military service his parents were taken hostage, thus increasing the burden of the choice he had made. His partisan experiences in 'il mondo della storia' were to prove as formative as those encountered in 'il mondo della natura'.

Calvino's initial choice to join the Communist brigades was prompted more by practical than by ideological reasons, as they were simply the best organised of the many partisan groupings of the time. However, after the Liberation his commitment to the Communist cause was strengthened, occasionally taking on the anarchist tendencies depicted in his earliest stories. In September 1945, like other veterans, he was allowed to enrol in the third year of a degree course at the University of Turin, graduating in English Literature in 1947 with a thesis on Joseph Conrad. In the meantime his first articles (on Ligurian socio-political issues) came out in local papers, before his most substantial piece, 'Liguria magra e ossuta' (*S*, 2363–70), appeared in *Il Politecnico* in December 1945, while his first short stories were published in 1946 (see Chapter 1). Also in 1946 he became a regular contributor of both articles and short fiction to the Communist daily *l'Unità*, sharing with Marcello Venturi at the end of that year the newspaper's prize for short fiction, for 'Campo di mine'. Encouraged by this success, he completed his first novel in December 1946, *Il sentiero dei nidi di ragno* (*The Path to the Spiders' Nests*), published in 1947, which went on to win the Premio Riccione, though it had failed to win the more prestigious Premio Mondadori (Dini, 1993).

As a young, unestablished author Calvino was unable to support himself full-time with his writing, but he was able to work in the contiguous fields of journalism (*l'Unità*) and publishing (he first joined the famous Turin publishing house of Einaudi in 1947). In February 1949 a collection of thirty short fictions, *Ultimo viene il corvo* (*The Crow Comes Last*) was published to considerable acclaim, though his subsequent attempts at a second novel were more problematic: *Il bianco veliero* (*The White Schooner*) was written between December 1947 and April 1949, but both Calvino and Vittorini felt it required rewriting – only one chapter of it was deemed publishable (as the short story 'Va' cosí che vai bene'). Similarly *I giovani del Po* (*Youth in Turin*) (January 1950-July 1951) and *La collana della regina* (*The Queen's Necklace*) (June 1952-December 1954), both dealing with urban realities of the time, were also considered unsatisfactory novels by the author. *Che spavento l'estate* (*What a Fright, the Summer*), started some ten years later in 1963, was a final abortive attempt at a realist novel and remained merely a fragment. It took Calvino eighteen months to finish *I giovani del Po*, and to compensate for this laboured work of socialist realism, he decided to write the kind of fantasy story he himself would have liked to read (I, 1307), composing *Il visconte dimezzato* (*The Cloven Viscount*) in little over a month (July-September 1951). In late 1951 he spent two months in the USSR as correspondent for *l'Unità*, the articles being published early in 1952; in a curiously symmetrical way, at the end of the decade he went to the USA (in 1959–60), where his stay would have an even more profound effect. The death of his father in October 1951 was also to affect him deeply, eliciting the homage to his parent in the final paragraph of the autobiographical trilogy, *L'entrata in guerra* (*The Entry into War*) (1954), and in the semi-autobiographical work, *La strada di San Giovanni* (*The Road to San Giovanni*) (1962), written just after the tenth anniversary of his father's death.

From 1954 to 1956 Calvino was engaged on the collection and then rewriting of *Le fiabe italiane* (*Italian Folktales*) (1956), an experience which was to confirm his own taste for non-realist fiction, as well as alert him to the structural similarities of all stories. Destalinisation and the violent suppression of the Hungarian uprising in 1956 caused him at first to dissent and then to resign (in August 1957) from the Italian Communist Party (the PCI). Shortly after his resignation, his satirical allegory against the PCI's *immobilismo*, 'La gran bonaccia delle Antille', appeared in the dissident left-wing journal *Città aperta*: both actions provoked the ire of the party leader Togliatti and his supporters. From April 1956 he had been working on *La speculazione edilizia* (*A Plunge into Real Estate*) and finished it in July 1957, but in the meantime, again to 'compensate' for its socio-political content, he wrote between December 1956 and February 1957, a second fantasy novel, *Il barone rampante* (*The Baron in the Trees*): both novels were published in 1957, and both register in different ways the political upheavals of those times. In 1958 he collected in *I racconti* a corpus of over fifty of his short stories and novellas. The following year, just before going to the USA on a Ford Foundation grant, he completed the third part of the fantastic trilogy, *Il cavaliere inesistente* (*The Non-Existent Knight*). Also in 1959 he became co-director with Vittorini of *Il Menabò*, a cultural journal which explored the role of literature in the new industrial age. There now followed four years in which he published no major work, and letters of the time testify to his growing dissatisfaction with the contemporary novel and his anxiety about having nothing more to say (*ILDA*, 365, 367, 378, 380–81, 473).

The period 1963–64 proved to be a turning point for Calvino in many ways. In 1963 he published: his last traditional 'novel' (though, consisting of fewer than 100 pages, it is more a long short story), *La giornata d'uno scrutatore* (*The Watcher*), which he had begun ten years previously; his last militant essay as a Marxist, 'L'antitesi operaia (The Working Class as Antithesis)' (*S*, 127–42); and his first work in the new serial or modular manner, composed of a series of microtexts forming a macrotext, a format that was to be used for the rest of his output: *Marcovaldo ovvero le stagioni in città* (*Marcovaldo, or The Seasons in the City*). In 1964 he bade farewell to his realist phase by reissuing his first novel, with an important new preface which explains the neorealist context of its genesis. Another important change around this time was his wedding in Cuba in February 1964 to Esther Singer, an Argentinian translator for UNESCO whom he had met in Paris. Initially they settled in Rome, but in 1967 the family, including a daughter,

Giovanna, born in 1965, moved to Paris, where they remained until 1979. At least one critic (Perrella 1991, 8) has adopted a psychoanalytical approach in this context, suggesting that there is a connection between the author's new married state and the fact that all his fiction from this point on also has a kind of barrier or frame surrounding it, whether in the scientific epigraphs of *Le cosmicomiche* (*Cosmicomics*) (1965), the structural grids of *Le città invisibili* (*Invisible Cities*) (1972) and *Palomar* (*Mr Palomar*) (1983), the Tarot cards in the margin of *Il castello dei destini incrociati* (*The Castle of Crossed Destinies*) (1973), or the elaborate 'cornice' surrounding *Se una notte d'inverno un viaggiatore* (*If on a Winter's Night a Traveller*) (1979). Perhaps more objective than this hypothesis are Calvino's own words, that once he had decided to be a full-time writer and to abandon his work in the adjacent fields of journalism and publishing, he had no more 'screens' to put between himself and the world (*Eremita a Parigi* (*Hermit in Paris*), 256–7): this is, no doubt, one of the reasons that frames begin now to appear in his fictions, but there are, of course, others. Perhaps the most significant transformation around this time, as he admits in an interview with Ferdinando Camon, was the fact that he also lost interest in direct political action, cultivating instead an innate instinct to be a bookworm (*S*, 2784).

In 1965 *Le cosmicomiche*, the first work in his new style, appeared, a style aimed at expanding the confines of literature by attempting to put it on a par with the advances being achieved in contemporary science. It is no coincidence that this was the period of the first satellites, space shots and the first men on the moon: the moon is one of the dominant themes of the cosmicomic tales. *Ti con zero* (*Time and the Hunter*) (1967) was in the same mode, but in its last four stories it embraces a rapprochement not so much between literature and science as between literature, mathematical logic and deductive reasoning: this coincided with the writer's move to Paris in 1967, and his interest in the mathematical-combinatory enthusiasms of Raymond Queneau (whose *Les Fleurs bleues* (*I fiori blu*) he translated in this same year). Through Queneau Calvino came to know Roland Barthes and the members of the Ouvroir de Littérature Potentielle (OULIPO), including Georges Perec: an association that would strongly influence his subsequent output. He followed the European student upheavals of 1967–70 with detached interest, his own ideas moving in a utopian direction through his reading of the French utopian Charles Fourier, a selection of whose works he prepared for Einaudi in these years. In 1969 he agreed to write a text, 'Il castello dei destini incrociati', to accompany Franco Maria Ricci's lavish edition of the fifteenth-century Bergamo Tarot cards: this text eventually was published along with its sequel illustrating the ordinary tarot cards ('La taverna dei destini incrociati'), with the title *Il castello dei destini incrociati* (1973). But in the meantime he wrote and published *Le città invisibili* (1972) which united his interests in utopias, the city and the Orient. In 1973 he became a full foreign member of OULIPO. There then followed an unparalleled period of six years in which he wrote no major work: not surprisingly, when his next volume did appear, it was a novel about writer's block and creativity, *Se una notte d'inverno un viaggiatore* (1979). However, as early as August 1975 Calvino had written for the *Corriere della sera* the first tales centring around a new character, Mr Palomar, who would be the protagonist of the last book to be published in the author's lifetime. Although the newspaper articles involving Palomar were often different from those eventually included in the homonymous book (1983), what emerges clearly from all of them is that in the late 1970s the author was deliberately trying to write completely contrasting kinds of work, shifting from the globe-trotting hypernovel to the minutely localised analyses of *Palomar*. In 1980 Calvino selected his essays from the period 1955–79, some political, most literary, in *Una pietra sopra* (1980, some of which are translated in *The Literature Machine*), a volume which amounts, as its title suggests, almost to a valedictory to a particular phase of his committed journalism.

In his final years Calvino's writing was stimulated particularly by the other arts. He wrote serious and ludic pieces inspired by photography, paintings (notably works by Domenico Gnoli, De Chirico and Arakawa – see Ricci 1989b, Belpoliti 1996, 113–231) and music, including a libretto for Mozart's *Zaide* and libretti for his friend Luciano Berio. He continued to work on more cosmicomic tales reissuing an expanded corpus of them, *Cosmicomiche vecchie e nuove* (1984), and published another collection of essays, mostly cultural rather than political or literary articles, *Collezione di sabbia* (*Collection of Sand*) (1984). He also wrote three of a projected five tales about the five senses (posthumously published as *Sotto il sole giaguaro* (*Under the Jaguar Sun*)). He had completed five of the six Norton Lectures for Harvard when he suffered a stroke on 6 September 1985, and he died two weeks later during the night of 18–19 September.

Chapter 1

The Apprentice Artisan

The Early Short Stories

Italo Calvino was a precocious as well as prolific writer. He began writing his first fictions at the age of 17 in the spring of 1941, had a collection of stories ready by May 1942 to which he gave the title *Pazzo io o pazzi gli altri* (*Either I'm Mad or The Rest Are*), but these were rejected by Einaudi in that year and have never been published (III, 1299–1300). Between spring 1943 and autumn 1944 he then wrote at least twenty-six 'Raccontini giovanili', mostly existential and antifascist apologues, which had provisional titles of *Raccontini di dopodomani* (*Brief Tales for the Day After Tomorrow*) or *Apologhi esistenzialistici* (*Existentialist Fables*) (III, 1300–16). Some of these were published clandestinely before the fall of Fascism, but he never considered them suitable for collective publication in his lifetime. He felt they contained 'a vision of humanity on the lowest rung of its descent, humanity-as-anthill, a humanity which retains only a latent and confused memory of its former individuality' (III, 1300). These twenty-six early stories were only published posthumously (in III, 767–830).

Instead Calvino regarded his first stories as those written immediately after the Liberation of Italy (25 April 1945). Since he considered himself as more a writer of short stories than a novelist (*S*, 671; *Six Memos*, 49), it seems appropriate to begin this study by examining his prolific output in this genre over the first twenty years (see Appendix), the genre in which both his earliest and final fictions were written. In order to chart his early development accurately, the most instructive approach is to enter this apprentice's workshop and observe him at work on some early postwar fictions which he later found deficient for one reason or another, either rewriting them or removing them from later collections. After this, I shall examine the more successful tales which are indicative of the burgeoning of a prodigious and precocious talent, and which contain some of his masterpieces in what was to remain his most congenial genre. Finally the chapter will examine the complex structures of the three short-story collections which contain the *racconti* written between 1945 and 1963. In fact, even leaving aside the twenty-six stories written before 1945, Calvino wrote between the end of the war and the end of 1963 at least 117 short fictions as well as ten novels. The stories written after 1963 were of a different kind, as we shall see below (Chapters 6–9), and were later inserted into organic collections such as *Cosmicomics*.

Calvino's first short-story collection, *Ultimo viene il corvo* (*The Crow Comes Last*), was published in 1949. Of these thirty tales, five were suppressed from both his later collected *Racconti* of 1958 and the 1969 edition of *Ultimo viene il corvo.* Calvino defined these five tales as 'stylistically incongruous' ('fuori stile'), three of them because they were too emotional in their evocation of the Resistance ('Angoscia in caserma', 'La stessa cosa del sangue', 'Attesa della morte in un albergo', his earliest postwar stories, all written in 1945), and the other two ('Alba sui rami nudi', 'Di padre in figlio', both 1946) because they were too steeped in 'a kind of rural, naturalistic regionalism' (I, 1262–3).

The three war tales are worth considering in some detail. 'La stessa cosa del sangue' ('In the Blood'), his first postwar story, is a microcosm of all Calvino. Set in Liguria during three days of the Resistance, the story is about two brothers who discover that their mother has been taken hostage by the Germans, and who eventually decide to abandon their armchair antifascism to join the partisans in the hills. The story contains many of the motifs of early Calvino: the Ligurian landscape (pine forests, olive groves, the port city, the sea), commitment to the Communist cause, and the contrast between the two protagonists. The older brother, the first self-portrait (Falaschi, 1976, 96–151), is the absent-minded intellectual, 'always with a book in his hand . . . like someone from another planet, probably not even capable of loading a pistol' (I, 224), while the younger one always has a gun in his hand, continually courting the country girls (I, 224). It also opens with a typically crisp sentence: 'The evening that the SS arrested their mother, the two brothers went to the Communist's house for dinner' (I, 221). In addition there are elements that were later recycled in his first novel, *Il sentiero dei nidi di ragno* (*The Path to the Spiders' Nests*) (1947), which also account for the story's suppression in the 1950s and 1960s: the pine woods, the partisan camp, the meal, the woman cook, the little boy, the Communist, his tirade against the wasted coffee in Brazil and wasted sugar in Cuba similar to Mancino's in the 1947 edition of *The Path to the Spiders' Nests* (I, 1250–1), the pet falcon named after a communist hero (Langàn here, Babeuf in the novel) and the solitary partisan (here Giglio, Lupo Rosso in *The Path*) who is also similar to the self-destructive Dritto in the novel in praying for his own house to be bombarded first.

There are also harbingers of the later Calvino, notably the final 'cosmicomic' paragraph about the ages of the earth and the layers of rock: 'And while the two brothers, sitting on the edge of the ravine, waited for Giglio, the Communist went around wondering how the rocks, the ravines and the mountains had originally formed, and how old the earth was' (I, 227). Another theme to achieve later prominence, but first adumbrated here, is the contrast between life and literature, already apparent in that portrait of the two brothers:

> The struggle, the hatred they felt for the Fascists, were no longer what they had been previously, in the older brother's case something he had learnt from books, and which he had rediscovered in real life. (I, 225)

There is the first example of the image of flux: a vortex of cloud concealing and revealing the bombarded city (I, 226 – cf. Hume, 1992a), and even the first example of a favourite listing device, *enumeraciòn caotica* or chaotic listing: 'bombs, pistols, gun-magazines, rifles, medicines, propaganda sheets' (I, 222). Yet despite the many good things in the story, Calvino in 1958 and 1969 rejected this first-born postwar tale, partly because of its autobiographical content (the Calvino brothers' mother then father were taken hostage by the ss – for the psychological damage this caused see Calvino's article written on the fortieth anniversary of the Liberation, 'Tante storie che abbiamo dimenticato': *S*, 2912–19), partly for its total realism and absence of fantasy (there are none of the fairy-tale or mannerist elements of *The Path*), but mostly because of its climax, the emotional consciousness-raising speech by the older brother:

> 'I can't stand it any longer, this life of arm-chair rebels. Either we become partisans or we don't. One of these days we shall just have to take the road into the mountains and join the partisan brigade.' (I, 227)

In later stories Calvino would learn to achieve a more detached, understated closure (Deidier 1995, 18–19). As he was to say later in a typically ironic way, his main ambition as a young man was to become a minor author, since he has always remained 'an artisan writer rather than a member of the avant-garde: I like constructing things which close well' (*S*, 1788–9).

The second rejected story, 'Attesa della morte in un albergo' ('Waiting for Death in a Hotel'), also contains autobiographical elements and an overemphatic ending. The motif of the hotel used as a prison is autobiographical, occurring here for the first time and being reused in other tales as well as in his first novel; the old prisoner with the white beard and the hunter's jacket is the first portrait of Calvino's father; the setting is again Liguria, the seaport probably San Remo and the Marassi stadium at the end clearly in Genoa. There are also a number of similarities with characters in *The Path to the Spiders' Nests*: Michele's baldness and tendency to spout slogans (I, 233) resemble similar aspects of Mancino in the novel; and the informer Pelle-di-biscia shares the name, role and physical characteristics of the double agent in *The Path*. The former is described as:

> a thin youth . . . with parched lips flecked with saliva. He had an incipient moustache of blondeish hair, and was always pale, with a permanent cold which made his nostrils and eyelids red. (I, 231)

Exactly the same four elements are picked out in the first description of Pelle in the novel: 'a slim youth with a permanent cold, the shadow of a moustache, and his parched lips flecked with saliva' (I, 72; *The Path*, 104), and act as his leitmotif throughout (I, 101, 141, etc.). The original Italian makes the similarities more explicit: '*gracile ragazzo* . . . le *labbra sbavate dall'arsura* . . . *dei baffi incerti* . . . *col raffreddore*' (I, 231) is recycled in the novel as 'un *ragazzo gracile*, sempre *raffreddato*, con *dei baffetti appena nati* sopra le *labbra sbavate dall'arsura*' (I, 72). Perhaps also the mannered repetitive dialogue (I, 229), and the vision of the incontinent old man as a universal father figure owed too much to Vittorini. But two elements stand out. One is the extremely high frequency of similes in this very short story – much of it animal imagery: the Germans' shouts are inhuman, like those of werewolves (I, 230), Pelle plays cat and mouse with the prisoners (I, 231), Michele's 'bovine eyes' are stressed twice (I, 233). The other is the sequence of Dantesque echoes that permeate the tale: each man awaiting the Nazi verdict on whether he is to remain alive or die is described as 'hovering between life and death' ('come sospeso tra vita e morte': I, 230), recalling Dante's use of the adjective 'sospeso' to describe those in Limbo (Dante, *Inferno*, 2.52, 4.45), while Pelle the informer is a Minos figure with the power to save or destroy and is surrounded by a crowd of the damned (I, 231). Despite these positive qualities, the coda condemned the story in Calvino's eyes. When the two men realise that they are not to be killed but to be taken to a stadium – again an autobiographical detail – the narrator intervenes to end the tale on a consolatory note of anticipated return:

> The rough taste of life would stay with them from then on, whether in the howling passageways of the Marassi stadium, or in the desolate barracks of the North, all the time until their return home. (I, 235)

As has been pointed out (Milanini, 1997), this viewpoint-disrupting prolepsis, as well as the flashback to the old prison at the beginning of the tale, infringe Calvino's cult of linear writing and abhorrence of flashbacks (*S*, xxvi–xxvii), and probably also account for the author's uneasiness with this tale.

The third story, 'Angoscia in caserma' ('Nightmare in the Prison Barracks'), was the first to be accepted for publication, though it did not appear in print until December 1946, while 'Andato al comando', though written later in 1945, came out in December of that same year (*S*, 2715). Autobiography is again present: the young partisan is rounded up but then escapes while being transferred from prison, participates in the battle of Baiardo, his father is taken hostage, and San Remo hotels and villas are used as prisons. Motifs that would resurface in *The Path* are: the mystique attaching to words such as *sten*, *mitra*, *machine*; the execution of Fascist spies in the mist; the ambush of Nazi-Fascist convoys; and the plate of chestnuts shared round the partisan campfire. The most striking aspect of this tale is its precocious, self-reflexive discussion of symbols (Watson 1996): the young partisan is haunted by a tendency to see everything around him in symbolic terms. This sophisticated motif, however, is not enough to render the conclusion less emphatic and obvious:

> The grass and the sunlight and the two of them walking with their coats unbuttoned in the midst of that grass and sunlight, were what men often call, without really understanding why, freedom. (I, 245)

This finale, with its conclusive emphasis on 'libertà', clearly contained that 'emotional appeal' which caused Calvino to eliminate the tale from his short-story collections of the 1950s and 1960s. The earliest postwar short stories, then, evince little awareness of the importance of avoiding an overemphatic conclusion: not by chance one of the planned Norton lectures, which would have been part of Calvino's legacy to the next millennium, was to have been entitled 'Cominciare e finire (On Beginnings and Endings)' (*S*, 734–53). Nor is it an accident that he felt dissatisfied with these three war stories: apart from their flawed tone, they were the most autobiographical in terms of content, and contained a high number of narrative elements recycled in *The Path to the Spiders' Nests*.

By contrast, Calvino discovered that by eliminating or submerging ideological elements, his short stories functioned more successfully and acquired 'lightness'. Two tales which are regarded as high points of *The Crow Comes Last* are 'Andato al comando' ('Gone to Headquarters', 1945) and 'Ultimo viene il corvo' ('The Crow Comes Last', 1946). 'Andato al comando', the first Calvino story to appear in print, was the one, on the author's own admission, which established his name as a writer of fiction. The version published in Vittorini's journal, *Il Politecnico* (January 1946), contains a number of significant differences from that printed three years later in *The Crow Comes Last*. The story opens with an alternation between landscape description and staccato dialogue that is reminiscent of Hemingway in general, and of 'Hills like White Elephants' in particular: confirmation that Calvino was fascinated by this particular story comes from Natalia Ginzburg's memoir of how she and Calvino visited Hemingway in Stresa in 1948, where they were able to tell the old man how much they admired this story, and indeed Ginzburg mentions it in the same breath as 'Andato al comando' (*Enciclopedia*, 188–91; see also *S*, 2905). But more important than the opening is the story's ending: unlike the hagiographic allusion to the partisans at the end of 'La stessa cosa del sangue', here Calvino, when rewriting the story for the 1949 collection, even omits the only two mentions of the word partisan in the first version in order to produce a starker contrast between characters he simply terms 'the armed man' and 'the unarmed man' (I, 1289–90). He also cuts one lengthy retrospective paragraph about the Fascist spy and his double dealings with both Germans and partisans (I, 1289), and omits corresponding details about the partisan's precise knowledge of how, when and where each fascist spy had been executed, 'some shouting that they had done nothing, others wide-eyed with terror, some crying, some without even noticing' (I, 1290). The motives for such omissions are certainly to do with economy of narrative and a desire to maintain the geometric quality of the tale by minimising psychology and character, but as with similar omissions from other neorealist tales and *The Path*, Calvino also abhorred excessive emphasis on violence and death. Even in 'La formica argentina' ('The Argentine Ant', 1952) the only omission between its publication in *Botteghe Oscure* and its appearance in *I racconti* is the violent sequence about Capitano Brauni's sadistic elimination of the ants (I, 1314–15).

But the clearest example of Calvino's achievement of narrative economy in this Hemingwayesque tale is in the item of clothing exchanged by the two men. In the *Politecnico* version the armed man gives the spy his partisan jacket, in order to reassure him that he will not be shot for the sake of his jacket on entering the camp. In fact, the partisan does shoot the spy before reaching headquarters, the original ending running like this:

> He fell face downwards on the ground and *the final shot blended with a vision of feet* stepping over him. So he remained, with his mouth full of pine needles. Later he was black with ants.
> (Cascò con la faccia al suolo e *il colpo di grazia lo colse in una visione di piedi* che lo scavalcavano. Cosí rimase, con la bocca piena di aghi di pino. E poi fu nero di formiche.) (I, 1291)

However, in rewriting the story, Calvino has the men exchange boots not jackets, so that final vision of his own boots stepping over the spy has added force:

> He fell face downwards on the ground and *the last thing he saw was a pair of feet shod in his own boots* stepping over him.
> So he remained, *a corpse in the middle of the woods,* with his mouth full of pine needles. Two hours later he was already black with ants. (My translation, since that in *Adam, One Afternoon*, 67, the English translation of *The Crow Comes Last,* is not equivalent to the definitive version.)
> (Cascò con la faccia al suolo e *l'ultima cosa che vide fu un paio di piedi calzati coi suoi scarponi* che lo scavalcavano.
> Cosí rimase, *cadavere nel fondo del bosco,* con la bocca piena d'aghi di pino. Due ore dopo era già nero di formiche.) (I, 265)

The insertion of the other detail about the body lying deep in the woods helps recall the landscape of the story, which had moved, in parallel with the gathering tension in the tale, from the clearing at the beginning ('It was a sparse wood', I, 260; *Adam*, 61) to ominous emphasis on the depths of the wood both in the middle ('Down below the woods were lost in the dark . . . the wood was getting thicker and thicker, and it seemed they would never emerge from it' I, 261–2; *Adam*, 62–3), and at the end ('Now they were out of the glades and undergrowth and entering thick green woods, untouched by fire; the ground was covered with pine-needles' (I, 264; *Adam*, 65). Thus, although the conclusion is longer in the number of words, the exchange of boots and the mention of the depths of the woods tighten the story's narrative coherence and economy.

Even more economic closure is achieved at the end of the title story from *The Crow Comes Last* (written December 1946). Critics rightly stress the story's affinities with *The Path* and interpret it, as Calvino himself suggested, as a modern transposition of Flaubert's *St Julien l'Hospitalier* (*S*, 2921; Re, 1990 163–9). But it is worth adding that this was the first Calvino tale to contain a child protagonist, and to blend successfully fairy-tale motifs with a war-setting (Carter III, 1987; Cerina, 1979): its success is due to this blending, which determines its serio-comic close. The story's prominence is also due to the remarkable symmetry that structures the tale, the symmetry that becomes a guiding aesthetic principle for Calvino's output. The young boy who borrows the partisan's rifle hits an extraordinarily high number of targets. He uses the firearm initially against animals of the three other elements of water, air and earth (trout, falcon, pine tree and hares). The transition to him shooting at German soldiers' buttons and epaulettes is signalled by his firing at a road-sign, thus moving from the world of nature to that of human artefacts; a sequence of small military targets (the German soldier's rifle butt, helmet tip and belt loop) is followed in the finale by a return to victims from the natural world (thrushes, woodcocks): the final target, which for reasons of narrative symmetry has to combine satisfactorily the natural and artificial worlds, is the Nazi eagle sewn on the breast of the soldier's uniform.

The ending of this story, like that of 'Andato al comando', is also illuminating, and the manuscript shows that this was the most heavily worked part of the tale. The movement from manuscript to its first printing in *l'Unità* and its final redaction in the 1949 collection shows a progressive lightening and streamlining of detail. In the manuscript version, after the young boy shoots the German soldier, the final three paragraphs of the story are these:

> The bullet hit him in the middle of an eagle with spread wings embroidered on his tunic.
>
> *The boy went up to the huge stone, checked if his aim had been true, then without moving sought another target. He saw a cricket leaping amongst the leaves, and aimed.*
>
> Slowly the crow came circling down.
>
> (Il proiettile lo prese giusto in mezzo a un'aquila ad ali spiegate che aveva ricamata sulla giubba.
>
> *Il ragazzo s'avvicinò alla pietra, controllò se aveva colpito giusto, poi senza muoversi cercò un altro bersaglio. Vide un grillo che saltava tra le foglie e mirò.*
>
> Il corvo s'abbassava lentamente, a giri.) (I, 1293)

The *Unità* version is this:

> The bullet hit him in the middle of an eagle with spread wings embroidered on his tunic.
>
> *The boy went up to the huge stone, checked if his aim had been true.*
>
> Slowly the crow came circling down.
>
> (Il proiettile lo prese giusto in mezzo a un'aquila ad ali spiegate che aveva ricamata sulla giubba.
>
> *Il ragazzo s'avvicinò alla pietra, controllò se aveva colpito giusto.*
>
> Il corvo s'abbassava lentamente, a giri.) (I, 1293)

The definitive version merely contains two brief sentences:

> The bullet hit him in the middle of an eagle with spread wings embroidered on his tunic.
> Slowly the crow came circling down. (*Adam*, 73)
> (Il proiettile lo prese giusto in mezzo a un'aquila ad ali spiegate che aveva ricamata sulla giubba.
> Il corvo s'abbassava lentamente, a giri.) (I, 271)

Again the author has pursued a progressive lightening of the material at the end of the tale: not for nothing was 'leggerezza' one of the key qualities that Calvino postulated in all good literature (*S*, 631–55).

The structure of Calvino's earliest stories is always based on the contrast between two central characters, with the exception of the problematic 1945 partisan tale, 'Come un volo di anitre (Like a Flight of Ducks)' (II, 849–54), which was excluded from *The Crow Comes Last*. In 'La stessa cosa del sangue' there were the two brothers, in 'Attesa della morte' Diego and Michele, in 'Angoscia in caserma' the protagonist and the boy from Oneglia, in 'Andato al comando' the armed partisan and the disarmed spy, in 'Di padre in figlio' the two protagonists of the title, in 'E il settimo si riposò' (1946) the country worker Ramún and the city man Vinsé. 'La fame a Bèvera' (1947) like 'Di padre in figlio' contains the interplay between the protagonist and his animal. However, in 'Paura sul sentiero' ('Fear on the Footpath', 1946), for the first time we find an exclusive concentration on the sole protagonist, Binda, though there are deuteragonists in his subconscious: fear of the German Gund and desire for the girl Regina. Along with its exclusive concentration on a single protagonist, there is also effective symmetrical imagery in the tale: at the beginning and the end Binda is described in images of strength, having a face 'shut like a fist' and 'muscles like stones' (I, 246; *Adam*, 47). By contrast the middle of the tale is dominated by menacing animal imagery: the war revolving around the valleys like a dog biting its tail, fear like bats' wings inside Binda or like a monkey clinging to his neck, mines drifting like enormous subterranean spiders, Gund's eyes 'like those of the dormice' in a scene reminiscent of Conrad's *Heart of Darkness* (I, 247–51; *Adam*, 48–52). There is also the first hint of Calvino's interest in the metamorphic quality of men–animals–plants (*Fiabe*, 12–13; *S*, 637–38):

> There was a German in every thicket, a German perched on the top of every tree, with the dormice. The stones were pullulating with helmets, rifles were sprouting amongst the branches, the roots of the trees ended in human feet. (I, 250; *Adam*, 51)

'Campo di mine' ('Minefield', 1946) develops this motif of the solitary figure crossing hostile terrain, though there is an initial contrast between the protagonist and the old man at the beginning. Again we find the same menacing imagery and the same suspense-building structural technique which informs all these stories and which Calvino mentions in a letter to Marcello Venturi (I, 1288). The climax of carnage when he finally steps on the mine appears to be indebted to Hemingway's descriptions of death. This story was important to Calvino both because it won him the 'Premio de l'Unità' (jointly with Marcello Venturi) and because he had to write an article in the Communist daily (*l'Unità*, 5 January 1947) about his victory in which he reflected on the similarities and differences between himself and Venturi. He says that they both favour dramatic themes which allow an intense, pacy rhythm, and both favour 'a harsh, bare language, made up of solid words and rough syntactical links' (*S*, 1477; see also Surdich, 1988). But the young author went on to contrast himself with the veteran writer of authentic partisan tales, and to criticise himself for being 'really only one of those old individualist writers who nevertheless manage to represent themselves externally in "symbols" that are of contemporary and collective interest' (*S*, 1478). A letter to Venturi from the same period reveals a similarly precocious self-awareness. In it Calvino notes the similarity of structure in tales such as 'Andato al comando' and 'Campo di mine': 'It's the usual process of a sequence of states of mind that become more and more anguished . . . until they end with a shooting, a mine exploding, or something similar' (I, 1288). 'Andato al comando' was both his fortune and his ruin, he says, because he seems to have recycled its structure five or six times in other stories, and even regrets having infected Venturi with 'Andatocomanditis' since all Venturi's partisan tales now end in the same way.

Apart from the structure, the figurative elements also contribute effectively to the tension Calvino acknowledged in 'Campo di mine'. The opening comparison of the old man's vague gesture compared to someone 'wiping a steamed-up window' (I, 288) has a figural consistency with the opaque central images of the landscape of rhododendrons as an impenetrable, uniform sea concealing the mines in its depths (I, 290). The other opening simile of the protagonist's smile, which freezes over his teeth as if caught by an unripe prickly pear, leads coherently into the bristling imagery that follows: the old man's tone and look is as unhelpful as the bare landscape on which the grass grows 'like a badly shaven face' (I, 288), the mines themselves are 'huge sleepy animals liable to waken at his footsteps' (I, 289) and the air is 'pierced by the noise of marmots as though by the cactus prickles' (I, 291), clearly anticipating the lacerating explosion at the end in which the man is ripped apart 'as a piece of paper is torn up' (I, 293).

If these Resistance stories contain perhaps the most successful of those written between 1945 and 1949 and constitute a definitive 'cycle' recognised by the author himself, there are at least five other groups of tales in this period. The second group is what could be termed 'problem tales', ones which have neither a war setting nor peacetime memories; instead they are rather derivative of Pavese or Italian regionalism, often set in the city and dealing with love, and were later found wanting by the author himself. Calvino rejected 'Vento in una città'

('Wind in a City', 1946; III, 952–9; *Numbers in the Dark*, 47–53), his first urban tale, when it was already in proofs for the 1949 edition of *The Crow Comes Last*. Despite the humour of the fantasy about the FIAT boss's toilet, he probably deselected it because of the derivatively Pavesian contrast of city and country, and perhaps because of too autobiographical a portrait in the narrator, who is a writer who used to live in a large villa by the sea before transferring to Turin.

Another story removed at proof stage was 'Amore lontano di casa (Love Far from Home)' (1946; III, 960–8; *Numbers*, 38–46). Like 'Vento in una città', this too is set in the city, with contrasting memories of the protagonist's life in a villa in the seaside town. The similarities of both these tales to the short novel which Calvino also regarded as defective, *I giovani del Po (Youth in Turin*) (1950–51) suggest that in 1949, when *The Crow Comes Last* was already at proof stage, Calvino removed these stories because of their predictable, Pavesian antitheses of city and country, and – in the case of 'Amore lontano da casa' – he probably also felt dissatisfied with the misogynistic (again Pavesian) division between men and women and the Vittorinian dialogue. The story is interesting for its coherent marine imagery, its motif of the intellectual narrator reading before his girlfriend arrives (a motif that will resurface in *La giornata d'uno scrutatore* (*The Watcher*)), and that first view of the city roofs and the description of the waves which will reappear in one of his last works, *Palomar*. But the flaws of 'Amore lontano di casa' outweighed its virtues. These two stories also have in common the sexual liaison between the male and female protagonists: like the later portrait of himself, Usnelli in 'Avventura di un poeta', Calvino found it difficult to write positively about love.

Also at this time he found fault with at least one Resistance tale. 'Come un volo d'anitre' ('Like a Flight of Ducks', 1945; III, 849–54; *Numbers*, 31–7) was not included in *The Crow Comes Last*. Despite the protagonist Natale being an anticipation of Gurdulú of *The Non-Existent Knight*, particularly in his failed sexual encounter with Margherita, Calvino rejected the story, like the three earliest war tales, for its facile denouement describing the awakening of consciousness in Natale:

> He came to understand it all when he found himself with the Germans just beneath him climbing the road to the Goletta and firing their flamethrowers into the bushes. (III, 854; *Numbers*, 36)

Presumably he also withdrew the story for its echoes of *The Path*, which had been published in 1947, especially the echoes of Chapter IX of the novel: at the conclusion Natale understands that the men on both sides are made up of men like himself, beaten by his father, exploited by the landowners and humiliated by fellow soldiers, though he cannot work out precisely why he was on the right side and the Fascists on the wrong one.

The pattern that emerges in Calvino's first twenty stories is that about half of them have a Resistance setting, but with many of those that do not have a war setting he felt some dissatisfaction, excluding them from his 1949 collection ('Vento in una città', 'Amore lontano di casa', 'E il settimo si riposò', 'Ragionamento del cugino'). He tended to keep in his collections only those non-war tales that paid memorialistic homage to his father in the prewar days ('Uomo nei gerbidi', 'I fratelli Bagnasco', 'L'occhio del padrone'). These 'peacetime' autobiographical *racconti*, then, form a third strand of writing, and are grouped as 'Le memorie difficili' in the 1958 *Racconti*. 'Uomo nei gerbidi' ('Man in the Fallow Fields'), a slight tale about hunting, contains another early portrait of Calvino's father as a hunter and of himself as the inept son. 'I fratelli Bagnasco' (1946) marks a return to the motif of the double as opposed to the single protagonist. The two bourgeois brothers are detested by the *contadini* because they are bourgeois, even though when they are in the city they share cigarettes with the workers and affect left-wing standpoints. This story is narrated entirely in the present tense, like his first novel. 'L'occhio del padrone' ('The Master's Eye', 1947) is also largely autobiographical (again the lazy son is contrasted with the work ethic of the father), but contains the first appearance of the protagonist as eye (which will receive fullest development in *Palomar*), not just in the title, but in the fourfold repetition of 'eye' in the opening paragraph:

> 'The master's eye', his father said to him, pointing to his own eye, an old lashless eye between wrinkled lids, round as the eye of a bird. (I, 192)

But here the protagonist's eye, unlike Palomar's, does not attempt to catalogue the universe, it does not even see clearly what is going on, so alienated is the son from the father's rural world. 'I figli poltroni' (1948) also contains autobiographical elements. The two lazy brothers, their hard-working parents and the family land at San Cosimo will receive fuller elaboration in the extended autobiographical account, *La strada di San Giovanni* (*The Road to San Giovanni*, 1962; III, 7–26), as will the theme of the father's sense of waste ('perhaps his whole life has been like this, a waste of his energies, a huge pointless effort', I, 198), while the rest of the opening description of the father will resurface at the end of 'Le notti dell' UNPA' ('The U.N.P.A. Nights', 1953) in an act of literary *pietas* for the man who died in October 1951 (I, 545). Perhaps the most autobiographical of all these early tales is 'Pranzo con un pastore' ('A Goatherd at Luncheon', 1948), as is suggested by the author's excision, when rewriting the tale, of phrases which could have offended his parents: mentions of the 'aristocratic condescension' of the mother and the 'servile affability' (I, 1282) of the father are both removed between the 1949 edition of *The Crow Comes Last* and the later collections.

'Furto in una pasticceria' ('Theft in a Cakeshop', 1947) was Calvino's first humorous tale and inaugurated the fourth type of story, those of low life recounted in a comic, picaresque manner. This one is replete with animal imagery and a delight in lists of the different verbs of eating and names for cakes.

Falaschi (1988b, 128) suggested that the three picaresque tales 'Furto in una pasticceria' (1946), 'Si dorme come cani' ('Sleeping Like Dogs', 1947) and 'Dollari e vecchie mondane' ('Dollars and the Demi-Mondaine', 1947) were possibly inspired by Calvino's first reading of Queneau, whose *Pierrot mon ami* was published in Italian by Einaudi in 1947, but this cannot have been true of the first of these tales, since although it initially appeared in print in June 1947, it had been written in 1946 (according to Calvino's own index to *I racconti*). In fact the title as well as the grotesque characters of 'Dollari e vecchie mondane' may have been more directly inspired by Conrad's grim tale 'Because of the Dollars', remarked upon in Calvino's university thesis (p. 93). Falaschi (1988b, 124–5) also shows that around 1949–50 Calvino, struggling to write his second novel, experiences a similar crisis in his shorter fiction, and the rate of deselection of his stories seriously increases. Ferretti confirms this, pointing to a general decrease in the number of stories written in this period, as well as a reluctance to commit himself to explicit statements of his own poetics until 1955 (Ferretti, 1989, 17–19). 'Va' cosí che vai bene (Go On, You're Doing Fine)' is a fragment from the failed second novel, *Il bianco veliero* (*The White Schooner*), which Calvino wrote between 1947 and 1949. Set just after the end of the war, this tale has two physically contrasting protagonists, Foffo and Nasostorto, who respectively try to get the better of two apprentice black marketeers, the girl Costantina and the streetwise urchin Adelchi, the latter a postwar version of Pin, the boy protagonist of *The Path*. Perhaps another reason for the failure of *Il bianco veliero* as a novel was its similarity to *The Path*: in future Calvino would learn never to write two similar novels in succession, but would specialise in writing an opposite kind of fiction to the one just written – so much so that by the time of *Se una notte d'inverno un viaggiatore* (*If on a Winter's Night a Traveller*) he could make the paradoxical claim that his novels were so different from each other that it was this very variety that was his hallmark (II, 619).

'Un bastimento carico di granchi (A Boat Full of . . . Crabs)' (1947) is important as the first *racconto* to be exclusively about children and – unlike 'Ultimo viene il corvo' or the first novel – to have a postwar setting. This represents a fifth, separate group of stories: tales in which either children or nature or animals are the protagonists. The most successful here are 'Un pomeriggio Adamo (Adam, One Afternoon)' (1947), 'Il giardino incantato (The Enchanted Garden)' (1948) and 'Pesci grossi, pesci piccoli (Big Fish, Small Fish)' (1950).

The sixth and final group are what Calvino termed 'favolistica politica' ('political fables'). These were neo-expressionist political allegories such as 'Impiccagione di un giudice' ('A Judgment'), 'Il gatto e il poliziotto' ('The Cat and the Policeman') and 'Chi ha messo la mina nel mare?' ('Who Put the Mine in the Sea?'), all written in 1948 and all firmly tied to the bitter and disillusioned political context in which they were composed – the defeat of the Left in the April elections and the assassination attempt on Togliatti in July 1948.

Alongside the political fables of the late 1940s Calvino tried what he called 'a freer, more articulated kind of writing' (I, 1267). The first example in this vein was 'Avventura di un soldato (Adventure of a Soldier)', the only 1949 story to be included in that first edition of *The Crow Comes Last*, one that was to prove the harbinger of perhaps his most successful set of short stories, the adventures of the different lovers in *Gli amori difficili* (*Difficult Loves*).

One war story that best exemplifies Calvino's eclectic poetics is 'Uno dei tre è ancora vivo' (1947). Set in an unnamed country, three men are tried and condemned to death for war crimes. They are shot and dumped down a kind of natural well, the Culdistrega, but one of them survives, eventually managing to find an underground passageway which leads him to a safe shore. The description of the protagonist's loss and regaining of consciousness recalls Hemingway's description of the protagonist being wounded in *A Farewell to Arms*:

> A cloud of pain in the back like a swarm of stinging bees prevented him from losing consciousness at once; he had fallen through a briar-bush. Then tons of emptiness weighed down on his stomach. (I, 274; *Adam*, 76)

There is also a hint of Poe's *The Narrative of Gordon Pym*, one of Calvino's favourite texts (*S*, 1733–4), when the prisoner in the cavern first shelters in 'a niche in the rock' (*Adam*, 77) and then slips through 'a narrow, horizontal crack in the rock' (*Adam*, 80), running the risk of being buried alive. But the contemporary flavour of war and horror are blended with an antithetical source to Hemingway and Poe, Dante. This is clearly an infernal scenario which becomes more Dantesque as the tale progresses. The three political traitors at the bottom of the pit immediately suggest the three traitors in Satan's mouth (*Inferno*, 34); another scene recalls the angels preventing the entry of Virgil and Dante into the city of Dis (*Inferno*, 8–9):

> Up there, against the sky, there were good angels with ropes, and bad angels with grenades and rifles, and a big old man with a white beard who opened his arms but could not save him. (I, 277; *Adam*, 80)

The protagonist crawls through the bottom of the cavern 'like a snake', and this satanic image of the rotten worm or serpent at the earth's core is continued in the bats' wings that graze his face in the cavern. The allusions to the *Inferno* extend to many precise microtextual details, echoes of famous lines from those favourite intertextual areas, the beginning and the end of the cantica. Of these many echoes, a few will suffice: 'La vista del cielo lo disperò: certo era meglio fosse morto' ('The sight of the sky plunged him in despair; it would certainly be better to be dead', *Adam*, 77) recalls 'Tanto è amara che poco è piú morte' (*Inferno* 1.7), 'ch'io perdei la speranza dell'altezza' (*Inferno*, 1.54) and 'Non isperate mai veder lo cielo' (*Inferno* 3.85); similarly 'stava per morire. Ma non si sentiva venir meno' is close to: 'Io non morii e non rimasi vivo' (*Inferno* 34.25); while the waters of

Culdistrega gather at the bottom of the pit like those of Dante's Hell, and the narrow passage underground is called 'un budello sotteraneo' like the 'natural burella' at the end of *Inferno* (34.98). When finally the survivor remerges 'sotto il cielo', the landscape is more reminiscent of the wood of the suicides (*Inferno*, 13) or of the dark wood at the beginning of Dante's journey:

> Intorno c'era un bosco fitto d'alberi deformi, nel sottobosco non crescevano che stecchi e spini. L'uomo era nudo in regioni selvagge e deserte. (I, 279)
> (Around it was a wood full of twisted trees; all that grew in the undergrowth was thorns and brambles. He was naked in wild and deserted parts.) (*Adam*, 81)

This recalls Dante's descriptions: 'Non pomi v'eran ma stecchi con tosco', (*Inferno* 13.6); 'Esta selva selvaggia e aspra e forte . . . la piaggia diserta' (*Inferno*, 1.5, 1.29). The final paragraph is a fitting conclusion to this allusive tale, in which the heavily hendecasyllabic rhythm of the prose as well as the sense of the last sentences all reinforce the intertextual allusions to *Inferno*, *Paradiso* and even to the close of Virgil's first *Eclogue*:

> La vallata era / tutta boschi e dirupi cespugliosi, / sotto una fuga grigia di montagne. / Ma in fondo, a una gobba del torrente / c'era un tetto d'ardesia e un fumo bianco / che s'alzava. La vita, pensò il nudo, / era un inferno, con rari richiami / d'antichi felici paradisi. (I, 279)
> (The valley was all woods and shrub-covered slopes, under a grey hump of mountain. But at the end of it, where the torrent turned, there was a slate roof with white smoke coming up. Life, thought the naked man, was a hell, with rare moments recalling some ancient paradise.) (*Adam*, 82)

That these poetic lines are not fortuitous is confirmed both by their frequency in this tale and by the author's own observation later that he consciously used the hendecasyllabic rhythm in his prose (*Il barone rampante*, school edn., 213). As that final sentence suggests, although many of the allusions in the tale are to the *Inferno*, the story has also been about the protagonist undergoing a kind of purgatory: when he immerses himself in the torrent he is able to cleanse himself: 'poteva nettarsi dalla crosta di fango e sangue proprio e altrui' (cf. *Purgatorio* 1.95: 'che li lavi 'l viso, / sí ch'ogni sucidume quindi stinghe'). As in Joyce's *Dubliners* story, 'Grace', the protagonist of Calvino's tale undergoes modern equivalents of Dante's Hell and Purgatory before being granted a glimpse of Paradise. This motif of reality being another Inferno will resurface at the close of one of Calvino's most celebrated later works, *Invisible Cities* (II, 497–8), where, however, there will be no proleptic glance forward to Paradise.

In general as regards the changes made between the newspaper or journal redactions of these stories and later editions, Falcetto (I, 1274–6) has stressed three constants:

1. the elimination of over-explicit ideological content, notably in 'Andato al comando' and the conclusion of 'Il gatto e il poliziotto';

2. the attenuation of the harsher tones, usually as regards sexual detail; and
3. the pursuit of greater stylistic homogeneity.

But it is worth looking in more detail at the implications of Calvino's own selections of his earliest tales. By February 1949, when he made the definitive selection of thirty stories for *The Crow Comes Last*, he had written over forty *racconti*, and we have already seen that stories unconnected with the five broad themes outlined above (war, peacetime autobiographical memoirs, children and nature, the black market, political apologues) were more likely to be excised. The structure of Calvino's first collection of short stories, something over which he always took great care, repays analysis. In the 1949 collection these tales were not explicitly divided into groups, but it is clear that they fall into three bands of about ten stories each. The first ten deal with: child protagonists ('Un pomeriggio Adamo', 'Un bastimento carico di granchi', 'Il giardino incantato'), the regional landscape ('Alba sui rami nudi', 'Di padre in figlio') and autobiographical tales ('Uomo nei gerbidi', 'L'occhio del padrone', 'I figli poltroni', 'Pranzo con un pastore', 'I fratelli Bagnasco'). Then comes 'La casa degli alveari', which is a transitional tale containing the landscape of Ligurian idyll but also the theme of violence which will be the common denominator of the next group of ten stories, those set during the Resistance ('La stessa cosa del sangue', 'Attesa della morte in un albergo', 'Angoscia in caserma', 'Paura sul sentiero', 'La fame a Bèvera', 'Andato al comando', 'Ultimo viene il corvo', 'Uno dei tre è ancora vivo', 'Il bosco degli animali', 'Campo di mine'). Lastly come nine stories about the problems of postwar Italy, six dealing with black marketeers ('Visti alla mensa', 'Furto in una pasticceria', 'Dollari e vecchie mondane', 'L'avventura di un soldato', 'Si dorme come cani', 'Desiderio in novembre') and three political fables ('Impiccagione di un giudice', 'Il gatto e il poliziotto', 'Chi ha messo la mina nel mare?'). The thirty stories thus chart the move from edenic innocence in the world of nature (not for nothing does the first title include 'Adamo', the third a 'garden'), to adolescent experience of history and war, to the bleakness of contemporary reality in the period of postwar reconstruction. We can also infer from an important letter of 1958 (*ILDA*, 262–4), which discusses the structure of his later collected *Racconti*, that Calvino indeed thought of this first collection of thirty stories in 1949 as falling into three sections, since he terms the first three subsections of that later anthology 'La natura', 'La guerra', 'Il dopoguerra', and these correspond largely to the stories of the 1949 *The Crow Comes Last*.

Between 1945 and 1958 Calvino wrote just over one hundred short narratives, of which his collected *Racconti* represent almost exactly fifty per cent, since it contains fifty-two tales. The collection retains nineteen but de-selects eleven of the thirty from the original *The Crow Comes Last*. Those rejected are: the five he would eliminate also from the 1969 *Ultimo viene il corvo* (the two examples of regionalism, 'Alba sui rami nudi', 'Di padre in figlio', the three earliest emotional partisan tales, 'La stessa cosa del sangue', 'Attesa' and 'Angoscia') and six others: 'La casa degli alveari' (in an awkward transitional place in the 1949 edition too, neither idyllic nor a war tale), 'La fame a Bèvera' (the weakest war story), 'Visti alla mensa' and 'Desiderio in novembre' (the least picaresque tales of the black market group) and two of the three political allegories ('Il gatto e il poliziotto' is retained and grouped with the black market tales as the most humorous of the political fables). The major pillars of the architecture of the fifty-two stories in *I racconti* are the four books into which the collection is divided: 'Gli idilli difficili' 'Le memorie difficili', 'Gli amori difficili', and 'La vita difficile'.

The most substantial book is the first, containing thirty-two 'difficult idylls'. It begins with six tales about 'natura' (the first three of the 1949 collection plus three new ones, written around 1950: 'Pesci grossi pesci piccoli', 'Mai nessuno degli uomini lo seppe', 'Un bel gioco dura poco'), then seven stories on 'la guerra' (the six war tales remaining after the removal of the three early partisan stories, and in place of 'La fame a Bèvera' another war story, written in 1953, 'Paese infido'), then six about 'il dopoguerra' ('Furto', 'Dollari', 'Si dorme', with the addition of 'Va' cosí che vai bene', 'Un letto di passaggio' and 'Il gatto e il poliziotto'). There then follow ten Marcovaldo stories about 'la natura in città' and three humorous industrial tales, embodying 'il mondo delle macchine' ('La gallina di reparto', 'La notte dei numeri', 'La signora Paulatim').

The second book consists of two sections relating to memories: the five autobiographical tales, beginning with 'Uomo nei gerbidi', plus the trilogy 'L'entrata in guerra' (1953), thus opening and closing the sequence with portraits of the author's father. The third book contains just nine 'Amori difficili', with 'L'avventura di un soldato' now promoted from a picaresque tale of low life to something more autonomous, the first of Calvino's successful tales of sexual desire; this series of 'Difficult Loves' ends, significantly, with 'L'avventura di un poeta', a tale that is self-referential both in its metaliterary questioning of the written word's capacity to deal with positive aspects of nature and beauty, and in its self-portrait of a writer who finds it almost impossible to write positively about sexual desire and love. In fact the aesthetic question of beauty becomes a preoccupation of the writer in the late 1950s, from *La nuvola di smog* (1958) to *La giornata d'uno scrutatore* (1963).

The fourth book contains the substantial realistic trilogy, 'La formica argentina' (1952), 'La speculazione edilizia' in an abbreviated, depoliticised version (see Chapter 4) and 'La nuvola di smog' (1958). Confirmation of the careful planning of the structure of the volume is to be found in the detailed letter of 2 September 1958 to Pietro Citati (ILDA, 262–4). In it Calvino stresses that the theme of the first section, 'Difficult idylls', is 'the impossibility of harmony with nature, with things and with other men' (ILDA, 262), and that he found it difficult to place 'Le memorie difficili' in the collection, since he thought of the collection as divided into three books, and a book on 'Difficult Memories' would ruin the sequence of idyll–love–life; in fact he feels that the real novelty in the collection is the group of 'Difficult Loves'. The overall architecture of the volume, in its move from idyll and memory to the difficulties of loving and living, deliberately implies a journey from communion with nature to solitary alienation, and the characters develop from geometric two-dimensional figures to the more complex protagonists of *A Plunge into Real Estate* and *Smog* (Ricci, 1990).

In the 1969 edition of *Ultimo viene il corvo*, the author's index visibly groups the thirty tales into four parts: the first contains eight Resistance tales (the same seven as in *Racconti* and the reinstated 'La fame a Bèvera'); the second has eight picaresque black market tales (the six of the 1949 edition plus 'Va' cosí che vai bene' and 'Un letto di passaggio', both added in 1958); the third has eleven tales in which nature, children or animals predominate (the three opening tales from 1949, the five autobiographical ones, 'La casa degli alveari' and two of the three added in 1958, 'Un bel gioco' and 'Pesci grossi, pesci piccoli'); the fourth part contains the three tales of 'favolistica politica'. The only story to be omitted between the 1958 and 1969 selections is 'Mai nessuno degli uomini lo seppe', which is a hunting tale without child protagonists or strong autobiographical memories. In this process of selecting and deselecting stories over twenty years Calvino expended considerable care, and the overall architecture of all these collections of stories reflects his evolving poetics over two decades as well as his conviction that the structure of any collection of texts is an integral part of its meaning.

In the first postwar decade of writing, Calvino establishes himself as a fine craftsman of short stories, helped often by being a rigorous self-critic – indeed even if he had written no novels at all, Calvino would have remained a major exponent of this favourite Italian genre. The stories that he either refuses to collect or at times deselects from his authorised collections of 1949, 1958 and 1969 are those that belong to none of the five categories outlined above (war, peacetime memories, child-centred or nature tales, postwar low life and political allegories). His predominant textual strategy is to represent problematic contemporary reality, by adopting one single or two contrasting intertexts, assuming a comic-picaresque tone in the portrayal of the poor or adopting a fairy-tale code when dealing with political or Resistance issues. When he tries to write about the city, industrial reality or love, without any of these contrasting or deforming devices, the result is unsatisfactory, as we have seen in 'Vento in una città', 'E il settimo si riposò' or 'Amore lontano di casa'. The problems he encountered with such stories on a small scale reflect the larger difficulties he experienced when attempting to write a novel on any of these topics. As a ruthless self-editor, Calvino suppressed the publication in book form of these less convincing narratives; at the same time, however, his critical intuition allowed him to see the potential for a full-blown novel in the boy protagonist and present-tense narration of one of his most succesful short stories, 'Ultimo viene il corvo': it is no accident that the story and the novel were written within weeks of each other.

Chapter 2

A Small-scale Epic

The Path to the Spiders' Nests

Il sentiero dei nidi di ragno (*The Path to the Spiders' Nests)* (1947) occupies a problematic place in the history of postwar Italian literature. Because of the status the author was later to acquire, and because of the important Preface about its neorealist genesis which he wrote for it in 1964, it has become a canonical text of neorealism, though recent criticism has rightly underlined the extent to which it is eccentric rather than central to that movement. Neorealism was a movement embracing literature, cinema and other arts, which extended at its broadest from 1941 (publication of Pavese's *Paesi tuoi*) until 1955 (publication of Pratolini's *Metello*), though most critics limit its extent from 1943 (the release of Visconti's film, *Ossessione*) to 1950 or even 1948 (the defeat of the Left and 'involution' of Italian culture – see Corti, 1978b, 25–31; Milanini, 1980, 10–11). In literature the movement was characterised by three broad objectives:

1. a new realism of content, new because in narrating the unexplored reality of antifascist and then postwar Italy, it was different both from late nineteenth-century realism and from the censured or 'hermetic' literature written under Fascism;
2. a new realism of style, which implied a more authentic representation of 'natural' Italian, including a closer mimesis of the spoken language as well as of regional and dialect forms;
3. a committed socio-political message (Corti, 1978b, 32–7; Falcetto, 1992, 120–6; Falaschi 1976, 105; Milanini, 1980, 8–9).

Examined under the first two headings Calvino's first novel was certainly a neorealist work, though even the content is defamiliarised by the author's technique of adopting contrasting narrative codes such as that of the fairy tale (Re, 1990) and the style contains only a few dialectalisms (Mengaldo, 1989). Where it was clearly anomalous to the movement was in its modification of the message about *impegno*: even at this early stage Calvino was non-conformist, preferring to avoid the hagiographic approach encouraged by the Communist Party, which favoured 'socialist realism' and 'positive heroes'. Instead he went against the grain, eschewing the Manichaean portrayal of the antifascist struggle as a battle between good and evil (a portrayal found, for example, in Vittorini's *Uomini e no*) and stressing instead how similar the men were on both sides, how their joining the Fascists or partisans was often fortuitous rather than the result of political consciousness, and opting in fact to portray the least positive partisans imaginable (I, 1192–3; *The Path*, 16–17). For Calvino the overriding objective was to portray men at the problematic stage *before* they achieve the political consciousness that would allow them to arrive at total commitment to the cause.

The chronology of the novel's composition is also important. Calvino wrote the first chapter with great slowness and hesitation in the autumn of 1946, interrupted work on it for a while then finished it in the space of three weeks in December of the same year. Ferretti (1989, 38–42) has argued for the relevance to the novel of the key article 'Le capre di Bikini' (*S*, 2131–6), in which Calvino maintains that man owes an explanation and apology to the animals for destroying their world and ours with wars or atomic weapons. The boy protagonist Pin is thus caught between two alterities, that of the natural world and that of the adults, but at the end he achieves a facile reconciliation with both in the figure of Cugino, who is like Pin a misogynist, and in that sense still a child, and who accompanies him along the path to the spiders' nests teaching him that fireflies, like women, are repugnant close up but beautiful if seen from a distance. Ferretti argues that the ecological sympathy of the article informs the novel which was written in the same year. In fact the chronology bears closer examination: *The Path* was mostly written immediately after the article, since the latter was published on 17 November 1946, while the novel was completed in twenty days in the following month. Equally as important contextually are the two stories Calvino wrote in that same month of December 1946: 'Ultimo viene il corvo', in which, as we have seen, another young boy meets up with partisans and, in a similar present-tense narration, undergoes a *Bildung* that initiates him from the world of innocent nature to the world of violence and war; and 'Cinque dopodomani: guerra finita!', an account of the model Russian partisans which becomes the coda to Chapter IX of the novel. I will return at the end of this chapter to the significance of these two tales after discussing the other aspects of this first novel.

The more general context in which Calvino wrote this book has been fully outlined by Lucia Re. She notes the relevance of Sartrean existentialism and of the 1946–47 debate about the autonomy of culture from politics, a debate conducted in Communist circles and in the pages of Vittorini's *Il Politecnico*. Other motifs of neorealist narratives are also present in the work but Re argues that the novel deliberately demythifies specific problematic aspects of the Resistance: the lone agents (Lupo Rosso, Pelle, Cugino), the execution of Fascist prisoners (Chapter VII), the achievement of political consciousness.

Most critics have stressed the felicity of Calvino's solution to the question of tone and 'point of view' by filtering the narrative through the eyes of a naive, child focaliser, the urchin Pin. What they have said less about is structure, though they have mentioned the use of the present tense and its consequent 'degerarchizzazione degli eventi', and the shifts in point of view. But little attention has been paid to the overall architecture of the material. The twelve chapters can be grouped in threes: Chapters I–IV take the action from the alleyways of Pin's home town to his escape from prison and his rescue by Cugino; Chapters V–VIII change the scene, introducing Pin to the woodland setting of the partisan camp; Chapters IX–XII begin with another shift of perspective in the appearance of Kim and Ferriera, then move to the climax of Dritto's and Giglia's lovemaking while the battle rages 'offstage', and this 'Iliad' of battle is then followed by Pin's 'Odyssey' back to the spiders' nests. Within these three major sections there is also careful, alternating structuring of the material. Chapter I is static in scene, introducing both everyday life in the *carrugio* and the arrival of 'Comitato', the activist whose advice to the men to form their own GAP (Gruppo di Azione Patriottica) will set in motion the whole chain of events; by contrast, Chapter II has more movement, narrating Pin's theft and concealment of the pistol. In Chapter III again the action remains in one place (the prison), while Chapter IV contains the dramatic escape; Chapter V is lively in recounting Pin's arrival at the hut in the woods and his vision of the arrival of the motley crew of partisans, while Chapter VI instead is once more static, giving us backgound detail of the most important characters: Dritto, Pelle, the four Calabrians, Zena-il-Lungo. Chapter VII is the dramatic account of the hut exploding in fire and the evacuation, while in Chapter VIII the partisans again are stationary in their new camp, offering their (eccentric) views on the causes of the war. In the last third of the novel, we again find that alternation between static and dynamic chapters: after the speculations of Kim (Chapter IX) comes the partisan battle and the lovemaking of Dritto and Giglia (Chapter X); and after the sedentary discussions about the future of the band in Chapter XI we reach the dramatic final chapter recounting Pin's return home and the vengeance exacted on his sister by Cugino. Alternating contrasts, which Milanini (1990, 62) sees as the structural principle underlying the 1950s trilogy, are clearly already at work in this first novel.

Even within chapters there is careful, symmetrical organisation: Chapter I opens with the description of the sun's rays slanting down the *carrugio* and Pin shouting insults at its inhabitants, and ends in the same alley but with Pin in isolation in the gathering darkness. Chapter X is also symmetrical, beginning with speculation on whether the blankets the men carry into battle with them will keep them warm the following evening or be their bloodied shroud, but it ends with another blanket, the one under which Dritto and Giglia are making love while the partisans open fire. Chapter I ends on a topos of closure (night), as does Chapter VI (Zena closing his book and blowing out the lantern to go to sleep), Chapter VII (Dritto leading the men away from the burning hut as in a retreat), Chapter XI (Pin escaping and Dritto being led away for execution) and of course the final chapter (Pin going off into the night hand in hand with Cugino). Calvino provides a particularly effective, understated ending to the revenge killing scene, when the three Calabrians force the two Fascist spies to dig a tomb for Marchese and also for themselves: 'Then the others leave the brothers-in-law standing there with their bared heads and their cocked pistols; and the mist comes up, a thick mist that blurs outlines and muffles sounds' (I, 81; *The Path*, 113). Other chapters close more dramatically: Pin being arrested and seeing the German sailor pointing an accusing finger at him (Chapter I); the bombing of Dritto's home town (Chapter VIII); Chapter III and V end with Lupo Rosso's slogans, but are separated by the ending of Chapter IV with Cugino's hendecasyllabic leitmotif: 'la guerra è tutta colpa delle donne' (I, 54; *The Path*, 85). However much filtered through the naive perspective of Pin, the author even in this first novel clearly used a logical, rational scheme for organising the varied matter of the text: though no visual diagram survives, such as those for *Invisible Cities* or *If on a Winter's Night a Traveller* (II, 1360, 1394–5), it is clear from this careful architecture that Calvino had a precise plan of the structure of the novel during its composition.

The most controversial area for discussion of the novel's structure has been the awkward status of Chapter IX, in which the commissar Kim, an intellectual, and the military commandant, Ferriera the worker, arrive to deal with the problems in Dritto's camp. Calvino himself admitted in the 1964 Preface that he felt that the chapter disrupted the stylistic unity of the whole in order to provide the ideological message that would otherwise have been impossible to convey through Pin's perspective (I, 1189; *The Path*, 12–13). In fact the simplistic discussions about the causes of the war in Chapter VIII (Carabiniere blames the students; Mancino the bourgeoisie; Cugino women) do lead naturally into the more sophisticated analyses of Kim in the next chapter, and it is worth adding that these are also anticipated both by Giacinto's naive definition of Communism (Chapter VIII), and by the contrast between the flawed commissar and commandant of Chapter VIII (Dritto and Giacinto) and the upright ones of Chapter IX. One of the main aims of Chapter IX is to emphasise that Calvino does not embrace a Manichaean view of the antifascist struggle; for him the same kind of men make up both sides, and it takes very little for one to opt for one side or the other, as is evident in the case of Miscèl il francese, Pelle and Pin. Kim is described as having a tremendous desire for logic, clarity and serenity, always wanting to divide things up into *a*, *b*, *c*, yet in the middle of this paragraph he acknowledges that there is a crucial 'dark area' where individual choices assume collective significance, and this can lead to monstrous deviations. Similarly when explaining to Ferriera what motivates men to fight, he divides them logically into groups, *a*, *b*, *c* (the peasants, the workers, the students); nevertheless when he is on his own, Kim's logic starts to cloud over, he is not serene (I, 142–3), and his conclusion is that men take sides for obscure not clear reasons: 'We all have a secret wound which we are fighting to avenge' (I, 109; *The Path*, 143). The whole chapter revolves around a dialectic between clarity and confusion, and although its last words sound a note of clarity: 'Kim is serene. "A, b, c", he'll say. Again and again he thinks: "I love you, Adriana." That, and that alone, is History' (I, 111; *The Path*, 146), nevertheless the rest of the chapter suggests that this certainty will again shift dialectically into uncertainty. Despite the author's admission of the ideological nature of this chapter, that stress on serenity chimes in with the young writer's own aspirations at the time: as he puts it in a letter to his friend Eugenio Scalfari, written on 3 January 1947 soon after completing the work, *The Path* is 'un romanzo terribilmente mio, una rischiosa aspirazione di serenità (a novel that is horrendously my own, with its dangerous aspirations towards serenity)' (quoted in Deidier, 1995, 20).

As for characters, Calvino's predilection for doubles has been noted (Ponti, 1991; Milanini, 1990): Pin's prostitute sister, la Nera, has a double in the less than lily-white Giglia; Pin is parallel to the traitor Pelle, the only one to discover the pistol hidden in the spiders' nests; Lupo Rosso is comparable to the other loner Cugino; Dritto, the defeatist leader, is contrasted with the outstanding Baleno; Kim the medical student with the worker Ferriera; but there are no facile contrasts between partisans and Fascists. Yet there are many other oppositions: Lupo Rosso's slogans are contrasted with Mancino's; Lupo is also contrasted with Pelle, the other young loner, who is interested not just in arms, but also in women and the spiders' nests; Dritto and Giacinto are compared unfavourably with the other commandant and commissar, Ferriera and Kim; Pin is contrasted with Lupo Rosso, who is also only a boy; and of course there is a contrast between the 'omone' Cugino, and the 'omino', Mancino. There is a clear link in terms of nomenclature between Pin and Kim (their monosyllabic names, as Weiss (1993) suggests, probably derive from other famous child protagonists, such as Huck and Tom, as well as the more explicit models, Collodi's Pinocchio and Kipling's Kim): both are observers, one naive, one sophisticated, but in the end neither of them change or develop.

Calvino's penchant for dialectical contrast is apparent even within individual characters: Pin is a boy-man; the German sailor has a 'fleshy bottom, like a woman's' (I, 7; *The Path*, 33), and 'a shy nature, deep down, like a girl's' (I, 16; *The Path*, 43); even a minor character like the German officer has a 'baby-like face' (I, 27; *The Path*, 55); and Giglia's man's shirt is mentioned several times (I, 59, 114, 121; *The Path*, 90, 149, 156). These antitheses extend at times to places: the prison is an ex-villa (I, 32; *The Path*, 61), and the idyllic countryside is invaded by memories of the squalid city (I, 88–9; *The Path*, 121). Calvino's fondness for contrasts and symmetries pervades every aspect of the novel.

In psychological terms, the characters are deliberately superficial. As the author admitted, he had deformed his one-time companions into expressionist caricatures (I, 1190; *The Path*, 13), mostly by developing these into leitmotifs which he repeatedly applies to each of them: Cugino's grotesque fountain-mask face (Chapters IV, V, VIII, XI), and his huge hand, warm and soft, which 'seems made of bread' (*Path*, 85), used both the first time he rescues Pin in Chapter IV, and the second time, at the very end of the novel (*Path*, 184); Lupo Rosso's shaven head and Russian beret (Chapters III, V, XI); Dritto's lowered eyelids and constant complaints of being ill (Chapters V, VI, VII, IX, X, XI); Pelle's permanently cold and cracked lips (Chapters VI, IX, XII); Duca's irascibility symbolised by his huge Austrian pistol (Chapters VI, VIII, X); Zena's laziness (Chapters VI, VIII, XI). Even minor characters who only appear once or twice have their 'epic' epithet: Pietromagro's yellow eyes and black beard (Chapters I, IV), the Southern sentry with the badly shaven cheeks (Chapters IV, VI). But no characters have positive or even neutral physical characteristics except Kim and Ferriera: the former is thin, always nervously biting his moustache, the latter stout with a small white beard and clear, cold eyes.

The descriptions of Pin are the most significant for the import of the entire novel. His freckles are often mentioned (Chapters I, II, III, IX), as are his constant shouts, cries, insults (Chapters I, II, III, VI, XI) and songs (Chapters I, VII, X, XI). But more important is the very first description of him as wearing a man's jacket that is too big for him (I, 5; *The Path*, 31), symbolising his unsuccessful integration with the adult world. A 'bambino vecchio', he is fascinated by the things that characterise grown-ups: wine, women, song, violence. The computerised concordance of the novel (Alinei, 1973), despite Calvino's ironic allusion to it in *Se una notte d'inverno* (II, 795–6; *If on a Winter's Night*, 187), does confirm illustrative lexical trends. The adjective applied most to Pin is 'solo': of the eighty-eight occurrences of the adjective, no fewer than thirty-six refer to Pin (five to Cugino, three to Pelle, two to Kim, two to Lupo Rosso, one to Miscèl francese). The solitude of the hero, typical of fairy tales and of Conrad's narratives, is evident in Calvino's first novel (Falcetto, 1988). Pin thinks he is the friend but is in fact the plaything of the adults, but he is equally unable to play with children his own age. Sex and violence are constantly used to characterise the adult world: in his sister's bedroom the adults hit and embrace each other naked (I, 16; *The Path*, 43); but animals are referred to in the same way, killing and coupling, thus are equally repulsive to him (I, 24; *The Path*, 53); Pin's desire to kill is like a distant desire to love, like smoke and wine (I, 71; *The Path*, 102); sexual desire and bloodlust are 'common to all grown-ups' (I, 78; *The Path*, 110). When defecating, Pin thinks of men and women chasing each other or prisoners being killed, and later he thinks of 'the rest of humanity, male and female, rubbing themselves against each other on the ground, others attacking and killing' (I, 122–3; *The Path*, 159). His final fantasy, also violent and sexual, is of killing the German captain who is his sister's current boyfriend, and of Giglia allowing him to touch her breasts (I, 140; *The Path*, 176). For Pin sex and violence are always linked, and are both attractive and repulsive to him at the same time.

The character Pin also allows Calvino to solve the neorealist problem of the ethical message, for moralising can be avoided by filtering views on adult behaviour through the child focaliser. The condemnation of the men's cowardice in reneging on setting up a GAP is undercut by linking it to the child's concept of games: 'Grown ups are an untrustworthy treacherous lot, they don't take their games in the serious whole-hearted way children do' (I, 22; *The Path*, 50). This recurrent *gioco/serio* antithesis, which is one of the most important thematic contrasts in the novel, probably derives from another intertextual source, the Great Game (of war and espionage) in Kipling's *Kim*, as do many other motifs such as poverty, friendship, songs. Although *gioco* and its cognates are used occasionally of innocent child games such as hide-and-seek, it is mostly used in more sinister contexts: Pelle's game which has death as its stake, Miscèl's 'doppio gioco' and the partisan leaders playing a cat and mouse game with Dritto. It occurs twice in Chapter IX, again suggesting that the chapter is not as extraneous as even the author claimed: Ferriera will play games of cunning and daring in his mountains, and Kim argues that to kill a German requires a game of mental transposition so complex it addles the brain.

Pin's point of view permits other ways of understating the critique of the men's actions: when Miscèl francese deserts and decides to join the Fascists, Pin does not condemn him for his treachery, he is simply 'annoyed with Michel, not because he thinks Michel has behaved badly and become a traitor. What annoys Pin is getting it wrong every time and never being able to foresee what grown-ups will do next' (I, 31–2; *The Path*, 60). The questions of good and evil can thus be deliberately attenuated and reduced, in Pin's perspective, to the level of consistency in games and predictability. Instead of being categorised as good or bad, at most adults are criticised for being 'ambiguous', though the adjective is always linked to another negative adjective such as 'incomprehensible' (used of all men five times), 'treacherous', 'distant': the men in the tavern are 'ambiguous and treacherous' (I, 22; *The Path*, 56), 'ambiguous and incomprehensible' (I, 52; *The Path*, 82), all adults are 'ambiguous and lying' (I, 63; *The Path*, 94), and even the partisans are 'ambiguous and stand-offish' (I, 132; *The Path*, 168) and even more incomprehensible than the men in the tavern, with their desire to kill and make love (I, 132; *The Path*, 168). In any case Pin has no time for good people: 'Pin has always been embarrassed by good people' (I, 56; *The Path*, 86); 'Pin is not used to dealing with people who are good' (I, 140; *The Path*, 177). Even the few mentions of Mussolini are devoid of moral overtones, always occurring in comic or ironic contexts: first in a quotation of a Fascist song in Chapter III (I, 32; *The Path*, 61), then when Lupo Rosso explains that he will put a 'Mussolini helmet' on the guard in Chapter IV (I, 42; *The Path*, 72), and finally in the comic discussion on who caused the war in Chapter VIII (I, 92–4; *The Path*, 124–6).

This conscious pursuit of understatement is confirmed by the careful use of morally loaded terms. *Tradire* and its cognates are used several times of both men and women: five times, appropriately, of the traitor Pelle, twice of Cugino's wife, once of la Nera, once of Giglia. By contrast, just before Miscèl's treacherous decision to join the Fascists, it is twice stressed that Pin will not betray the men of the tavern. Thus only the adults are treacherous, not Pin, and their treachery embraces both sex and war. Similarly with the adjective *buono/a*: it is used three times of Cugino; once of Comitato as the only good man in the tavern; once of Dritto when he is teaching Pin to clean the guns; Pelle predictably is described as 'not a good comrade'; but Pin cannot decide whether Mancino and Giglia are good or not; a land where everyone is good is a utopia imagined by Pin, but there is also the more realistic thought in Pin's mind that men are a mixture of something repulsive and something good. *Bravo/a* is used once of the political prisoners, twice of Cugino, once of Dritto, once of Lupo Rosso, and three times on the last page to describe the mothers of Pin and Cugino. *Cattivo/a* is used six times of Pin himself, three times of Pelle (and of Dritto's teeth!), once of the German sailor, once of la Nera, and parallel to Pin's fantasy about a land where everyone is good, Kim dreams about a world in which men will not be bad.

The haphazard nature of men's decisions to become Fascists or partisans, stressed by Kim, is also crucial in undercutting moral judgments and is symbolised by the vicissitudes of the pistol stolen by Pin. The gun, which originally belonged to the German sailor, was removed in la Nera's bedroom by Pin who then hides it in the spiders' nests. Pelle later steals it, and returns it to Pin's sister; in the last chapter Pin takes it from la Nera again, gives it to Cugino who kills her with it (presumably in the place where it was first stolen, the bedroom), and then returns it to Pin. The P.38 thus moves from the Nazis to the as yet uncommitted boy, then to the Fascist double agent, then back to the boy who now has partisan experience, before becoming the weapon of execution by a partisan, and finally being restored definitively to Pin. The passing of arms from side to side is part of the reality of war, but particularly part of its celebration in literature, as Calvino says of Ariosto's *Orlando furioso* and of Fenoglio's *Una questione privata* (I, 1202; *The Path*, 27).

Through Pin we are shown that the real centre of the book is the adolescent's difficult initiation into adult life. Pin requires a father figure, a friend, someone who will be interested not so much in women as in the place where the spiders make their nests: one day he will find a true friend and he will tell him, and only him, where the nests are (I, 23; *The Path*, 51–2). Time and again he fantasises about going off with one of the adults to perform heroic deeds, usually with the repeated formula 'E' bello' (or 'E' una cosa bellissima'), but each time he is let down: he imagines Comitato leading him against the Germans (I, 22; *The Path*, 51), then rescuing him from them (I, 28; *The Path*, 56–7); he fantasises about joining the Fascists, telling them about the spiders' nests, then all going to his sister's place to drink, smoke and watch her dance (I, 29; *The Path*, 58); he dreams about going around with Lupo Rosso: 'sarebbe bello andare in banda con Lupo Rosso' (I, 37; *The Path*, 67); later he thinks: 'è una cosa bellissima stare insieme a Lupo Rosso, non c'è differenza tra il gioco e la vita' (I, 46; *The Path*, 76); but he decides Lupo is too serious, and resolves not to tell him about the spiders' nests (I, 47; *The Path*, 77); at one stage he even finds it 'bello' to peel potatoes with Mancino and Giglia (I, 63; *The Path*, 94); then he decides that Pelle is the long-sought friend, who knows evrything about women, pistols and spiders' nests (I, 73; *The Path*, 105); later he finds cleaning pistols with Dritto to be 'una cosa bellissima' (I, 90; *The Path*, 123). But in each case Pin's hopes are deceived: Comitato never reappears, Lupo Rosso abandons Pin, Mancino and Giglia are untrustworthy, Pelle betrays the partisans and Dritto is led away to be shot. In the final chapter the identity of his real friend is revealed, still using the same formula: 'E' bellissimo aver trovato il Cugino . . . Cugino è il Grande amico tanto cercato, quello che s'interessa ai nidi di ragno' (I, 146; *The Path*, 184). Even here there is a moment of hesitation when Cugino asks for la Nera's address: Pin would have preferred him not to be interested in women, but he sees that Cugino is like all men; disillusioned, he would not mind if Cugino were killed, for he is now no longer 'il Grande Amico' (I, 146–7; *The Path*, 184). However, when Cugino returns after killing his sister, merely telling Pin he was repelled by the idea of having sex with her, Pin concludes: 'E' davvero il Grande Amico' (I, 147; *The Path*, 184).

Pin is also used as the filter for descriptions of nature. These are never idyllic, except for one brief moment in the mountains, when he is sent for water or firewood to the stream or the forest: there he sees unusually coloured mountain butterflies, wild strawberries, yellow-brown mushrooms, red spiders on invisible webs, young hares all ears and legs. However, this does not last – all it needs is for Mancino to curse him 'to draw Pin back into the squalid, ambiguous world of human beings' (I, 88–9; *The Path*, 121). This is a unique passage since every other animal mentioned in the book is either repulsive or aggressive: spiders, frogs, lizards, falcons. That is also the reason why the novel ends on the mention of the fireflies, since they resolve this dichotomy by being both repellent close up and beautiful from a distance. There are few lyrical passages, mostly because Calvino finds it impossible to write poetically about his own landscape except when it is infested by the violence of war (I, 1188–9; *The Path*, 11–12). The two areas of nature and the adult world are linked by a number of passages: when first mentioned, frogs are said to be 'smooth and naked as women' (I, 14; *The Path*, 41), and the link is enforced at their last mention, when Pin's sister is described as 'that hairy frog' (I, 146; *The Path*, 184); and since Pin has fantasised about killing a frog with his pistol in Chapter II, that is in a sense what happens in Chapter XII when Cugino kills la Nera. The natural and animal world are never otiose elements in this or any other Calvino novel.

In stylistic terms, *The Path*, like other neorealist texts, contains dialect and regional words (*beudo*, *smiccia*), folksongs, technical terms (*sten*, *gap*, *sim*, etc.), and the expressionist techniques of description outlined above. It also deploys imagery consistent with Pin's world-view, and a dialogic style reminiscent of Vittorini deriving from their common model Hemingway (Ponti, 1991). The computer analysis of the text shows that there is an abundance of strong, expressionist terms (*grugno*, *guercio*, *muso*, *narici*, *zazzera*), as well as many words for 'allegria', 'ridere', 'scherzare' – these latter epitomising the text's stylistic brio and the author's fondness for contrasting emotions which emerges elsewhere, for instance his citing of Ungaretti's famous title, *Allegria di naufragi* (III, 875).

Re (1990) and other critics have established the broader stylistic implications of this novel. Despite its precocity, the work is already a sophisticated, self-conscious text in its concern with language (Pin is confused but fascinated by terms such as *comitato*, *sim*, *gap*, *sten*, etc.), in its techniques of defamiliarisation (the codes of partisan novel and fairy tale are constantly alternated), and in its mannerist narrations (both the introduction of Lupo Rosso and his escape with Pin from prison have the flavour of boys' adventure albums, while Lupo's account of Pelle's execution is a verbal equivalent of *film-noir* killings). Everything is seen, even the opening street scene, through the limited, distorting filter of Pin's gaze, and is narrated in the present tense, thus collapsing the distinction between routine and significant events, again consistent with Pin's perspective; even the superficial, expressionist character descriptions can be linked to the protagonist's viewpoint.

The recurrence of fairy-tale elements means that the *fiaba* is the other main narrative code adopted throughout: Re (1990, 202–5) details at least twenty-one of Propp's functions in the tale, such as absence of parents, appearance of the helper, the magic talisman, etc. Benussi (1989) mentions the three tasks Pin has to accomplish (steal the pistol, escape from prison, return home). Similarly, Lucente (1986) notes the fairy-tale motif of the orphan child and of the women either being idealised, barred (the dead mothers of Pin and Cugino discussed at the end) or evil (Nera and Giglia). But there are many other folk-tale elements: in the very first chapter there is a self-reflexive allusion to the nature of the whole novel, when Pin's stories are defined as 'fables the grown-ups tell amongst themselves' (I, 10; *The Path*, 38). There is also the 'scenario incantato' of the villa transformed into a prison (I, 37; *The Path*, 61), the fantasy about leaving cherry stones so that Lupo will find him (I, 51; *The Path*, 81), Cugino's huge boots which he has worn for the last seven years (I, 58; *The Path*, 89), Mancino's resemblance to a little gnome living in the hut in the woods (I, 57; *The Path*, 88), Giglia's role as a fallen Snow White (I, 60; *The Path*, 90–1), the motif of the partisans resembling an army lost in the forest like something out of Ariosto (I, 64; *The Path*, 95), the direct reference to the fairy tale when Pin imagines following the revived falcon to a magic land where everyone is good (I, 123; *The Path*, 159), the old, rural couple with the goats who offer Pin shelter like Ovid's Baucis and Philemon (I,

140; *The Path*, 176–7), Pin's appearance as shepherd boy looking for a lost sheep (I, 140–1; *The Path*, 177), and when he finally returns to the spiders' nests, the area is described as a 'posto magico' (I, 141; *The Path*, 177), the pistol is like a wand and Cugino who has magically reappeared is like a great wizard (I, 144; *The Path*, 181). Generally what these motifs do is to point up the author's consciousness of genre, to render the text more self-conscious by mingling two opposite codes, the war story and the *fiaba*, or, as he says in the later preface, mixing Hemingway's *For Whom the Bell Tolls* and Stevenson's *Treasure Island* (I, 1196; *The Path*, 20).

In a number of ways Calvino's first novel is a left-wing homage to Stevenson's masterpiece: Mancino's tattoos are obscene versions of the old sea captain's nautical ones; Mancino himself, the cook, is a politicised version of the ship's cook, Long John Silver, while his pet falcon, Babeuf, is named after an anarchist hero of the French Revolution, as Silver's parrot, Cap'n Flint, derives his name from an infamous pirate; the partisans are rough diamonds, like the rum crew aboard the *Hispaniola*; Pin's songs are political equivalents of the old sea shanties quoted in *Treasure Island*. But the crucial reference amongst all these elements of fairytale is the explicit one which suggests that a land where everyone is good is a fairy-tale utopia (literally no place), and that the real world inhabited by Pin and the others is one in which the only good people are those who kill, like Cugino and Lupo (I, 53–4; *The Path*, 84). The seeds of Calvino's later utopian concerns are already here.

Recent criticism has alerted us to the intertextual significance of Pin's song about Godea in Chapter VII: like Godea's son, the Oedipal Pin returns from war to cause the death of his sister (Re, 1990; Milanini, 1990; Pedriali, 1998). But in addition all three songs mentioned in the first chapter have an intertextual function, and are thus not merely elements of local colour: the prison song anticipates Pin's time in prison; the old anarchist song *Torna Caserio* alludes to the political violence of the action to follow; Pin's obscene song is linked to the erotic activity of his sister, la Nera.

This is, then, a composite text, but the plot is 'not meaningful in any unified sense' (Lucente, 1986, 270) because it never resolves the problem of how to live without other men or women. Re (1990) sees it as an open text, of which no totalising reading is possible, as the novel continually estranges each narrative code that it employs: history may be the subject, but the *fiaba* is the narrative mode. The reader is invited to pass from surface reticence to the significance of Pin's (and our own) emergence over what Conrad called the shadow line (Re, 1990; Milanini, 1990; Ponti, 1991). Although because of the composite nature of the text no single reading is possible, it is clear from the above that the story is primarily about Pin's 'iniziazione mancata' (Milanini, 1990, 19). It is significant that the novel ends at a point before maturity, underscoring the parallel between Pin and the men, who are also portrayed at the point before achieving political maturity – not for nothing did Calvino send a copy of the 1964 edition of the novel to Paolo Spriano with the Pavesian dedication 'Precedendoti nella maturità' (Scarpa, 1993).

However, I would argue that the epic code plays as important a role as history and the fairy tale in this composite text. For all its attempts to underplay the seriousness of its thematics, the novel is intended – in a paradoxical way, typical of the author – as both a modest and yet epic account of the Resistance. In twelve chapters, like the twelve books of the *Aeneid*, it narrates Pin's involvement in the Iliad of war and the Odyssey of his return home. This epic aspiration is confirmed both by the epic leitmotifs attached to the characters and by Calvino's references to Homer's relevance to the Resistance at the time of the composition of the novel. On 15 September 1946, when just beginning the book, he wrote a crucial article 'Omero antimilitarista' in *l'Unità* (*S*, 2118–19) in which he argued the Marxist line that the *Iliad* represents the criticism of the troops against the officers' arrogant quarrels, and the *Odyssey* portrays the problematic return that awaits all soldiers and partisans. In another article, of 1 December 1946, the month in which the bulk of the novel was written, he claimed that the proletariat did not need the bourgeois theatre, as they had a more epic mentality consonant with the victorious period through which it was living (*S*, 2139). He is also aware of the Homeric qualities in his favourite author, Conrad, as he mentions in his university thesis, written in 1946–47 (thesis, p. 141). In the same period (1945–46) he contributed to a collective volume about the partisan war with the antithetical title *L'epopea dell'esercito scalzo* (Milanini, 1997, 175, n. 5). Later in December 1948 he would write another important article, 'Saremo come Omero' (*S*, 1483–7), in which he would articulate the aspiration of contemporary writers to achieve an epic 'coralità realistica e storica' (*S*, 1485). Similarly in the 1964 preface to *The Path*, he would define his own novel as a 'collective epic' (I, 1194; *The Path,* 18), and align it with other postwar 'fragmentary epics' of the Resistance (I, 1201; *The Path,* 27). The epic aspects of the Resistance were present in a paradoxically understated way in Calvino's first novel and were acknowledged in his theoretical essays.

Even one of the explicitly nominated intertexts, Aleksander Fadeev's *The Rout* (I, 1195; *The Path,* 19), was seen by Calvino, in an essay written in 1947, as being more epic than documentary:

> It has something of the flavour of an epic poem, all cavalry charges, unsaddling opponents, battles, solitude and human problems; and all around this is a taste for the marvels of landscape, woods and marshes, trunks of bethel trees, squirrels and birds. . . . Far from being portrayed as models of discipline and virtue, the partisans are studied in all their colourful liveliness, in their numbing and shapeless resentments. And their commander, Levinson, is a man who wants to be a new man, but who still contains within him the burden and uncertainty of a hidden crisis. (*S*, 1309–11 (1310))

Most of this passage could in fact be a definition of Calvino's own first novel.

However, there is a problem of compatibility between a realistic novel about partisans and an epic tone. The more modern epic of Ariosto, already one of Calvino's favourite authors, helped resolve that contradiction. We have already seen that the movement of weapons across enemy lines and the motif of the partisans marooned in the forest derive from this classic text, and Pelle's twin obsessions of 'armi e donne', apart from symbolising the two themes of sex and violence which inform the novel, are to be found in the famous first line of the *Orlando furioso* (itself a rewrite of the first line of the *Aeneid*: 'Arma virumque cano'): 'Le donne, i cavalieri, l'armi, gli amori'. This link between the partisan epic and Ariosto is explicitly made by Calvino in the case of Fenoglio's *Una questione privata* (I, 1202).

Lastly let us return to the two contemporary short fictions mentioned at the outset of this chapter as shedding crucial contextual light on the aims and achievements of *The Path*. 'Ultimo viene il corvo', written in the same month as the novel, is also a present-tense narration about a young boy who encounters partisans and is initiated from the world of 'natura' to that of 'storia', though Pin, like all the characters in the novel, is a more flawed character by comparison with the unnamed boy of the short story. These two boys are the first child protagonists in Calvino's fiction, and it is likely that the success of the one in making the *racconto* work encouraged the author to try the formula out in a full-scale novel. But despite the many similarities between this story and the novel, the other tale written at this time, 'Cinque dopodomani: guerra finita!' seems even more relevant. Published on 7 November 1946, a month before completing the novel, it contains many parallels: the foul-mouthed cook, the undisciplined, lice-infested Italian partisans, coughing from the damp wood they lazily burn, and the contrast between them and the Russian group who escaped from Briga where they had worked as German prisoners on the fortifications. The comparison between the Russian and Italian partisans is in a key sequence in the short story:

> [The Italian partisans are] people who don't wash, are lice-ridden, go about in rags, quarrel amongst themselves, don't understand why they are on this side and not on the other, and yet they fight to the death, full of frenzy. The Russians are a world of *serenity, they have* already *decided everything*, and now know how to *fight the war*, and continue to do so *with enthusiasm* and hatred *and method*, but without surrendering themselves to its violence. (III, 846, my italics)

But there are important differences between this passage and the corresponding passage in the novel: 'The Soviets are *serene, they have decided everything*, and *are now fighting the war with passion and method*, not because war is a fine thing, but because it is necessary' (I, 108; *The Path,* 142; my italics). The omission of *odio* in this sentence in the novel also shows to what extent Calvino attenuated polemical details, but the insistence on how easy it was for Italians to fight on one side or the other and the 'furore' inside them illustrates how central this theme was to the novel. In an analogous way the novel distances itself from the events by never specifying place names: Briga becomes merely 'the border area' (I, 111; *The Path,* 146). But there is the same character Aleksej, an engineering student, son of a mujik, who always shouts 'sale e tabacchi' and 'cinque dopodomani' ('five days after tomorrow'); there is the fascination with the hybrid language that evolved amongst the men ('luki luki' meaning to look, 'comsí comsà' to steal, 'retura' to return – once again the *Odyssey* theme), similar to Pin's fascination with language. In another episode in the story, the narrator and another Russian go for heat and food to an old couple in the mountains, who at a certain point get down on their knees to say the rosary – this episode is recycled in Chapter XII of the novel when Pin arrives at the old couple's house. The Sicilian cook's song, however sentimental, was the song of all partisans, no matter their contry of origin, and it united them all in nostalgia for the return home (the character of the cook and the songs are important in the novel). The last paragraph of the story tells proleptically how Aleksej did eventually return home after all his 'dopodomani': 'he eventually made the good day after tomorrow come, the one when he finally left the mountains' – again this proleptic 'happy ending' is not permitted in the novel which is written mostly from Pin's limited point of view.

Calvino's first novel stands out as a largely successful neorealist fiction, but it was not without its flaws: Salman Rushdie noted that although *The Path to the Spiders' Nests* had 'one of the great titles in 20th-century literature, . . . the last sentence appears to have dipped its feet in slush' (Rushdie, 1981, 16). But the rest of Rushdie's review proves that Calvino was soon to learn how to write more effective final sentences. The subsequent editorial vicissitudes of Calvino's first novel also shed light on its achievements and limitations. Published in October 1947, it won the Premio Riccione that year and sold 6,000 copies, an unusually high level of sales for the time. But the author soon turned his back on his first book as he modified his early neorealist poetics, and only authorised a re-edition in 1954. A whole decade later, in 1964, as he prepared to abandon realism altogether and embark on the fictions that were to make him internationally famous, Calvino went back to his first book and authorised a third, definitive edition. And this time, to accompany the novel he composed a preface which remains his most substantial and revealing self-commentary, as well as an indispensable analysis of Italian neorealism.

Despite its length, however, the preface makes no explicit mention of the substantial changes that Calvino made in the text of both the 1954 and 1964 editions: in both cases he excised or toned down certain passages depicting Cugino's and Pin's antifeminism, Mancino's political extremism, as well as some violent details (see Chapter 10). However, reading between the lines we can see that there is a hint of these changes, when the author criticises the youthful extremism of the novel in its exaggerated emphasis on sex, violence, political ideology and expressionist characters, and then adds: 'The uneasiness this book caused me for so long has, in part, been attenuated; in part, it remains' (I, 1190; *The Path*, 14). Only late in life and nearly twenty years after writing the preface did Calvino explicitly acknowledge the changes and their motivation (see Chapter 10, p. 151).

Calvino's 1964 preface provides a typical sample of his elegant essay writing, and allows us a glimpse of how he matured as a writer in the two decades between the 1940s and the 1960s. It displays some typically Calvinian symmetries and dialectics. Consisting of twelve sections like the twelve chapters of the novel, the first section deals with external elements of the context in which the book emerged (the anonymous oral tradition of narrative in postwar Italy as people were allowed to speak freely again and recount their adventures); the second with the book's Italian literary ancestry (Verga, Vittorini, Pavese). This alternation between external and literary elements informs the whole preface: the next three sections return to non-literary factors (the question of commitment), while the two central ones establish international literary influences (Hemingway, Russian writers, Stevenson). Finally Calvino returns to other external factors (the discussions with 'Kim', his own meditations on violence, his identification with Pin), before concluding with further literary discussion (of Fenoglio and of the cost of writing one's first novel). The main emphasis thus falls on this favourite dialectic between lived experience and literary texts: even the young bourgeois Calvino's desire to prove to his partisan comrades that he 'could cope' ('all'altezza della situazione' (I, 1199; *The Path*, 24) – a phrase that recurs often, for example in *S*, 2917) has a literary antecedence as it is the phrase he continually used of Conrad's heroes as well (*S*, 39, 43, 815 etc.). The other ideas stressed in the preface are the young author's feelings of 'remorse' (mentioned no less than six times) at having deformed the physical and psychological features of men with whom he shared the risk of death, and his unease not just with the themes of sex and violence but also with his exacerbated treatment of them. The preface ends with an insistence on how one's first novel defines and, by de-fining, limits the writer. But if the novel's conclusion is rather anodyne (Pedriali, 1998), the more mature preface ends with one of those elegant Calvinian paradoxes that are typical of the writer at the peak of his powers: 'A completed book will never compensate me for what I destroyed in writing it: namely that experience which if preserved throughout the years of my life might have helped to compose my last book, and which in fact was sufficient only to write the first' (I, 1204; *The Path*, 30).

Calvino had written his first novel at the age of twenty-three, in a few weeks in December 1946. But when it came to writing the follow-up novel to *The Path*, like other writers, Calvino was to find the second novel even more difficult to write than the first. The crisis was also due to the fact that after the electoral defeat of the Left in 1948, to continue to adopt a non-hagiographic approach to the Resistance and its values would have meant running the risk of seeming to have changed sides (Milanini 1997). Calvino's incapacity to produce a satisfactory 'socialist' novel, notably in the failed experiments of *Il bianco veliero* (1947–49) and of *I giovani del Po* (January 1950–July 1951), led to the first of a few but significant moments of creative block in his literary career. Confirmation of the crisis of the late 1940s is to be found in the words that introduced the short story 'Pesci grossi, pesci piccoli' in the journal *Inventario* (Autumn 1950). There he discusses the difficulties of writing now compared with the youthful élan of his first narratives: that early work has defined him too much and he feels constrained, whereas 'Pesci grossi' represents an area in which he moves with greater ease, an area which deals with 'encounters with elements of nature and human beings, attitudes that hover between confidential secrecy and reserve, between compassion and ruthlessness' (I, 1267–8). Even at this early stage of his literary career Calvino takes stock of his own limitations as a writer: what he really wants to achieve now is to represent 'rounded, adult characters [and] genuine female characters' (I, 1269). By the end of the 1940s Calvino was in crisis as he reached this impasse, and only by writing the kind of book he wanted to write was he able to obviate this obstacle and rediscover himself as a writer of fantasy. The protracted genesis of the slight novella of urban realism, *I giovani del Po* was followed immediately by his rapid writing of *Il visconte dimezzato* (*The Cloven Viscount)* in a few weeks at the end of the summer of 1951. As we shall see, his periods of creative crisis always turned out to be the prelude to a dazzlingly original resolution.

Chapter 3

From Neorealism to Fantasy

Our Ancestors

After two prolonged but unsuccessful attempts at writing a second novel between 1947 and 1951 – *Il bianco veliero* (*The White Schooner*) (1947–49) and *I giovani del Po* (*Youth in Turin*) (1950–51) took respectively two years and eighteen months to write – Calvino turned in the summer of 1951 to writing the kind of book he 'would have liked to read' (I, 1307), and between July and September 1951 completed *Il visconte dimezzato* (*The Cloven Viscount*) which was published the following year. Subsequently Calvino would go on to write *Il barone rampante* (*The Baron in the Trees*) in 1957 and *Il cavaliere inesistente* (*The Non-Existent Knight*) in 1959, before collecting all three novels into the trilogy *I nostri antenati* (*Our Ancestors*), published in 1960. The problems encountered in writing *I giovani del Po* are crucial to an understanding of the thematics of *The Cloven Viscount*, so the author's own testimony is worth quoting at length:

> My objective [in *I giovani del Po*] was to provide an image of human integration with the world. Instead I ended up with a work that was uncharacteristically grey for me: in it the fullness of life, despite substantial discussion of it in the novel, does not come across much at all – that was why I never wanted to publish the work in book form . . . What happened next was that in the two months immediately following completion of *I giovani*, to compensate for the punishment that had been inflicted upon my imagination, I wrote *Il visconte dimezzato* (in which I also tried – in a more arbitrary and approximate manner – to write about man's mutilation and alienation and aspirations towards wholeness). It turned out, of course, to be a more amusing book compared with *I giovani del Po* which faded even more into obscurity. (III, 1342)

The theme of wholeness and integration thus subtends both Calvino's realist and fantasy works of the 1940s and 1950s.

It is, once more, instructive to begin by considering the structure of this deliberately geometrical tale. Divided into ten brief chapters, the first three recount the departure for war of the young Medardo, his severing in two by a cannonball and the return of one half to Terralba – though even in this most fantastical tale there are autobiographical elements, since 'Terralba' was the name of the villa in which Calvino's father had been born (see III, 1204). The second three detail the sadism of the Bad Half who has returned and who after the death of his father institutes a reign of terror over Terralba. Chapters VII to IX concentrate on the actions of the Good Half who also returns and tries to make amends for the mutilations inflicted by the Bad Half on humans, animals and the natural world. The final chapter tells how the two Halves fight a duel and are finally sewn together by the eccentric Dr Trelawney so that the whole Medardo can be married to the whole (and wholesome) woodland girl Pamela. It is this symmetrical structure that qualifies the story for the adjective 'geometrical' which the author applied to it (I, 1211). As in his first novel, here again there are some effective closing passages. Chapter II ends with the right half of Medardo being sewn together, and put back on his one foot, alive and cloven (I, 375; *Our Ancestors*, 10); the next ends with the death of his father, the strange bird-man Aiolfo, who dies in his bed in the huge birdcage with all his birds fluttering round and finally settling on his deathbed 'as if it were a floating tree-trunk in the midst of the sea' (I, 380; *Our Ancestors*, 14). If the grotesque details of battle in the first two chapters owe something to the paintings of Hieronymus Bosch, this closing scene of the third chapter seems a secular, literary equivalent of Giotto's Deposition of Christ in the Arena Chapel in Padua. It is also probable that here again biographical elements lurk beneath the text, since the eccentric father's name, Aiolfo, contains the same vowels as Mario Calvino's first and second names, and the author's father's capacity for imitating bird sounds is remarked upon several times in other works (see, for instance, *La strada di San Giovanni*, III, 12; *The Road to San Giovanni*, 11).

However, this superficial symmetry is complicated by some deliberately asymmetrical features. Calvino's mind, as he often admits (*S*, 217; *The Literature Machine*, 17–18; *S*, 2789), is always inclined to consider the value of opposite strategies instead of univocally adopting one approach. As in *Six Memos for the Next Millennium* he has words of praise both for rapidity and for delay in narration, both for precision and for vagueness, so here this symmetrical tale is complicated by asymmetry. This, then, is not unequivocally an allegory in praise of human wholeness, since the complete Medardo at the beginning is a naive and inept character, and the whole Medardo at the end does not inaugurate 'an era of marvellous happiness; . . . obviously a whole Viscount is not enough to make all the world whole' (I, 443; *Our Ancestors*, 71). In fact each Half makes a paradoxical speech in favour of the halved but intense existence. To confuse the issue further, the left side is the Good Half and the right side the Bad, and the book is not directly about good and evil, since both Halves are shown to be equally burdensome to the people of Terralba. The fact that both Halves pronounce a eulogy of the halved existence (I, 403, 421–2; *Our Ancestors*, 34, 51) also implies that paradoxically this half-life represents some kind of intense totality. A further hint of the complexity and literary sophistication of this superficially naive narrative resides in the allusions to signs and signifiers in the text. In the first chapter the protagonist has to have various signs decoded by his more experienced squire, Curzio: the storks rather than birds of carrion flying to the battlefield, then other 'signs' of battle, including the severed fingers which seem to point in a certain direction (I, 369), and finally on reaching the camp, the emperor and his marshals communicate by grunts rather than speech since their mouths are full of map-pins. The most spectacular instance of this motif is the grotesque system of signification used by the Bad Half in Chapter VI to communicate with Pamela: the severed remains of a bat and a jellyfish mean she has to meet him at dusk by the seashore, the cockerel tied to the top of a mulberry tree means a meeting in the woods at dawn, and so on.

Although the author claims that this is a *divertimento,* not a work with a moral message, it is not entirely without an ethical dimension and it certainly reflects the divided atmosphere of the Cold War in which it was written (I, 1209–11). The motif of returning from war to find one's home country divided in two clearly alludes to the condition in which Calvino and many other ex-partisans found themselves in the first five years after the Liberation. Not just the protagonist, but all the subjects are divided in two: Pietrochiodo the carpenter is torn between on the one hand constructing instruments of torture, for which he possesses a greater facility, and on the other devising machines beneficial to man (an allegory of the practical scientist in the nuclear age); his opposite, the eccentric Dr Trelawney, is caught between pursuing his otiose researches into will-o'-the-wisps, or a rare disease suffered by one cricket in a thousand, and curing the sick (the pure research scientist); similarly the decadent hedonism of the colony of lepers is contrasted with the work ethic of the community of Huguenots.

Falcetto has shown that a passage describing the decadent leper colony on Molokai in Stevenson's *In the South Seas* resides behind Calvino's invented leper colony (I, 1308–9), and certainly the departure of the nurse, Sebastiana, owes something to the Scottish writer's description of the departure of one of the female islanders for Molokai. But the Stevensonian roots of this novel go even deeper. The contrast between hedonist lepers and Huguenot workaholics may also have derived from the Scottish author's *Father Damien*, in which Calvino's favourite author defended the Catholic missionary from the accusations made of him by the Protestant Dr Hyde, amongst which was that of having 'contracted the disease [leprosy] from having connection with the female lepers' (Stevenson, 1922, 498), and Stevenson's mention of Captain Cook's voyages to these islands probably also inspired the figure of Dr Trelawney, who at the end of the novel rejoins Cook on his travels. The only whole and wholesome characters are the two women, the elderly nurse Sebastiana, and the young woodland girl Pamela. Finally there is the narrator, Medardo's young nephew, a boy on the verge of adolescence, who explicitly emerges in the tale only in Chapter IV: he too is caught between the role models of the good and evil halves of his uncle, as well as between wholeness and the halved existence. His sudden emergence as narrator a third of the way into the novel complicates the point of view, and his concluding remarks in the final chapter also render this more than a fairy tale. The story does possess many of the traditional fairy-tale functions (as outlined by Propp), beginning 'Once upon a time there was a war against the Turks . . .' (I, 367; *Our Ancestors*, 3), and telling us towards the end of the final chapter that Medardo married Pamela, had 'a happy life, many children and a just rule' (I, 443; *Our Ancestors*, 70). Nevertheless the narrator then adds the more realistic details that everyone's life did not become instantly marvellous, and he himself felt more lonely and incomplete, telling himself tales in the woods. He is eventually abandoned by his friend Dr Trelawney to face growing up alone 'in this world of ours full of responsibilities and will-o'-the-wisps' (I, 444; *Our Ancestors*, 71). This final page serves as a frame enclosing the narration of the story proper and suggests that the tale itself was just one of many which the narrator told himself in those woods on the verge of adolescence, a self-reflexive story about storytelling. The conclusion also confirms that, as in his first novel, so here Calvino was more interested in the process of maturing and integrating with the rest of humanity than in those who have already achieved a final good or evil status. As in *The Path to the Spiders' Nests*, any moral message is understated. Yet there is a progression: if the first novel ended with the child and adult walking hand in hand amidst the fireflies, the conclusion to *The Cloven Viscount* takes us a stage further with an adolescent facing the path to maturity alone, and the final sentence has acquired an ambiguity that avoids the 'slush' at the close of *The Path*. The second novel of the trilogy goes further still, as we shall see, portraying a full life and representing a *Bildung* that takes us from the protagonist at the age of twelve to his senility and final demise.

A letter to a Marxist critic, Carlo Salinari, of 7 August 1952 confirms some of the above interpretations. Calvino informs the critic that *Il visconte dimezzato* was not really an allegory about good and evil in Medardo and hence in contemporary man; rather any ethical message was in the marginal characters:

> The lepers (i.e. decadent artists), the doctor and the carpenter (science and technology detached from humanity), those Huguenots portrayed both sympathetically and ironically (they are a kind of autobiographical allegory of my family, a sort of imaginary genealogical epic of the Calvino clan) and they are also an image of the whole idealist tradition of moral philosophy from the Reformation to Croce. (*ILDA*, 67)

The author's conclusion is that his ideal would be to continue to write in equal doses (and ideally with equal facility) things that are both useful and amusing, especially if he could write something that was both at the same time. The Horatian ideal of combining *utile dulci* clearly underlies the whole trilogy. And Calvino's solution in terms of genre was simply to reverse the formal strategy adopted in *The Path*: if the first novel had been largely realistic but undercut by elements of fable and epic, then this second novel was broadly fantastic, but with a number of allusions to contemporary reality. In both cases, Stevenson acted as a catalyst to creation: in the figure of the split protagonist Medardo, Calvino explicitly acknowledged the influence of *Dr Jekyll and Mr Hyde* and the two brothers of *The Master of Ballantrae* (I, 1211), and it is obvious that Dr Trelawney derives from his namesake in *Treasure Island*, though here too Calvino indulges in small-scale creative inversion: the opening words of Stevenson's novel are 'Squire Trelawney, Dr Livesey . . .', so Calvino inverts the titles of the two men to produce his new creation, Dr Trelawney.

Il barone rampante (*The Baron in the Trees*) was, like *Il visconte* and *Il sentiero*, written in a rapid creative burst. Calvino had begun the realistic novel, *La speculazione edilizia* (*A Plunge into Real Estate*), on 5 April 1956 but it took him a full fifteen months to complete, the final words being written on 12 July 1957 (see Chapter 4). In the midst of the prolonged creation of *La speculazione*, in the space of a mere two and a half months between 10 December 1956 and 26 February 1957 (I, 1329), he managed to complete his longest, and some would argue his most successful, full-length novel (only *If on a Winter's Night* is longer, but it is not a single novel). As the protracted genesis of *I giovani del Po* generated the contrasting *divertimento* of *Il visconte dimezzato*, so the roots of this later burst of creative fervour lie in the author's antipathy towards the realist novel he was labouring with contemporaneously, as well as in his reaction to the momentous political events of the time: Calvino began to dissent more and more from the attitude adopted by the Italian Communist Party towards the riots in Poland and the uprising in Hungary in late 1956, a dissent that was to lead eventually to his resignation from the party on 1 August 1957. In September 1956 he writes to Leonardo Sciascia that this was for him 'a time for serious rethinking of positions' (*ILDA*, 192). On 14 November he talks despairingly of the 'last few weeks of political anguish which shows no sign of abating, and which are even more numbing for any kind of creative activity' (*ILDA*, 198), just before embarking on *The Baron*. Soon after completing it, on 22 May 1957, he talks of himself as a 'hermit of socialism' (*ILDA*, 221), and a week later, just before the novel is published, the final paragraphs of a letter to Franco Fortini encapsulate his ironic pessimism exactly:

> We are living in dark times, absolutely nothing is going right, and the only consolation is the idea that life is short. I feel perfectly at home in this situation, I have to say, and I can at last indulge totally in that misanthropy which I am now discovering fits my true nature precisely. . . Ha! Ha! It can only get worse.
>
> I've written a book, the one I mentioned to you, *Il barone rampante*, in which I have, I think, partly managed to express these concepts . . .
>
> The better things get, the better one writes! Hurrah! (*ILDA*, 226)

This pessimism, misanthropy and sense of hermetic solitude are evident throughout the novel, and at times there appear to be indirect allusions to the events of

1956–57, notably when Russian soldiers chase remnants of Napoleon's army back into Western Europe (Chapter XXIX). Once again Calvino found it easier to write about political dissent in a genre that owed more to fantasy, the adventure novel and the historical novel than to traditional realism.

This second volume of the trilogy is a unique work by Calvino. Consisting of thirty chapters, like one of its literary models and intertexts, Voltaire's *Candide*, it recounts the life of the protagonist Cosimo from the age of twelve, when he first rebels against the absurdities of his family existence and climbs up into a tree, until his final disappearance from his arboreal kingdom in old age. It opens with a sentence – 'It was on 15 June 1767 that Cosimo Piovasco di Rondò, my brother, sat among us for the last time' (I, 549; *Our Ancestors*, 77) – that deliberately recalls the first sentence of another favourite intertext, Stendhal's *La Chartreuse de Parme*: 'On the 15th of May 1796, General Bonaparte marched into the city of Milan' (Stephens 1995; for Calvino's enthusiasm for Stendhal's novel, particularly its opening, see *S*, 959–60). Despite the length of the book, the organisation of the material displays the by now familiar symmetrical architecture. The thirty chapters divide again into three equal sections. The first ten chapters recount the initial episodic moments of the first days of Cosimo's rebellion: the flight into the trees (I), the first meeting with Viola (II), the fruit thieves (IV), the defeat of the wild-cat (VI), the encounter with his father (VIII), all take place within days of his rebellion. Chapter X is a more substantial and transitional chapter, denser in style as well, dwelling in compact, detailed paragraphs on the characteristics of the various trees of Cosimo's new world and thus suggesting the passing of more than just a couple of days which had been the average diegetic span of the previous chapters, and narrating the appearance of his faithful companion, the dog Ottimo Massimo. The second group of chapters (XI–XX) recounts the more substantial, formative experiences of his adolescence: his similarity to but ultimate divergence from potential role models such as the Cavalier Avvocato (XI), Gian dei Brughi (XII), the Abbé (XIII); then the defining events: the fire in the woods (XIV), the death of the Avvocato (XV), the death of his father (XVI), the episode with the Spaniards (XVII–XVIII), his love life (XIX) and the death of his mother (XX). With both his parents dead, the narrative of the last ten chapters centres on the exploits of Cosimo's maturity: the return and departure of his childhood love Viola and Cosimo's subsequent madness (XXI–XXIV), his interest in freemasonry (XXV), the attempted revolution at Ombrosa (XXVI), the invading French army (XXVII), the meetings with Napoleon (XXVIII) and with Prince Andrej (XXIX), and his final illness and departure on the balloon (XXX). The three thirds of the novel correspond respectively to Cosimo's childhood, adolescence and maturity.

Once again, though, as in the *Visconte*, the protagonist is not an unequivocal hero: Cosimo encounters both the advantages and disadvantages of the isolated intellectual existence, and the plot allows Calvino to debate his own sense of belonging to or severing himself from the Communist movement and party which had been like a family to him since his coming of age, with all the anachronistic and institutionalised rigidities of any family. In fact the author is working out a series of dialectical choices in the novel: the active or contemplative life, public or private, community or isolation, enlightenment or restoration, realism or fantasy, literature or reality. As in the first novel of the trilogy, again there is an obsession with the excesses of religion and war, and with the dangers of literature interfering with life: as the Good Half had nearly been killed while reading Tasso's *Gerusalemme liberata* (I, 425–6), so here Gian dei Brughi is reduced by his passion for reading to an ineffectual bungler who finishes his days, like the protagonist of the last book he is reading, Jonathan Wild, dangling at the end of a rope. In one of his prefaces to the novel, Calvino himself raised the question, without answering it, of whether Cosimo represented an allegory of commitment or its opposite (I, 1230), though he certainly believed he exemplified not a flight from human society but someone who paradoxically distanced himself from others in order better to devote himself to the improvement of society: his interest in technology and crafts, in local government and his full love life show that he too is an emblem of that ideal of 'pienezza' (I, 1214) that had haunted Calvino from the early 1950s and the writing of *I giovani del Po*, from the time, in other words, that Calvino's own life had moved away from partisan and political activity to a more sedentary, literary existence. A typically Calvinian paradox, expressed in his 1960 'postfazione' to the trilogy, sums up Cosimo's achievements: 'the only genuine way to live *with* others, is to live separately from them, . . . this is the vocation of the poet, the explorer, the revolutionary' (I, 1214). What the author called his 'true narrative theme' characterised both the *Visconte* and the *Barone*: 'a character willingly invents a difficult rule for himself and follows it through coherently to its ultimate consequences' (I, 1213), a phrase that echoes that used by Calvino to describe the ethos of Conrad's novels (thesis, p. 126; *S*, 808–9, 815).

Most critics have interpreted the book along these lines, seeing it as a critique of alienation, class barriers and inhibitions (Woodhouse, 1968). Yet Cosimo is not completely victorious: his attempts to reorganise society function only in the short term, and by the end of the novel the restoration has fully taken place and the ideals of the revolution are in tatters. In fact it is his conformist brother Biagio who, according to the fiction of the novel, manages to compose the one text, the novel itself, which does survive, unlike Cosimo's unread utopian and political writings. But even Biagio calls into the question the referential status of the written word in the famous final, lengthy sentence of the novel, in which he compares the vegetation of Ombrosa to the book's dense foliage of words and phrases, and wonders if it is only the latter that exists, though even the text's existence is called into doubt as he calls the work a pattern 'embroidered on nothing' which finally 'so ends' (I, 777; *Our Ancestors*, 284). This darker interpretation chimes in exactly with the months in which Calvino wrote the work, a time of rethinking the ideals of the Resistance and the place of the intellectual in society. The mention of Napoleon's disastrous Russian campaign and the evils perpetrated by invading armies are also contemporary references to the brutal Soviet suppression of the revolts in Poland and Hungary in autumn 1956.

Equally important to Calvino in this period is the question of the role of literature and the function of the writer in society. Literature is seen in the novel as an ambivalent force. It can improve, when read in the right frame of mind as it is by Cosimo and not by Gian dei Brughi, and always so long as it does not supersede reality – hence Cosimo's interest, immediately after the Gian dei Brughi episode, in Diderot's and D'Alembert's *Encyclopédie* and practical treatises. In fact the image of Cosimo with a book in one hand and a rifle in the other is both a composite image of the two brothers of 'La stessa cosa del sangue' (examined above, in Chapter 1), only here one character possesses both gun and rifle. It is also an emblem of Cosimo's resolution of the problem that exercises Calvino throughout the 1950s: the conflict between the active and contemplative lives. On the other hand, literature can also be remote from reality, as illustrated by the useless utopian tract he writes (XIX), the ignored written constitution (XXVIII) and the other 'victim' of literature, the inert poet Agrippa Papillon (XXVII). The novel reaches no univocal, unambiguous synthesis as regards the status and values of the literary text.

Despite the novel's overall success (along with *If on a Winter's Night* it is Calvino's best-selling novel), many critics complained about the 'tired' feel of the plot in the second half of the novel (Pullini, 1959, 354; De Tommaso, 1965, 203–26; Gatt-Rutter, 1978, 48), and even before publication, Citati advised Calvino to cut out an otiose episode involving a boar hunt (*ILDA*, 224) while Vittorini objected to the stylistic disunity between the early and later chapters (*ILDA*, 222). These criticisms suggest that once again, even in this novel Calvino found it more congenial to write of children and nature than of the larger themes of the last third of the book: sex, society and politics. Yet despite this thematic flaw, the novel remains something of a tour de force in Calvino's oeuvre. It is an extraordinarily successful attempt to reproduce a utopian, philosophical *conte* for the 1950s, with a whole range of intertextual allusions and a sophisticated parody of the poetics of the early English moralising novel as practised by Richardson and parodied by Fielding (Cannon 1981, 40). Chapter XII is an almost self-contained miniature of the eighteenth-century novel, with a vast range of allusions to contemporary texts from Lesage's picaresque novel *Gil Blas* to Richardson's *Clarissa* and Fielding's *Jonathan Wild*. Other critics have shown that the novel 'is about the text's relation to other texts', not least that of *Genesis*, and that Cosimo's ascent is a visualisation of what was becoming a much debated narratological question, that of 'point of view' (Carlton, 1984). Similarly the

Abbé is unable to benefit from the books that Cosimo makes him read; instead the most powerful image of the old cleric is when he is distracted from his reading in the tree by the flight of a butterfly (I, 613), an image that will recur more famously in the episode where the female reader prefers the butterfly to the book she is reading in *Se una notte* (II, 780; *If on a Winter's Night*, 172).

Stylistically, Calvino's bravura at understated death scenes is again in evidence, not just in the striking visual images at the end of the chapters recounting the deaths of Gian (XII), and the Avvocato (XV), but particularly in the minimal, paratactic sentences which describe the last moments of Cosimo's mother: 'Una bolla giunse fino alle sue labbra e restò intatta. Ci chinammo su di lei. Cosimo lasciò cadere la ciotola. Era morta' (I, 700; 'A bubble even reached her lips and stayed there intact. We bent down over her. Cosimo let the bowl fall. She was dead': *Our Ancestors*, 215). The opening paragraph of Chapter II is a typical example of Calvino's prose artistry. It begins with very brief, one-verb sentences, the third one a hendecasyllable ('Cosimo era sull'elce. I rami si sbracciavano, alti ponti sulla terra. Tirava un lieve vento; c'era sole': I, 560). Then the sentences gradually become longer as Cosimo's vision extends further over his new habitat, the longest one ending with his gaze on the distant harbour. The last sentence of the paragraph is once more beautifully short and visual, and ends again poetically with two alliterative hendecasyllables: 'In fondo / si stendeva il mare, alto d'orizzonte, / ed un lento veliero vi passava' (I, 560; 'In the background was the sea, with a high horizon, against which a sailing boat passed by': *Our Ancestors*, 87).

The Baron in the Trees also contains a kaleidoscope of eclectic, intertextual allusions. A *conte philosophique* like the thirty-chapter *Candide*, it has also been shown to have links with Rousseau which go beyond the allusions to his texts in the novel (Bryce, 1989). The appearance, in the penultimate chapter, of a character such as Prince Andrej Bolkonsky, from Tolstoy's *War and Peace* (another favourite text of Calvino – see *S*, 28–30), also suggests that this is a novel that attempts to bridge the gap between the world of the eighteenth-century *philosophes* and that of the great nineteenth-century novel. But at the same time it is a text that stands as a modern, secular version of Defoe's *Robinson Crusoe*, a favourite text with Calvino's Marxist mentor Vittorini (and also Pavese). Like Cosimo, Crusoe argues with his ancient father, spends his first night (after shipwreck) in a tree, skins animals for clothes, finds a dog as a companion, rescues another man (Friday) from his captors and educates him (as Cosimo rescues Gian dei Brughi and teaches him to read), hears of Spanish shipwrecks nearby, and towards the end survives the attack by the wolves who are infesting a village, as Cosimo does in Chapter XXIV. Again confirmation of this comes not just from Calvino's lifelong fascination with this text (cited in many essays, and reduced to a virtuoso fifteen-line summary in 1982 – *Enciclopedia*, 118), but particularly from the article on Defoe written in the same year as the novel (*S*, 831–6). In it he notes Defoe's desire to provide 'a moral education . . . sound moral backbone' (*S*, 832) in the book, and his wish to give details of the protagonist's life from birth to old age (as Calvino does in *The Baron*). In particular the economy of Defoe's style is praised in describing the basic manual tasks and importance of every object (Gaetani, 1994), and this precise stylistic brio is something that Calvino also achieves in his rewriting of Defoe's text.

Il cavaliere inesistente (*The Non-Existent Knight*) was written between March and September 1959 (I, 1365). Calvino himself felt that despite being set in a more remote time (the age of Charlemagne, the ninth century), it possessed potentially a more modern relevance than the other two parts of the trilogy, since its main polemical target was the contemporary 'organisation-man' in consumer society (I, 1362; *Our Ancestors*, x). Once more, presumably because of the epic material, the work is organised in twelve chapters, like the twelve books of the *Aeneid*. Again there is the familiar symmetrical structure: Chapters I–IV take us from the parade of the paladins before the walls of Paris to the battle in which the young Rambaldo tries to avenge his dead father and is saved by the warrior maiden Bradamante with whom he falls in love. Chapters V–VIII move from mealtime in the army to the journeys of Agilulfo (the non-existent knight), Torrismondo, Bradamante and Rambaldo in search of Sofronia. The last four chapters continue the journeys of all four until the final denouement of their stories: Torrismondo finds that Sofronia is not his mother but his half-sister, which means that he can marry her and settle in Curvaldia; Agilulfo disappears believing Sofronia was not a virgin when he rescued her, thus losing his title and *raison d'être*; and Rambaldo then comes to collect Bradamante from the convent where she has, under the guise of the nun Teodora, been writing this very story.

Symmetry is also constituted by the six central chapters (IV to IX) which open with Teodora's speculations on narratological problems and the status of the fictional text. At first (Chapter IV) she discusses the problems of recounting as a cloistered nun the many things she has never seen before: an ironic list of the rape and pillage that she has witnessed then follows, debunking the whole question of whether the writer must always write from experience (I, 980; *Our Ancestors*, 308). Then (Chapter V) she claims that when she lacks inspiration, the sounds of lunch being prepared in the convent conjure up not the noise of battle as it had in the previous chapter, but simply the sounds of mealtime in Charlemagne's army. Next (Chapter VI) she argues that it is as difficult for a nun to write about love as about war, but she will do her best; but (Chapter VII) she feels that there is more life in the noise of young boys and girls larking about in the river outside the convent than in all the pages she completes. In narrating the wanderings of the protagonists she wishes that the white page would turn into a visual map of the journey (Chapter VIII), or even better into something three-dimensional, into the actual substance on which they travel: rocks, sand, vegetation (Chapter IX). The final intervention by the narrator comes only in the last chapter, when she claims that she has started to write at great speed, omitting her usual speculations on storytelling at the beginnings of Chapters X and XI because she is anxiously awaiting the arrival of Rambaldo who will gallop off with her towards an unknown future. These narratorial interventions, despite their relevance to contemporary debates on narratology, are also modelled on the intertextual source of the rest of the plot, Ariosto, who in the *Orlando furioso* not only narrated the deeds of Charlemagne's knights and damsels but also initiated each canto with a 'proemio' which meditated in general terms on the issues thrown up by the poem's content.

The themes of this third novel once again are those of the absurdities of war and religion, the difficulty of the maturing process, and the attempts to acquire consistency and avoid dissolution by the protagonist, especially at dawn, the hour when things lose their consistency and we doubt their existence: to combat this malaise Agilulfo has to indulge in an exercise of precision, 'counting objects, arranging them in geometric patterns, resolving problems of arithmetic' (I, 968–9; *Our Ancestors*, 298). Agilulfo does this with 'leaves, stones, lances, pine-cones'. This list suggests that he is linked on the one hand with the boy protagonist of 'Ultimo viene il corvo' and on the other with the elderly Palomar, and that avoidance of 'dissolversi' shows him to be the antithesis of a Conrad hero (cf. Calvino's discussion of the tendency to *cupio dissolvi* of Conradian heroes in *S*, 40). Indeed there are other striking anticipations of future works in this text: the theme of the void, so prominent in the works of the 1970s and 1980s, is already found in the 'vuoto' inside Agilulfo's armour, and the phrase used to describe the criss-crossing of the protagonists' journeys in the Bay of Biscay 'un tale pasticcio di linee che si intersecano' ('such a mess of criss-crossing lines', I, 1043; *Our Ancestors*, 363) resurfaces as the title of one of the micro-novels in *If on a Winter's Night*: 'In una rete di linee che s'intersecano'.

As in his first novel so in the fantastic trilogy as a whole, the characters are all exaggerated grotesques, ranging from the physical and moral extremes of the divided viscount himself and his terrorised subjects to the bizarre family of eccentrics that surround Cosimo and the polar opposites of, on the one hand, Agilulfo, who is an invisible mental force inside a suit of armour, and, on the other, Gurdulú who is all too physical and threatens on every occasion to blend into the sea of objects that surround him. The only rounded characters, physically and metaphorically, are the females: Sebastiana and Pamela in the *Visconte* have already been mentioned; Viola is the specular opposite of Cosimo, everything that he is not – if he represents Enlightenment man, she stands for the baroque/romantic female who borders on the destructive (I, 1215); Bradamante (strong-lover) and Teo-dora (Given to God), as their names suggest, constitute one single, more complete character than any of the male characters. Hume (1992a) rightly observes that the problems even in the last novel of the trilogy are the same as in *The Path*: for Rambaldo and Torrismondo the problem of integration with others in general; for Agilulfo and Gurdulú the particular question of integration with the feminine Other. But the protagonists of the earlier two books came closer to happiness than those of the *Cavaliere*.

Stylistically there are some familiar features. Apart from the opening two hendecasyllables – 'Sotto le rosse mura di Parigi / era schierato l'esercito di Francia' ('Beneath the red ramparts of Paris lay marshalled the army of France': I, 955; *Our Ancestors*, 287) – which recall the Ariostan intertext, poetic passages appear elsewhere, often linked to Bradamante as in these alliterations: '*V*olteggiando *v*eloce una *l*eggera *l*ancia tene*v*a di*s*costi i *s*araceni' ('Swiftly turning a light lance round the warrior kept the Saracens at bay': I, 987; *Our Ancestors*, 315), or when in a caricature of the first appearance of Ariosto's Bradamante by the river at the start of the *Orlando furioso* (1.59–64), Rambaldo comes upon her as she urinates into a stream, parodistically described in two straight hendecasyllables: 'Era una donna di armoniose lune, / di piuma tenera e di fiotto gentile' ('She was a woman of harmonious moons, tender plumage, gentle flow': I, 990; *Our Ancestors*, 317). The standard scene of male knight recognising female knight by the hair that emerges from her helmet, a topos in Italian romance epic, is here literally reversed and seen from the opposite angle.

However, this last book is really so different from the other two books as almost to hint at the disintegration of the trilogy (Bonsaver, 1995c). Not only is the reader's attention split between the paladin's deeds and the nun's narratological ruminations, but unlike the other two eponymous protagonists, Agilulfo is more deuteragonist than main character, disappearing as he does at the beginning of the penultimate chapter. In fact, as in the other two novels, the narrative focus is on the young man on the threshold of maturity, in this case Rambaldo who is seeking an identity for himself both in war and in love. The open ending pointing towards the future which still has to be conquered is clearly differentiated from the traditional closures of marriage and death that had haunted the conclusions to the previous two novels (and of Ariosto's text), and is in fact prophetic of Calvino's own radically different future as a novelist. In the 1960s he would abandon both the fantastic and realistic modes which characterised his writing up until the end of the 1950s.

As to what that different future would contain, a discarded preface to the trilogy, also written in 1960, provides some clues. It claims that although this cycle of fantastic tales was complete (I, 1220), the author was undecided what to write next (I, 1223). He had stopped writing realist fiction because each realist work had turned out to be negative and defeatist; only in these fantasy tales did he achieve an active thrust which was genuinely optimistic. Hence his love for Ariosto's optimism, irony and sadness: the Renaissance poet can be a model, he argues, even in the age of electronic brains and space shots, which are in a sense the continuation respectively of the knights' magic weapons and their travels over the globe and up to the moon (I, 1223–4). It is that mention of the moon which anticipates the lunar setting of his cosmicomic fictions of the next decade.

Of course Calvino does write some other works between finishing the trilogy and publishing *Cosmicomics*, but, as we shall see, they are all works that have their origins in the 1940s or 1950s. The open ending of *The Non-Existent Knight* and the many metafictional passages in the novel questioning the status of the written text are, then, the prelude to another period of crisis and transition extending from 1959 to 1964 (Scarpa, 1993). It is on this crucial quinquennium in Calvino's creative life that the next two chapters will concentrate.

Chapter 4

(Re)Writing Realism

A Plunge into Real Estate

The novel which cost Calvino most time and effort in both its initial composition and in subsequent rewriting and re-editions was *La speculazione edilizia* (*A Plunge into Real Estate*), a novel for which he had a considerable regard, as he tells Arbasino in a 1963 interview (*S*, 2764–75), but which was for a long time relatively neglected by critics. Recently, however, scholars have begun to take note of the considerable modifications to which it was subjected. The novel was begun, as we know from the original manuscript, now in Pavia, on 5 April 1956 and finished at 5.15 p.m. on 12 July 1957 (McLaughlin, 1989a, 95). The Pavia manuscript contains a complete initial draft, full of cancellations and interlinear insertions (*A*) and a fair copy (*B*). It was first published, in a redaction containing twenty-three chapters, in September 1957, in the journal *Botteghe Oscure* (XX, Autumn, 1957, 438–517, henceforth *BO*). A shorter version of only twenty-one chapters was printed in the *Racconti* (441–520), which appeared in November 1958 (henceforth *R*). Then a longer redaction, with twenty-four chapters but slightly shorter than *BO*, was published in 1963, in Einaudi's Nuovi Coralli series (henceforth *NC*), and this last is the edition which has become definitive, the source for all subsequent reprints. The novel thus exists in no fewer than five redactions (*A*, *B*, *BO*, *R*, *NC*).

While the final manuscript draft, the *Botteghe Oscure* version and the definitive Nuovi Coralli edition are similar in substance and length, though progressively moving towards greater narrative economy, the collected *Racconti* prints a radically shortened and reordered version of the story. Recently two critics have provided partial accounts of the variants and their significance (Ricci, 1990, 117–18, n. 5; Milanini 1990, 73–80). In the apparatus to the novel in the collected *Romanzi e racconti*, Milanini has listed nearly all the textual variants between the *Botteghe Oscure*, *Racconti* and Nuovi Coralli versions (I, 1338–51). However, given the broad scope of his monograph, Milanini understandably did not go into detail or discuss other, minor but not insignificant, omissions; nor does his textual apparatus in the Mondadori volume prove exhaustive. Neither Milanini nor Ricci considers two major questions:

1. the overall relationship of the manuscript redaction to the subsequent printed versions; and
2. the possible motivation behind the excisions made in the 1958 *Racconti* edition.

These are the questions which this chapter addresses in order to elucidate the whole of the complicated genesis of one of the key fictions of Calvino's realist phase. Because of the philological complexity of the material, and for the sake of clarity, the chapter will be subdivided into five sections and English translations will be largely omitted in order not to clutter the text (the only available English translation of the novel is in the volume *Difficult Loves. Smog. A Plunge into Real Estate*, 161–250, but it is based on the short version of the tale, of twenty-one chapters, in the *Racconti*).

1. FROM MANUSCRIPT TO *BOTTEGHE OSCURE*

Calvino finished writing his first, rough draft of *La speculazione edilizia* (*A*), as has been noted, on 12 July 1957. Presumably it was shortly after this date that he completed the fair copy (*B*), since *B* reuses some of the *fogli* of *A*. Some time between mid-July and September 1957, when the autumn issue of *Botteghe Oscure* appeared, Calvino evidently made a number of alterations to the fair copy, since *B* does not entirely correspond to BO. It has been pointed out elsewhere (McLaughlin 1989b) that the major differences between the final manuscript draft and the first printed version in *Botteghe Oscure* fall under three categories:

1. Changes of nomenclature, either (a) moving towards the more up-to-date or better known equivalent: 'Agipgas' and 'Finmeccanica' (*B*, 22r) become 'Italgas' and 'Finelettrica' (BO, 459) respectively, 'rincospermi' (*B*, 87r) becomes 'caprifogli' (BO, 517)) and so on; or (b) tending towards greater precision: '[Quinto] aveva rotto con tutti, s'era fatto tutti nemici' (*B*, 12r) is expanded to 'aveva rotto con tutti, *s'era iscritto al partito comunista*, s'era fatto tutti nemici' (BO, 450); the generic 'i rami bassi e frondosi degli alberi' (*B*, 48r) is changed to 'i rami delle mimose' (BO, 482); and 'a leggere Thomas Mann' (*B*, 82r) becomes 'a leggere il Felix Krull' (BO, 511]), an important alteration the significance of which will be discussed later.
2. Suppression of minor details about some of the characters, for instance: Caisotti's eyes are no longer described as 'acquosi, buoni' (*B*, 30r), merely 'acquosi' (BO, 466); Lina is described at first as 'bianca e rossa, con quegli occhi tutti ciglia' (*B*, 36r), later merely as 'con quegli occhi tutti ciglia' (BO, 471); Caisotti's 'ostinazione' is described initially as 'invincibile' (*B*, 39r), but the adjective is later dropped (BO, 473); and an entire sentence about Ampelio's dislike of Travaglia is omitted: 'Ampelio, che pure non sapeva di politica, raccoglieva tutte le voci contro di lui [Travaglia] e a stento nascondeva la sua disistima' (*B*, 34r, cf. BO, 470).
3. Most substantial of all, the elimination of two sizeable passages (printed in I, 1350, but see also McLaughlin, 1993b, 73, nn. 9–10). The first is a parodistic, pseudo-lyrical evocation of the mercantile activities of towns such as Alessandria, Pavia, Biella and others in the hinterland of Italy's 'triangolo

industriale' (it would have appeared at the end of Chapter XIV in NC). The other is a passage about the shift in Cold War attitudes after the French defeat at Dien Bien Phu and the failure of the European Defence Community initiative (it would have come at the end of Chapter XVIII of NC).

There was presumably a stylistic motive for the omission of the first passage: its unique pseudo-lyrical tone, unlike anything else in the whole of Calvino's oeuvre, would have been incongruous in the context of the objective documentary timbre of Chapter XIV. The geographical emphasis of the passage also appears to contravene Calvino's poetics in this period, as expressed in 'Il midollo del leone' (1955), where he claimed that the novel lives in the realm of history and should not amount to a mere geographical depiction of a locality (*S*, 19). But in terms of content both passages were too detailed for a novel which really only concerned the geography of San Remo, not its hinterland, and the history and politics of Italy, not those of Europe and Indochina. In addition, Calvino at this time argued, in a major review of *Dr Zhivago* in 1958, that the modern realistic novel had to deal with contemporary reality and to observe 'unity of time and plot, as in Greek tragedy' (*S*, 1364). The criterion of unity of plot was one of the few secure aesthetic principles to which his generation adhered, as he says in the later preface to *The Path* (I, 1189; *The Path*, 13).

To sum up this section, the changes made in the early phases of composition of *La speculazione edilizia*, from manuscript to first printed form, roughly from July to September 1957, aim at greater precision in terminology and greater narrative economy, while at the same time evincing a vigilant concern for thematic unity.

2. FROM *BOTTEGHE OSCURE* TO THE NUOVI CORALLI EDITION (1963)

The final draft in manuscript (*B*) is closer to the version that appeared in *Botteghe Oscure*, than to either of the two editions in book form. Both the manuscript and journal redactions contained twenty-three chapters (even the fair copy (*B*) in the Pavia manuscript contains only twenty-three chapters, but after Chapter VII (*B*, ff.18bisr–22r) Calvino mistakenly numbers the next chapter IX (23r), thus arriving at the number XXIV for the final chapter in the manuscript, though it is in fact only the twenty-third chapter). However, rather than compare them with the chronologically closer *Racconti* edition of 1958, it is more instructive to compare them initially with the version that is similar in terms of length, the 1963 Nuovi Coralli version, which is just a little shorter than BO.

The major differences between the first printed version (BO) and the final edition (NC) concern content and are mostly noted by Milanini (I, 1338–51). Here again Calvino excised two substantial passages. One of these is a lengthy sentence, providing background about the lawyer Canal in Chapter IV: it is suppressed, partly because it is not strictly relevant to the plot, but partly also because it is too close to the real-life model for this character (I, 1343; *BO*, 448; but see also McLaughlin, 1993b, 74, n. 14).

The other substantial sequence omitted occurred in Chapter XX (XIX of *BO*), a passage of dialogue relating the partisan experiences of the labourer, Angerin, and Quinto's claim that he too had struggled with the weight of a machine-gun on his shoulders in the war (I, 1346–7; *BO*, 502). If the first passage, about Canal, was removed so as not to offend a friend, this dialogic sequence was probably excised for being too autobiographical. On more than one occasion Calvino mentions his own difficulties in carrying the machine-gun and other munitions, 'Ricordo di una battaglia' (1974) being just one: 'il peso della cassetta di munizioni del mitragliatore che mi sbatte sulle spalle' (III, 51). Moreover, this autobiographical motif had already appeared in an early postwar short story, written in June 1946, in which Calvino had given the young labourer the same name he would later use for the protagonist of *The Path*: 'Ma Pin fa un viaggio dopo l'altro, su e giú per quelle scalette, sebbene il secchio gli stronchi la spalla piú che la cassetta di munizioni del Breda' ('E il settimo si riposò', 1946, now in III, 834).

Calvino's constant deformation of the personal reality that surrounded him is also evident in the chapter (VII) dealing with the intellectuals Bensi and Cerveteri and their projected journal. We know that in this period Calvino himself was involved with several left-wing periodicals: apart from being a regular contributor to *Il Contemporaneo* from 1954, he also closely followed the fortunes of other journals to which he subsequently contributed, such as *Città aperta*, *Tempo presente*, *Passato e presente* and *Il Menabò*. One critic has suggested that it is the setting up of this last journal, which Calvino and Vittorini established together, that is reflected in this chapter (Benussi, 1989, 53). But if indeed this chapter has any links with the author's activities in this period, it is chronologically more probable that Bensi, Cerveteri and their periodical on 'la società futura' (*NC*, 37) reflect Calvino's involvement with *Città aperta*. From February to May of 1957, while Calvino was finishing *La speculazione edilizia*, he was also enthusiastically anticipating the first issue of this new periodical, writing letters to two of the founders, Mario Socrate and Dario Puccini: 'Vi seguirò con interesse,' he writes to Puccini on 22 May, 'e spero anche che *Città aperta* valga a farmi uscire dalla posizione di eremita del socialismo che mi sono imposta' (*ILDA*, 211, 221). It could be that the contrasting fictional pair, the philosopher Bensi and the poet Cerveteri, were inspired respectively by the philosophically named Socrate and another co-founder of the journal, the writer Luca Canali, who was in correspondence with Calvino at this same time over his offer to translate for Einaudi the philosopher-poet Lucretius (see Calvino's humorous letter to Canali, on 11 July 1957 – the day before he finished writing *La speculazione* – in *ILDA*, 230). Bensi and Cerveteri's projected journal could thus reflect the difficult genesis of *Città aperta*, especially since in the Pavia manuscript the phrase at the end of Chapter VI, 'anni passati a far progetti sulla *società* futura' originally read 'anni passati a far progetti sulla *città* futura'(my italics, *B*,18r). However, although the discussions between Bensi and Cerveteri may reflect the troubled genesis of *Città aperta*, it is more likely that Franco Fortini is the original for Cerveteri and Renato Solmi is Bensi. (I am grateful to Luca Baranelli and Claudio Milanini for this information. Baranelli points out that the musical reference in the bisyllabic name Sol-mi is converted by Calvino into Ben-si, and the place Cerveteri, which has an Etruscan cemetery, probably alludes to Fortini's Tuscan origins.) This identification appears to be confirmed by Calvino's own reference in the autobiographical introduction to *Difficult Loves* (1970) to his discussions in 1954–55 'with the Hegelian Marxists from Milan, Cesare Cases and especially Renato Solmi, and in the background Franco Fortini, who had been and would continue to be for Calvino an implacable, antithetical interlocutor' (II, 1287).

A number of other briefer passages are omitted since they add very little relevant information, merely background details: again Milanini duly records most of these (I, 1343–9). Those not recorded by Milanini but worth noting are: Ampelio's attachment to San Remo, whose three syllables are alluded to in the text as '***' ('Un tempo Ampelio era molto piu legato a *** di Quinto, *non si sarebbe immaginata la sua vita se non tra quei caffé, tra quegli amici*; adesso non si faceva piú vedere . . .'; BO, 460); Travaglia's conformism ('coerente al costume *di conformismo* che l'ingegnere s'era imposto'; BO, 470); Bardissone's hieratic reading of the contract ('. . . e Quinto si domandò se non era davvero tonto. *Bardissone ci dava dentro a leggere con quel tono notarile che è parente di quello dei preti, per il modo in cui la cadenza del dialetto s'assimila alla terminologia rituale, e per il modo di correre su certi brani e di tirare il fiato. Caisotti ora sembrava diventato una spugna di diffidenza*, teso a non lasciarsi scappare nulla . . .'; BO, 476–7); and the second explicit mention of the year in which the story is set, 1954 ('. . . un antico compagno di lotte. *Dieci anni dopo: millenovecentocinquantaquattro!* Bella curva . . .'; BO, 497). This last mention of the date is important, since it underlines Calvino's ambition in this novel to chart the degeneration of Italian society in the decade that had elapsed since the Resistance.

In a couple of instances, the 1963 edition becomes more politically explicit than BO: Milanini records the passage about Bertellini ('la Bertellini era stata compagna d'idee politiche di Quinto' (*B*, 84r, BO, 513) which becomes 'compagna di partito' (NC, 132)). However, it is also worth registering the point made about Travaglia and not noted in Milanini's edition: 'si diceva che [Travaglia] si volesse far portare sindaco' (BO, 515) becomes 'si diceva che si volesse far portare sindaco *nella lista della maggioranza*' (NC, 135). Minor details of description are also suppressed, such as the site of Caisotti's office 'nella vecchia via delle botteghe' (BO, 463), and Caisotti looking 'come se guardasse Quinto *da una gran distanza e dovesse discernerlo in un puntolino* all'orizzonte' (BO, 474).

There are also some stylistic changes not without interest. At the end of the first paragraph of the novel 'una verifica di sensazioni' (BO, 438) becomes in the definitive edition 'una verifica di osservazioni' (NC, 9), no doubt because of the stress on the visual both at the beginning of that opening paragraph ('Alzare gli occhi dal libro . . .') and throughout the novel. There is also evidence of some more elegant phrasing: 'non si vide bene come fosse stato lo scontro' (*B*, 74r) becomes 'come fosse andato lo scontro' (BO, 503) and 'se fosse stato lo scontro' (*R*, 505, NC, 117); 'finita non riusciva a immaginarsela' (BO, 504) becomes 'terminata non riusciva a immaginarsela' (NC, 119); 'mise gli infissi, mentre tutto il resto della casa era ncora [*sic*] in aria, perché dovevano già venirci ad abitare' (BO, 508) becomes 'infissi, perché dovevano già venirci ad abitare' (NC, 124); 'non la vedeva mai' (BO, 512) becomes 'non la trovava mai' (NC, 130).

The major divergences, then, between the *Botteghe Oscure* version of the novel and the final Nuovi Coralli edition also concern content. These modifications are in the direction of a greater economy of detail about secondary characters (Canal and Angerin in particular), though the omissions are probably also determined by an attempt to distance the story from the author's experiences and acquaintances in San Remo. In descriptions, Calvino eliminates some precise temporal and geographical references, much minor detail and one allusion to a wing of a political party ('Canal era socialdemocratico *di destra*, consigliere comunale' (BO, 450) becomes 'Canal era socialdemocratico, consigliere comunale' (NC, 28)). On the whole, however, in moving towards the definitive version of the novel, Calvino does prefer to specify political details, for instance that Quinto joined the Communist Party (not in *B*, but in BO and NC), that Bertellini had also been in the PCI and that Travaglia wanted to be elected mayor for the Christian Democrats.

3. THE *RACCONTI* VERSION AND THE 1963 EDITION

According to Milanini (I, 1341–42) the major omissions in the substantially abbreviated and depoliticised 1958 edition of the story are:

1. the passage at the beginning of Chapter V about Quinto's past membership of the PCI and his unease with his old acquaintances in San Remo;
2. most of Chapter VI, in which Bardissone is revealed as a centre-left Christian Democrat, mildly sympathetic to the USSR;
3. two brief passages from Chapter XI about Travaglia's expedient conversion to the Christian Democrats, probably without the help of a religious crisis (though Milanini omits an important sentence which is also suppressed in *R*: 'S'era iscritto di recente al partito di maggioranza e v'aveva subito preso un posto locale preminente': NC, 62 – cf. I, 1342);
4. most of Chapter XIII, in which Quinto's past acquaintance with the Sindaco is recalled, from the days of the Liberation;
5. the whole of Chapter XIV, the sociological analysis of *** (San Remo);
6. the passage about the death of De Gasperi in Chapter XVIII (which thus

eliminates any reference to the temporal setting of the novel, since Calvino also suppresses all other temporal references as well as the date of composition at the end);

7. two brief passages from Chapter XXI in which Ampelio's dislike of Canal is stressed;
8. two short passages from the beginning of Chapter XXIV about Quinto's previous acquaintance with the lawyer Silvia Bertellini, when both were members of the PCI in the early postwar years (I, 1341–2).

But apart from listing them, it needs to be emphasised that all these passages, even the ones relating to the minor characters, have important elements in common. They deal not just with general details of the characters' past, but specifically with their political background: Bardissone in the omitted passage is revealed as a left-of-centre Christian Democrat not totally opposed to the Soviet Union partly because he had spent time there during the war; Travaglia becomes Christian Democrat in order to become Sindaco; the present mayor had started out as a member of the CLN (Comitato di Liberazione Nazionale); Bertellini had been a member of the PCI with Quinto in the early postwar years and had defended partisans' families against ruthless opportunists. The suppressed sequences illuminate either the characters' war experiences or their political affiliations or both. There is thus a whole range of characters who at one time had been in or connected with the partisan movement – from the intellectual Quinto and the speculator Caisotti to the Christian Democrat Sindaco and the giant labourer Angerin – though references to the latter two characters' partisan experience are omitted in *R*. Similarly the whole gamut of political stances is represented in the definitive edition of the novel: the Communist intellectuals, Bensi and Cerveteri; Communist workers, Masera and Martini; the centre-left Christian Democrat, Bardissone; the right-wing social democrat Canal; the mainstream Christian Democrats Travaglia and the Sindaco; as well as the ex-Communists Quinto and Bertellini. One of Calvino's aims in these passages seems to have been to emphasise the decline, in all political groupings, of the ideals of the Liberation in the decade since 1945 – indeed, from the manuscript it emerges that after a tentative writing of the first sentence on 5 April he had only seriously begun writing the novel on 25 April 1956 (McLaughlin, 1989b, 94), exactly eleven years after the Liberation – yet in the 1958 edition he suppresses much of this explicit political comment.

It is worth recording here a significant change in Calvino's own narrative perspective which is alluded to at the conclusion of the novel. In the early short story, 'E il settimo si riposò', published ten years previously, the young protagonist, Pin, works on a construction site with two older men, Vinsé (who lives only for Sundays when he can go to dances in pursuit of women) and Ramún (who lives only for Sundays when he can cultivate his exiguous patch of garden). Pin, initially torn between the two men and their leisure interests, concludes that in the new socialist world men will live not just for their escapist Sunday pursuits but will celebrate each new house built: 'il tempo non si conterà piú a domeniche, ma a case, finestre, piani . . .' The final paragraph contains a utopian epiphany that is worth quoting in full:

> Ramún ha detto a Pin che prima della guerra, quando finivano il tetto di una casa nuova, ci mettevano sopra la bandiera. Ora Pin vede già il tetto finito con la bandiera sopra, e loro muratori seduti sulle tegole, vestiti a festa, e altri tetti con altri muratori vestiti a festa, da tutte le parti della città, una festa di tetti fiammeggianti di bandiere. (III, 839)

Ten years later the motif recurs in the penultimate paragraph of *La speculazione edilizia*:

> La madre pensò che era piú bello quando facevano le case coi tetti di tegole, e quand'era finito il tetto ci mettevano sopra la bandiera. – Ragazzi! Ragazzi! – gridò verso le finestre della sala da pranzo. – Hanno finito il tetto!
>
> Quinto e Ampelio non risposero. La stanza, con le persiane chiuse, era in penombra. Loro, seduti con fasci di carte sulle ginocchia, rifacevano il conto di quando si sarebbe ammortizzato il capitale. (I, 890)

This time the work ends not with the utopian perspective of the idealistic labourer Pin, but with the nostalgic, depressing reality of the bourgeois protagonists turned property speculators. The story of Quinto's decline is thus charted from the opening phrase of the novel in which the intellectual lifts his eyes from his book, to the last words which depict him staring at pages of estimates of capital investment.

There is also at least one other, non-political, passage omitted in *R* but not mentioned by Milanini: a paragraph in Chapter XII which provides information on the 'scrittura privata' of the contract. The emphasis is on the contrast between the official contract with its falsified figures and the 'scrittura privata' which revealed the true nature of the partnership between the Anfossi and Caisotti. Clearly this detail, though part of a major preoccupation in Calvino about the inadequate status of the written word in reflecting reality, was felt to be superfluous in the 1958 version of the story.

On the question of the temporal setting of the novel, Milanini rightly points out that there is no subscript in *R* mentioning the dates of composition, unlike the Pavia MS, the *Botteghe Oscure* version and the *NC* edition. This, coupled with the omission of the year in which the story is set, which is specified as 1954 in the scenes in the lawyer's office and in Caisotti's office in the *Botteghe Oscure* version (*BO*, 479, 497) and is implicit in the mention of De Gasperi's death in all versions but *R*, thus makes the setting of the *Racconti* version similar to the undefined temporal backdrop of *La nuvola di smog* (*Smog*) and unlike the clearly specified dramatic date of *La giornata d'uno scrutatore* (*The Watcher*), which is alluded to both within the text and in the subscript.

4. MOTIVES FOR THE ABBREVIATED *RACCONTI* EDITION

Why did Calvino produce this politically desensitised version for his major collection of short stories? One motive, openly acknowledged by Calvino, was undoubtedly personal. A letter of February 1963 to his French literary agent, Franοis Wahl, represents the only occasion on which Calvino makes explicit mention of the cuts made in the 1958 *Racconti* edition. In it he claims that his reason for what he calls 'alcuni piccoli tagli' was that in moving from *Botteghe Oscure*, a journal with a relatively restricted readership, to his collected *Racconti*, the story would attract a larger audience and thus possibly offend those San Remo acquaintances who appear thinly disguised in the novel:

> In actual fact when it came to publishing the tale in the collected short stories, I had serious scruples about the possible offence that might be taken by the lawyer, the notary, the architect etc. – in fact by all my friends and relations from San Remo whom I had portrayed so faithfully in the story; so I made a few cuts. (*ILDA*, 419)

But there seem to have been at least two other possible motives, one aesthetic and one ideological. The aesthetic reason for the cuts was to make this version a more homogeneous *racconto* for the collection in which there is nothing so explicitly political as this novel, and in particular to accommodate it between two stories, *La formica argentina* (*The Argentine Ant*) and *La nuvola di smog*, which are devoid of specific details of time, place and political positions. Similarly, the more explicitly Communist partisan tales were omitted from the *Racconti* (see Chapter 1). The excision of political and sociological detail was presumably determined by Calvino's belief at the time that the novel should not usurp the functions of documentary cinema, journalism or sociological essays (*S*, 87). Calvino continued to be exercised by the problematic relationship between the novel and the essay at least until 1964. In that year, in an exchange of letters with Mario Boselli about *La nuvola di smog*, he defined the latter work in terms which could well be applied to the *Racconti* redaction of *La speculazione edilizia*:

> Perhaps there is an essay hidden inside the story, but it has been mostly cancelled out, only a few fragments remain . . . What aesthetic value can there be in the simple elimination of the essay element which nevertheless was meant to act as a prop for a network of images? (Calvino, 'Lettera a Boselli', 108–9)

The elements of the *saggio* were literally, not just metaphorically, cancelled in the 1958 edition of *La speculazione edilizia* partly to accommodate it alongside the politically inexplicit *La nuvola di smog*. The period from 1959 to 1963 was one of those rare periods of crisis and silence for Calvino (Ferretti, 1989, 89; *ILDA*, 365, 367, 378, 380–1), a period which came to an end with the publication of *La giornata d'uno scrutatore* (1963). By that time Calvino could return to explicit political comment both in that book and in the definitive edition of *La speculazione edilizia*.

But it is the political context which provides the most important clue to the abbreviated 1958 version of the novel. It is worth considering the dates of composition of the tale and examining in greater detail the political and cultural context within which it emerges. The novel is set in the summer of 1954. World politics that summer were dominated by the aftermath of the fall of Dien Bien Phu (8 May 1954), including the subsequent Geneva talks (July 1954), and by the question of the European Defence Community. Both items were present in one of the two passages omitted from the manuscript before publication in *Botteghe Oscure*. The major event in Italy was the death, on 20 August 1954, of De Gasperi, reflected in the passage in Chapter XVIII. From October 1955 to June 1956 Togliatti wrote a series of articles for *Rinascita*, the official journal of the PCI (to which Calvino also contributed), with the title: 'E' possibile un giudizio equanime sull'opera di Alcide De Gasperi?' (*Rinascita*, vols 12–13 (October 1955–May/June 1956)).

The following year, on Thomas Mann's 80th birthday in June 1955, Calvino wrote an important article for *Il Contemporaneo* on the German writer, pointing out the distance that separated him from the writers of Calvino's generation, but not renouncing his influence (*S*, 1339–42). In the same issue of the journal Cesare Cases wrote a fundamental appreciation of *Felix Krull*, seeing the work as a modern picaresque novel and its eponymous hero as a new Jonathan Wild (Cases, 1955). It is perhaps significant that shortly after this Calvino himself wrote his own 'picaresque' novel, *Il barone rampante* (1957), in which Jonathan Wild, as we have seen, is ironically alluded to in the figure (and name) of Gian dei Brughi, and in which class roles are often interchangeable, 'vagando dalla capanna al palazzo e poi ancora alla capanna o al covo dei briganti' (Cases, 1955, 8). Two months later, on 12 August 1955 Mann died. Between July and September 1957, Calvino became more specific about Quinto's reading matter in Chapter XXIII: in the final manuscript redaction he is merely reading Thomas Mann (*B*, 82r), but when the story first appears in print in *Botteghe Oscure* (511) Quinto is reading *Felix Krull*. There are a number of points of contact between the two novels, notably in the two protagonists' contradictory attitude to the world and society and the whole notion of the interchangeability of roles (see Thomas Mann, *Felix Krull*, 259–61). But the specific point of the intertextuality here is to portray Quinto as a confidence-man, a bourgeois trickster adept at assuming many different roles in his life: partisan and left-wing intellectual as well as would-be Don Giovanni, property speculator and bourgeois entrepreneur.

In the following spring, on 5 April 1956, Calvino wrote but did not complete the first sentence of *La speculazione edilizia* in the immediate aftermath of Khrushchev's denunciation of Stalin (February–March 1956). On 25 April, on the eleventh anniversary of the Liberation, Calvino resumed work on the novel, completing the first three chapters (McLaughlin, 1989b, 94): this anniversary seems connected with the insistence in the book on the degeneration of Italian society since 1945 (I, 862). In fact in July 1955 he tells Angelo Ponsi that he had been planning for months to write a short story, 'Il decennale', which would chart the downward curve taken by the country in the ten years since the end of Fascism (ILDA, 161): *La speculazione edilizia* is clearly intended also as a decennial balance sheet of the state of Italy ten years after the Liberation. Calvino's early optimism about destalinisation in the summer of 1956 soon turned to despair as events in Hungary unfolded. In September he admits to Sciascia that despite his attempts to look ironically on these historic upheavals, 'this is a period of serious rethinking for me' and by November he is gloomily alluding to 'the past few weeks of political traumas which show no sign of abating' (ILDA, 192, 198). In December, following the Soviet Union's violent suppression of the uprising in Hungary, Calvino signed a letter denouncing the actions of the Soviet troops, for which he was criticised by *l'Unità* (Spriano, 1986, 11–32; Ajello, 1979, 401). In May 1957 Calvino was still talking in pessimistic terms: 'we are living in dark times,' he writes to Fortini,' there is absolutely nothing that is going right . . . It can only get worse!' (ILDA, 226). It is interesting to note that it was in this dark mood that Calvino was writing not only *La speculazione edilizia* but also *Il barone rampante*: he interrupted work on his realistic novel, as we have seen, on 10 December 1956 to begin the second part of his fantastic trilogy which he finished by 26 February 1957. This historical context provides an appropriate perspective on the oscillations in *Il barone* between moods of optimism and resignation. Calvino finished writing *La speculazione edilizia* on 12 July 1957, but just a fortnight later, on 25 July, 'La gran bonaccia delle Antille', his satirical piece condemning the 'immobilismo' of Togliatti and the Communist party, was published in *Città aperta*, the journal of a breakaway group within the PCI (III, 221–5; Ajello, 1979, 440 ff.), even although it had been written some months before the journal was published (III, 1231). Soon afterwards, on 1 August, Calvino tendered his resignation from the Communist Party: the letter was printed in *l'Unità* on 7 August 1957, but it had been sent on the 1st (Spriano, 1986, 25). Around that time Calvino submitted the manuscript of *La speculazione edilizia* to *Botteghe Oscure*, since the issue in which the story appeared was printed in September 1957. The genesis and first publication of the novel is, therefore, inextricably bound up with Calvino's growing disillusionment with and detachment from the Italian Communist Party.

His resignation and the satirical article 'La gran bonaccia delle Antille' provoked polemical responses, including a furious letter from Togliatti (published in *l'Unità* on 29 September), and a satirical counterblast, 'La gran caccia alle Antille' by Maurizio Ferrara (*Rinascita*, vol. 14 (September 1957), 471–2). This last piece, which adopts the same allegory of maritime exploration used by Calvino in his article, sums up recent events by claiming that after the death of Captain Ahab (Stalin) there had been a mutiny in the Hungarian fleet which in turn had led to an uprising on Fratello Charlie's navy (the PCI) instigated by Antonio il Nipote (Antonio Giolitti) and Italo il Petalo: in case the identity of this last, botanical allusion was not clear, the article was signed by 'Little Bald' (Calvino). In the following year, 1958, when preparing his collection of short stories and in the aftermath of the polemics that followed his resignation from the party, Calvino eliminated many of the more explicitly political passages from his most realistic and autobiographical novel to date – a work which indeed he explicitly defines as one of the most Communist novels he ever wrote: 'However, I have now finally embarked on a phase of "realistic" literature, and the story which I have just finished is perhaps the most Communist thing I have ever written,' says the author in a letter to Spriano on the day of his resignation from the party, 1 August 1957 (Spriano, 1986, 25). In the first year or so after his resignation a number of polemical articles were written attacking Calvino, but the atmosphere cleared by 1959 (Spriano, 1986). The abbreviated and depoliticised version of *La speculazione edilizia* which appeared in his collected *Racconti* was written in the charged atmosphere of the twelve months which followed Calvino's resignation from the PCI, and this must also have accounted for his toning down of the political dimension of the story. By 1963 Calvino could feel that the polemics of 1956–58 were sufficiently remote and that a new political order had established itself in Italy, consequently in the Nuovi Coralli edition those political chapters and paragraphs could be reinstated. This is confirmed also by the letter to Fraņois Wahl of February 1963. There Calvino says he is about to restore the excised passages to the forthcoming Coralli edition for three reasons:

1. the bits I had excised are almost all rather good and are essential to the completeness of the picture drawn in the story;
2. by now my friends have read the tale, have made their comments, some of them got really angry, but time has now passed, so there should not be any more problems;
3. the increased length of the story, even if only by a few pages, is crucial as it provides more substance to the volume. (*ILDA*, 419)

By 1963, then, the time both for personal and political recriminations was past.

5. CONCLUSION

La speculazione edilizia undergoes a systematic pruning in the course of its genesis from manuscript to definitive version. Between the manuscript stage and the first printing of the novel in *Botteghe Oscure*, that is to say between mid-July and September 1957, Calvino omitted the industrial and political passages about the hinterland of the 'triangolo industriale' and about Dien Bien Phu. In moving from *BO* to *NC*, that is from 1957 to 1963, two more substantial passages are suppressed about Canal's career and about Angerin's partisan experiences. But between *BO* and *R*, in the year that followed his resignation from the PCI and the polemics that followed, he eliminated both these socio-political and the 'personal-autobiographical' passages, along with nearly all the political information about the secondary characters, the death of De Gasperi, the dating of the story and the lengthy sociological essay of Chapter XIV. Yet his motives for these excisions are not always uniform. The cutting out of the passages about the industrial hinterland and the aftermath of Dien Bien Phu was in order to avoid disrupting the thematic and geographical unity of the book. The omission of the passages about Canal and Angerin was in order to distance the story from Calvino's own personal world of San Remo and his partisan experiences, while the suppression of nearly all the political allusions in the 1958 edition was, as we have seen, motivated by aesthetic and ideological reasons as well as personal ones.

Behind the genesis of this novel lie Calvino's own increasing disillusionment with the Italian Communist Party, his views on what the contemporary novel could or should deal with, as well as the legacy of Thomas Mann, whose works he was discovering in this period. *La speculazione edilizia*, it must be remembered, is in at least one important way an original novel: Calvino had never before attempted anything so explicitly political and realistic in his fiction as this first novel in a projected trilogy of *Cronache degli anni Cinquanta* (*S*, 2922), and perhaps his anxiety about this new kind of fiction also accounts for the constant revisions of the text. Despite its protracted and difficult genesis, he regarded it as a kind of masterpiece – it is no coincidence that he chose for the cover of its definitive 1963 edition a reproduction of Picasso's design for Balzac's *Le Chef-d'oeuvre inconnu* (one of Balzac's most important novels for Calvino – see *S*, 711–13; *Six Memos*, 95–9). *La speculazione edilizia* is not a monolith, but like many of Calvino's texts, it is a stratified work which undergoes substantial modification and rewriting before reaching its definitive form (Milanini, 1990, and I, xxxviii–xl).

The publication of the definitive edition of *La speculazione edilizia* in 1963 came during what was already a problematic period for Calvino. The crisis extended from 1959 until 1964, a period in which he wrote no major new work, since *La giornata d'uno scrutatore* and *Marcovaldo*, though both published in 1963, had their origins in the 1950s (the first Marcovaldo stories were written as early as 1952 while the dates of composition placed at the end of *La giornata* are 1953–63). In fact the three years 1960–62 are uniquely barren for Calvino (see Appendix). In 1960 he published a chapter from the failed novel, begun in 1952, *La collana della regina* (*The Queen's Necklace*); in 1961 he withdrew at proof stage his book based on his recent trip to the USA, *Un ottimista in America* (*An Optimist in America*); in 1962 he published two short pieces, the unfinished film script 'Tikò e il pescecane' (III, 587–603) and the brief autobiographical memoir 'La strada di San Giovanni'; in 1963, although he completed the Marcovaldo cycle, composing ten new episodes, his projected realistic novel, *Che spavento l'estate* came to a halt. Apart, then, from *La giornata d'uno scrutatore* and *Marcovaldo*, both of which, as has been seen, have their origins in the 1950s, the only volumes

Calvino published in the early 1960s were three reissues: of the trilogy as a single volume entitled *I nostri antenati*, for which he wrote a special introduction in June 1960; of *La speculazione edilizia*, as we have just seen, in a fuller version than that published in the collected *Racconti*; and of his first novel, also with a new and important preface written in June 1964 (I, 1208–19). It was almost as though with the publication in 1963–64 of these five works which had their genesis in the 1940s or 1950s Calvino was clearing the decks of his previous fictions in order to embark on a completely new kind of narrative enterprise.

More explicit indications of the crisis emerge in his correspondence of the time. In April 1961, one year after his return from the USA, he tells of having destroyed when it was already in proof stage his next project after *Il cavaliere*, the book on his American travels, adding: 'The more I go on, the less sure I am about anything' (*ILDA*, 365). The following month, after telling Natalia Ginzburg that *Le voci della sera* is her best work to date, he ends the letter: 'As for me, I may not write again, but I'll live happily enough nevertheless' (*ILDA*, 367). By the end of 1961, he has not even an article to send to a journal and refuses to become a regular contributor to the *Corriere della sera* for similar reasons (*ILDA*, 378, 380–81). In May 1962 he again complains about having written long novels which in the end he feels unable to publish, but hopes that the alternation of periods of creativity and silence will eventually produce 'the word that I had always wanted to say, that I had always had on the tip of my tongue' (*ILDA*, 397). In January 1964 he tells the novelist Goffredo Parise that the triumph of 'Rome-centred petit-bourgeois realism' had hampered the development of all writers of the time (*ILDA*, 450). In May he declares that he now only reads astronomy books since he feels 'a massive weariness for literature, particularly for the novel' (*ILDA*, 473), and in October he announces that huge changes of taste and technique are taking place in fiction: for those over forty like himself this is a difficult time, 'both for those who write and for those in publishing who have to find new works to issue. Everything appears out of date, and what is not out of date is immature' (*ILDA*, 493–4).

However, the reading of astronomical texts which he mentions in May 1964 does eventually bear fruit, for in November of that year he publishes in the journal *Il Caffè* the first four cosmicomic tales: 'La distanza della Luna', 'Sul far del giorno', 'Un segno nello spazio' and 'Tutto in un punto' (*ILDA*, 429–30). Although this was to prove a fertile new area for Calvino, his impatience with the traditional novel continues. In January 1965 he notes that 'our kind of literature, with all its moral, political, lyrical levels as well as those of objective observation of internal psychology, is something that everyone now regards as antiquated' (*ILDA*, 502). By summer 1965 he is saying:

> I am now more than ever in favour of a literature that tends towards geometric abstraction, towards the composition of mechanisms that can function on their

> own, as anonymously as possible. And I feel very remote from everything that is existential, expressionistic, 'full of the warmth of life'. (*ILDA*, 522–3).

That 'warmth of life', that 'charge of vital immediacy' had certainly been an ingredient in *The Path* and the trilogy, but it was impossible to manufacture once the experience had passed (*ILDA*, 526). In October 1965 he claims to be still interested in politics and in literature, but he now believes that the political novel is no longer viable (*ILDA*, 528). By January 1966 he declares 'I feel a great intolerance for stories about political *mores* and psychology' (*ILDA*, 554): a decade after writing *La speculazione*, Calvino knew he would never write anything remotely similar again.

Chapter 5

Calvino's Thematics

Sex, Texts and the Secret Watermark of the Universe

This chapter examines how and why the cycle of Calvino's realist fictions came to completion, and offers an overview of the thematics which informed the first twenty years of his literary output. The author himself regarded the works of 1945–63 as forming a unit. In a major essay, written in 1976, 'Usi politici giusti e sbagliati della letteratura (Right and Wrong Political Uses of Literature)' (*S*, 351–60; *LM*, 89–100) he characterised Italian fiction between 1945 and 1960 as dealing primarily with political, ethical and social questions. But after 1960 this kind of literature came under attack from at least three different directions: from the literary avant-garde, particularly the Gruppo '63 (formed, as their name indicates, in 1963), who rejected this outmoded form of realism; from political theorists, who claimed that this kind of committed literature often amounted to patronising populism; and from the devotees of the 'new' disciplines capable of deconstructing literary texts, such as linguistics, information theory, semiotics and structuralism, which precipitated the crisis of realist fiction. After this, according to the author, fiction could no longer be a mirror of the world, but merely a concatenation of words and signs on the page. In terms of Calvino's oeuvre, the period he refers to as 'from 1945, right through to the 1960s and beyond' (*S*, 351) corresponds precisely to the period that extends from his earliest short stories and first novel to *La giornata d'uno scrutatore* (*The Watcher*) (1963).

The most explicit statement of Calvino's literary credo in these two decades is to be found in an article written in 1955, in the middle of this period, 'Il midollo del leone (The Lion's Marrow)' (*S*, 9–27): 'We believe that political commitment, taking sides on issues, compromising yourself in this way, is more than just a duty, it is a natural necessity for today's writers, and even more than for writers, for contemporary man' (*S*, 20). The works of this period are all informed by this active socio-political ideal. But although one critic (Petroni, 1976) has charted the development of commitment in Calvino up until 1976, his analysis stops at that date and ignores a number of key passages in earlier works. One of the aims of this chapter is to determine to what extent Calvino remained a politically committed writer throughout his career: even after he left the Communist Party in 1957 he still continued to have independent links with the PCI, and certainly considered himself a Marxist at least as late as 1967. The other objective is to show that the thematics of his works in the period that extends from 1945 until 1963 revolve not only around broad themes already well illustrated by critics (such as alienation, nature, maturity, etc.), but primarily around three linked topics: sex, literary texts and the question of political commitment.

It has often been noted that the figure of the reader appears in Calvino's texts at a precocious stage, long before the semiotic works of the 1970s, most critics pointing to the lazy reader Zena-il-Lungo in *The Path to the Spiders' Nests*. But, as was seen in Chapter 1, the older brother in his first postwar fiction, 'La stessa cosa del sangue (In the Blood)', was already portrayed as an intellectual and reader. There are also readers in four other short stories, all written shortly after the novel, in 1948. In 'Il giardino incantato (The Enchanted Garden)', two urchins sneak into the garden of a huge villa and, in the centre of the tale, catch a glimpse through a window of the small, sickly boy who lives there, leafing through an illustrated book in a room filled with butterfly collections (I, 171; *Adam, One Afternoon*, 22–3). That juxtaposition of the book and the butterflies is another antithetical emblem which will haunt Calvino's imagination and will resurface in an important chapter of *Se una notte d'inverno un viaggiatore* (II, 780; *If on a Winter's Night*, 172). But here the book, like the butterflies, symbolises the sterility of the rich child's existence, in contrast to the free mobility of the urchins outside. In 'Pranzo con un pastore (Goatherd at Luncheon)', the first-person narrator uses the newspaper as an instrument to underline the distance that separates himself and his bourgeois family from the illiterate goatherd who has been invited to lunch. In 'I figli poltroni (The Lazy Sons)', books symbolise the indolence of the older brother who spends his day reorganising his library, too lazy to read any more (I, 201). In 'Il gatto e il poliziotto (The Cat and the Policeman)', the policeman, who is searching for hidden weapons in working-class flats, thinks at first he has been ambushed when he hears a voice saying, 'Not a step farther . . . I've got you covered' (I, 357; *Adam*, 147), but these are only the words of a girl reading from an illustrated magazine a story about baronets in evening dress, which contrasts with the grey working-class housing in which Calvino's tale is set. In the early postwar period the written word, whether it is consumed by bourgeois or proletarian readers, is always problematically bound up with the question of social class.

In his first novel Calvino devoted a whole chapter to the ideological message. In that chapter the model partisan Kim concluded that since History is on his side, his every gesture is meaningful, even his love for his girlfriend Adriana, whereas any Fascist soldier's love for his girlfriend will be a futile gesture, cancelled out by History: 'I think "I love you Adriana" and that is History, it will have huge consequences; I'll behave tomorrow in battle like a man who has thought tonight "I love you, Adriana"' (I, 110; *The Path*, 144). Kim thus manages to reconcile Desire and History. In the next chapter we were offered a more concrete reverse image of the ideal partisan than the hypothetical Fascist soldier. The uncommitted partisan leader, i.e. Dritto, prefers in the end to stay at the camp to make love to Giglia rather than fight in battle with the rest of the men. He is the first instance of a type who recurs constantly in Calvino's fictions, the listless individual diverted from total commitment by sexual desire. Kim, on the other hand, is not only a model partisan and exemplary lover, he also adopts the correct approach to reading: his partisan code name comes from his boyhood reading of Kipling's homonymous novel and symbolises his emulation of the fictional Kim's search for purification. But as il Dritto was the foil to Kim the partisan-lover, so there is also an opposite of the model partisan-reader: Zena-il-Lungo literally cannot put down the *Supergiallo* (*Superthriller*) he is reading. When he is first introduced we are told that even when he goes into action he rests the open book against his machine gun. In the following passage the two foils to Kim are linked by reading:

> [Zena] reads out loud in a monotonous Genoese cadence; it's a story about men disappearing in a mysterious Chinatown. Dritto likes hearing him read and tells the others to keep quiet; Dritto has never in his life had the patience to read a book through, but once, when he was in prison, he had spent hours listening to an old convict reading *The Count of Monte Cristo* out loud and had enjoyed that very much. (I, 76; *The Path*, 107–8)

Here we have the two negative images of the committed partisan: Zena who is interested only in reading, and Dritto who has eyes only for the cook's wife. Unlike Kim, who was able to read a Communist significance even into a text written by a reactionary writer, Dritto is unable to see the relevance of Dumas' novel, even though he too, like its protagonist, is in prison. Time and again the texts read by characters in Calvino's fiction reflect their situation in Calvino's tale and underline their inability to apply the lessons of literature to life. So even that first novel was shaped by that 'esprit géometrique' which is such a characteristic feature of his mature works. There are three pairs of contrasting lovers (Kim and Adriana, the Fascist soldier and Kate, il Dritto and Giglia), three readers and books (Kim and *Kim*, Zena and the *Superthriller*, il Dritto and *The Count of Monte Cristo*). These contrasting pairs indicate that desire and literature, though they can be reconciled with commitment in idealised characters such as Kim, are more often impediments to *impegno*. In fact since Kim is merely the protagonist of a chapter not the whole novel, the emphasis in the rest of the book is on negative rather than positive ways of reading and loving. That this three-way dialectic is basic to this and many of Calvino's works, realistic or fantastic, up until 1964, is confirmed by the author's own grouping of the three themes in a key passage of the 1964 preface to the novel:

> I never managed to become what I had dreamed I would be before I was put to the test: I had been the most insignificant of partisans; I was an uncertain, unsatisfied and inept lover; the world of literature did not open up for me like a straightforward and objective apprenticeship, but was more like a journey which I did not know how to start. (I, 1200; *The Path*, 25)

I giovani del Po (*Youth in Turin*) (1950–51) treated the dialectic between love and commitment even more explicitly. The protagonist, Nino Torre, has just moved from the country to a factory job in Turin. Initially he is rebuked by a trade union activist for being more interested in his girlfriend than in attending a strike meeting, but on the whole Nino manages to reconcile his relationship with Giovanna and his devotion to the union's cause:

> Now I begin to see that there is an entire linkage connecting the city, the river, Giovanna, and my work in the factory and in the union meetings . . . And now I have something else: the river and my girlfriend, and everything compensates for everything else and fits in. (III, 1075)

But this idealistic solution to the problems of alienation from nature, desire and political commitment breaks down in the works of the later 1950s. Unlike Kim, Nino is the protagonist of the whole story, but since his foil is the country boy Nanin, the dialectical tension in the work revolves around the poles of city and country, not around conflicts between sexual desire and commitment: behind Calvino's general dissatisfaction with this 'uncharacteristically grey work' (III, 1342) lay no doubt these facile resolutions of the clash between emotion and commitment (Stephens, 1993).

Not only *The Cloven Viscount* but also the other two books in the trilogy *Our Ancestors* explore this theme of wholeness, so literature and love form an integral part of the development of each of the three protagonists. In the trilogy as a whole, reading, or rather certain kinds of reading, is considered dangerous. In the first book the Good Half of Medardo is declaiming Tasso's *Gerusalemme liberata* to Pamela when he is nearly killed by his rival, the Bad Half: here literature is seen as not just lethargic, but almost lethal (I, 425–6; *Our Ancestors*, 54–5). In *The Baron in the Trees* Cosimo is an avid reader, but Calvino is at pains to depict him as discerning and constructive in his choice of books. The whole of chapter XII is almost a self-contained story about the perils of passive reading. The highwayman, Gian dei Brughi, discovers literature through Cosimo, becomes a fanatical consumer of the lengthy novels of Richardson and Fielding, but unlike Cosimo Gian is never transformed by what he reads, he is not converted by the moral lessons of *Clarissa* nor by the satire of Fielding: in the end he no longer knows how to participate in the active life, not even in the form of brigandage, so he is captured by the police and meets the same fate as the hero of the last book he reads, Fielding's *Jonathan Wild*. Throughout the chapter Calvino stresses the similarity of life to literature: at the beginning Cosimo is reading *Gil*

Blas when Gian appears below him in the wood chased by policemen, and it is presumably the picaresque adventures he is reading that prompt Cosimo to lower the rope which allows the likeable rogue a miraculous escape. Later Cosimo progresses to more formative works such as Fénélon's *Télémaque* and Plutarch's *Lives*, while Gian becomes absorbed in Richardson and Fielding. The close correspondence between life and art (as well as Calvino's passion for narrative symmetry) is underlined at the end of the chapter when Gian is, like Jonathan Wild, hanged (the rope that had opened the episode by saving Gian's life now finishes it). Gian dei Brughi (John of the Wilderness in Italian) is thus the Italian equivalent of Jonathan Wild both in name and fate. In the next chapter Cosimo learns from Gian's demise to seek out texts not for escapism but for instruction, and turns now to Diderot's and D'Alembert's *Encyclopédie*: as the author claimed, the aim of the chapter was to illustrate the contrast between 'reading as escapism and reading as education' (*Il barone rampante*, school edn., 149).

At the end of *The Baron in the Trees* and throughout *The Non-Existent Knight* the literary emphasis shifts from reading to writing, as the author testifies in his introduction (I, 1218). The elegant final paragraph of the former questions whether the world of Ombrosa ever existed or was simply a thick vegetation of words on the page. In the final work of the trilogy such questions intrude into the openings of seven out of the twelve chapters of the book. By this stage Calvino seems to be as wary of his own role as writer as he had been cautious about the dangers of reading: the text registers increasing dissatisfaction with the inadequacy of the written word to convey reality, and in the end the nun who has been narrating the story, Suor Teodora, admits that she has been not only the writer of the tale but also an active participant in it; she is none other than her specular opposite, the warrior maiden Bradamante, who at the end of the book gallops off towards the future with her lover Rambaldo. This pairing of the sedentary writer and the woman of action will resurface in *The Castle of Crossed Destinies*, when the writer portrays himself as both St Jerome and St George. In both cases Calvino assuages his anxieties about having become a writer, a contemplative, by summoning up an image of the man of action he had been during the war.

If Teodora/Bradamante is both writer and lover, elsewhere the emphasis is on readers who are lovers. Cosimo in particular enjoys a full sex life both before and during his affair with Viola: indeed in *The Baron* sex is portrayed not as an obstacle to *impegno* but as an integral part of the active, committed existence epitomised by Cosimo. This is explicitly stated in Calvino's 'postfazione' to the trilogy: '[I wanted to portray Cosimo] not as a misanthrope, but as a man constantly dedicated to the good of his neighbours, in harmony with the historical movements of his times, someone who wants to participate in every aspect of the active life: from technological progress to local government, to a full love life' (I, 1214). The notion that satisfactory sex is an essential experience rather than a distraction is reiterated in *The Non-Existent Knight*, when Rambaldo finds, like

Kim, that commitment to the fight is enhanced rather than impeded by being in love: 'You can only fight well in war when in the midst of the lance-tips you glimpse a woman's mouth, and then everything, the wounds, the dust-cloud, the smell of the horses, taste of nothing but that female smile' (I, 1020; *Our Ancestors*, 344). When we recall that at the end of the first novel of the trilogy it was Medardo's love for and marriage to Pamela that acted as the catalyst for him becoming a complete man again, and that in the second novel it was Cosimo's love for Viola that fulfilled the protagonist, it becomes clear that in the trilogy sex is not so much an obstacle to as an integral part of the fully realised existence.

Even in less well-known works, such as 'Le notti dell' UNPA (The U.N.P.A. Nights)', the last part of the autobiographical trilogy *L'entrata in guerra* (*The Entry into War*) (1954), similar themes are evident in miniature. The opening two sentences dwell on the transition from childhood to adolescence in a typically Calvinian way:

> I was a late developer: at sixteen, despite my age, I was rather behind in a number of ways. Then, suddenly, in the summer of 1940, I wrote a comedy in three acts, had a love affair, and learned to ride a bicycle. (I, 525)

These three maturing experiences are once more concerned respectively with literature, sex and practical reality. In the rest of this symmetrical tale these three elements continue to interact. When the narrator spends the night on guard in a school, he reads an illustrated magazine which is 'full of photographs of English cities seen from the air, with clusters of bombs falling on them' (I, 531). He and his friends do not really grasp the propaganda significance of the pictures, being more interested in the magazine's story of King Carl of Rumania and his lover, 'la Lupescu'. The two boys then go out into the night in search of sexual adventure, but the squalid prostitutes they encounter are contrasted unfavourably with the romantic tale of 'la Lupescu'. After this exposure to carnal reality, the narrator is also confronted with military reality when the air-raid siren sounds and he has to rush back to the school. At the end of the tale, while the alarm continues, he sits on his bunk in the school, looking at the magazine with more experienced eyes: 'Flicking through the magazine, my eyes fell on the English cities gutted by bombs, and lit up by tracer bullets' (I, 544). There is no room for commitment in this tale of Calvino's youth under Fascism, but there is a clear contrast between the exotic Romanian love story and the seedy sexual encounters in the tale, as well as between Fascist propaganda about the bombing of English cities and the real threat posed by Allied bombers over San Remo.

In the trilogy and the earlier fictions of the 1950s the emphasis was on love rather than on sexual desire, and for Kim, Nino Torre and the protagonists of the trilogy love can be harmonised with commitment. The dialectic which animates other early characters such as Marcovaldo (the first tales were written in 1952) and the protagonist of 'La formica argentina (The Argentine Ant)' (1952) derives not from love and *impegno*, which they manage to reconcile, but from another source, their alienation from the world of nature. In their emotional lives both men are devoted to their wives and families. The first-person narrator of the latter tale is committed to protecting his wife and child against the ubiquitous ants, and he contrasts himself with his carefree, womanising uncle (I, 467; *Adam*, 176). For him, as for Kim, his emotional commitment is at one with his socio-political ideals.

In the stories written after 1956 the accord between the emotional and political lives of Calvino's characters breaks down: they are motivated more by carnal urges than by love, and they are mostly incapable of integrating desire with their political aspirations. The opening sequence of *A Plunge into Real Estate*, as we have seen, portrays the intellectual Quinto symbolically taking his eyes from his book and staring out at the increasingly built-up landscape of his home town on the Riviera. Significantly, the only other thing he reads are the local business newspaper, the evening paper announcing De Gasperi's death and Thomas Mann's *Felix Krull*, symbolising his confidence trick of conversion to the role of entrepreneur and his rejection of political commitment. Equally symbolic is the close of this symmetrical novella, when Quinto turns his eyes from his now diminished garden in the fading light to concentrate on the business accounts of the property speculation that now require all his attention. His failure to integrate properly with the world of business forces him to seek compensation in sex, first in his brief relationship with Nelly, the woman he meets in the estate agent's office, then with the French girl on the film set, and finally with a prospective tenant of the new building, la signora Hofer:

> He found himself summing up in her person everything he had missed, everything he had failed to bring off – his real estate plunge, the movies, the French girl. (I, 882; DL, 243)

Quinto, like many of Calvino's protagonists in the late 1950s, is lazy even about sex: when he first sleeps with Nelly we are told that 'for years Quinto had only gone with women who slightly repelled him physically. This was a deliberate program: he was afraid of ties, he only wanted casual affairs' (I, 851; DL, 216). Unlike the trilogy's protagonists, Quinto cannot find satisfaction either in his (corrupt) active life or in his (unfulfilled) sex life. That sex in this novella is equated with the active non-intellectual existence is corroborated by the pairing in the first two versions of the tale (printed in *Botteghe Oscure* and in the collected *Racconti*) of politics and literature as belonging to the world of his ineffectual left-wing friends, whereas the details of his affair with the French girl appeal to those steeped in 'reality', his business acquaintances: 'At last he could talk about something that everybody was interested in – Cinecittà, French actresses, and so on – unlike the days when he could only discuss politics and literature and never knew what to say to his old friends' (*Racconti*, 517; DL, 246). In *La speculazione edilizia*, then, Calvino has altered the terms of the antithesis established in previous works: hitherto political and sexual commitment were contrasted positively with the dangers of literature, but now in this deliberately negative tale politics and literature are seen as less tangible forms of reality than sex and property speculation.

In his next novella, *La nuvola di smog* (*Smog*) (1958), Calvino alters the terms of this triangular dialectic once again. The nameless first-person narrator is the antithesis of Quinto: he develops from being initially uncommitted into a journalist devoted to warning his readers about pollution and the atomic menace. The entire story, apart from being one of Calvino's most ironic essays on commitment, is an elegant disquisition on the relationship between reality and the printed word, whether in the form of journals, newspapers or colour magazines. In the end the protagonist prefers the greyness of the Communist daily newspaper to glossy magazines since it reflects more accurately the grey world around him. But in this story there is also room for the third term of the dialectic, sexual desire. Claudia, the narrator's glamorous girlfriend, comes to visit him in the polluted city in which he works, but even when she lies naked on the bed waiting for his embrace, he is portrayed as throwing himself onto her more for ecological than for sexual motives: 'I threw myself upon her in an embrace which was chiefly a way of covering her, of taking all the dust upon myself so that she would be safe from it' (I, 928; DL, 141). But this integration of *amore* and *impegno* is totally ironic and transitory: it does not last, nor does it eliminate the pollution problem. Fundamentally Claudia is seen to belong to the different world of wealthy escapism: in the central section of the novella, as the protagonist watches the smog gather over the city in a huge grey cloud, she can only perceive the graceful flights of birds (I, 926; DL, 139). At the end he rejects her beautiful but unreal world: as he notices that people prefer to read colour magazines rather than the grim atomic warnings in his own articles, one illustrated weekly appears with Claudia herself on the cover waterskiing (I, 948; DL 157). Although Calvino coupled *Smog* and *The Argentine Ant* as a city-country diptych about the environment (*S*, 2791, 2922), the former story is closer to, and indeed is a reverse image of, *A Plunge into Real Estate*. The protagonists seem dialectical opposites (Quinto moves from left-wing commitment to business speculation, *Smog*'s anonymous protagonist from indifference to total engagement with the problems of the urban environment), and the tension between sex, literature and reality is inverted: for Quinto, sex and property speculation were opposed positively to politics and literature, while for Claudia's partner the ecological commitment of the journalist outweighs erotic escapism. For the narrator these problems can be confronted only by political *impegno* and the printed word, thus the Communist daily and the anti-pollution journal on which he works contrast with the businessman's paper and the evening paper announcing De Gasperi's death in the 1957 story.

Gli amori difficili (*Difficult Loves*) was the title given by Calvino, initially to nine 'adventures' which formed the third, penultimate, book of his collected *Racconti*. Subsequently, in 1970, he published a whole volume entitled *Gli amori difficili* which contained the nine tales from the 1958 collection plus four other pieces: 'Avventura di un bandito' (1949), which had already appeared in *Racconti* with the title 'Un letto di passaggio'; 'Avventura di un fotografo', the narrative re-writing of an article on photography written in 1955 (Papa, 1980; Watson, 1988); 'Avventura di uno sciatore' (1959); and 'Avventura di un automobilista' (1967), which initially appeared as the penultimate tale in *Ti con zero* (*Time and the Hunter*) with the title 'Il guidatore notturno (The Night Driver)'.

This collection of tales, as the title implies, deals primarily with love and sex, and literature to a lesser extent, but the political dimension is largely absent. One of the most significant stories here is 'Adventure of a reader' (1958). The protagonist, Amedeo, is a young man with by now familiar (autobiographical) features: any enthusiasm he had possessed for the active life lingers on only in his appetite for lengthy nineteenth-century novels, from Stendhal, Dostoevsky and Balzac to Tolstoy, Flaubert and Proust. The six novels explicitly alluded to in this very short tale paradoxically represent the entire development of the European realist novel, and in a metaliterary way they underscore Calvino's marginal position to it: Calvino was always more a writer of short stories than of novels, and saw the former as the more appropriate form for his times (Badini Confalonieri, 1985). Despite having sublimated his youthful energy into reading (and to a lesser extent swimming), on the beach he is disturbed by the attractive woman who comes to sunbathe near him: there is a hint that because he likes big books, he only wants brief affairs, if any, with women. The appearance of this bikini-clad *signora*, whom initially he is determined to ignore by concentrating on his book, eventually threatens his solitary pleasure in reading. In the end Amedeo has to pay attention to life in the form of this woman who eventually seduces him, rather than to literature. Amedeo is capable of reading all the great love stories of the classics of the realist novel, but he is unable to read with any expertise the real erotic adventure which beckons. Although here emotional involvement forms part of the active existence, as it does in the trilogy, there is no social or political comment, and Amedeo is similar to Quinto Anfossi of *A Plunge into Real Estate* and other protagonists of *Difficult Loves* in his lazy approach to romance: like the protagonist of 'The adventure of a clerk', Amedeo is reluctant to embark on a long-term affair which would alter his routine existence.

Calvino, as we have seen, shifted his attention in the late 1950s from the reader to the writer, so it is not surprising to find that alongside 'Adventure of a reader' he also wrote, in the summer of 1958, 'Adventure of a poet'. Cosimo, Quinto and Amedeo were primarily readers, while Teodora and the protagonists of *Smog* and 'Adventure of a poet' are writers. The poet in this tale is, like

Calvino, a precise observer of the natural and human world around him, but we are immediately informed that 'ever since he began loving Delia, he had seen his cautious, sparing relationship with the world endangered' (II, 1167; DL, 104). This is confirmed when he and Delia row out to a beautiful cavern and she swims naked inside the cave. Usnelli is so overcome by the beauty both of nature and of Delia's body that he is poetically struck dumb:

> His mind, used to translating sensations into words, was now helpless, unable to formulate a single one . . . For him being in love with Delia had always been like this, as in the mirror of this cavern: in a world beyond words. For that matter, in all his poems, he had never written a verse of love: not one . . . Nothing that was there at this moment could be translated into anything else, perhaps not even a memory. (II, 1167–9; DL, 104–6)

A decade later, in a 1967 essay on eroticism (*S*, 261–5; LM, 65–70) Calvino is still convinced that aspects of eros largely lie beyond the power of words (Gabriele, 1994). The story ends with the poet only rediscovering his voice when he meets some poor fishermen and sees their weatherbeaten faces, the flaking paint of their boat and their crumbling village. Here, as in the trilogy, love and sex are seen as positive, vital elements of reality, whereas the written word, incapable of expressing these forces, is associated with potential sterility. The virtuoso sentence on which the story ends also suggests a critique of neorealism's facility in dealing with the negative rather than the positive aspects of existence (II, 1171–2). This beautiful, symmetrical tale, in which the shimmering colours of nature are skilfully picked out against extremes of light and darkness (McLaughlin, 1993a, 74–5), articulates a key statement about eros and the intellectual. In the first half of the story the poet utters only stammering, incoherent sounds in response to Delia's garrulous enthusiasms as they row into the beautiful marine cavern. In the centre of the tale, when to the splendour of nature is added the naked magnificence of her body as she swims in the cavern, his stammerings are reduced to total silence: gazing at her beauty was like staring at 'the most dazzling core of the sun. And in the core of this sun was silence' (II, 1169; DL, 106). This central synaesthetic mixing of sight and sound resurfaces at the close of the tale, when as the poet observes the squalor of the fishermen and their village, the words come tumbling into his mind and the white silence of that central paragraph now becomes a black scream:

> Into Usnelli's mind came words and words, thick, woven one into the other, with no space between the lines, until little by little they could no longer be distinguished, it was a tangle from which even the tiniest white spaces were vanishing and only the black remained, the most total black, impenetrable, desperate as a scream. (II, 1172; DL, 108)

La giornata d'uno scrutatore (*The Watcher*) (1963) is one of Calvino's most unusual texts. After the publication of *The Non-Existent Knight* (1959), there had followed four years of problematic silence (Scarpa, 1993) before his reappearance in print now with this deceptively slight volume. The work is also the one that marks the end of both the realist phase of Calvino's fiction and any attempt to write a traditional, continuous novel. From now on his fiction will always be in the format used for the other volume published later in 1963, *Marcovaldo ovvero le stagioni in città* (*Marcovaldo, or The Seasons in the City*): a series of microtexts structured into an overarching macrotext by a more or less complex grid or frame.

In *The Watcher* Amerigo Ormea, a Communist Party activist, is sent as election scrutineer in the 1953 general election to the Cottolengo in Turin, the hospital for the mentally and physically handicapped, and spends the day musing not only on political questions but also on how far the words 'human' and 'love' extend (even his own surname is an anagram of *amore* – see Usher, 1988). It is a work that celebrates complexity and eschews facile oppositions: the very first image is that of the many layers of the artichoke, evoked when the election posters are described as peeling off in the rain (II, 9) – Calvino used this very image in the same year to praise the artichoke-like reality conveyed by Gadda's complex novels (*S*, 1067). In the second chapter Amerigo is already thinking that to call his left-wing party the Communist Party and the religious institute the Cottolengo does not take him far on the road to exactness (II, 7) – one of the first signs of that obsession with precision that becomes a poetic principle in Calvino's writing from this point onwards, culminating in the Harvard lecture on 'Exactitude'. The chapter ends with one of his longest sentences, as Amerigo tries to define what it means to be called a Communist. The final chapter reiterates this complex reality: 'everything proved more and more complex, and it was increasingly difficult to distinguish the positive and the negative thing, and increasingly necessary to discard appearances and look for the essences that weren't makeshift: few and still uncertain' (II, 76; *The Watcher*, 71).

The protagonist, an active Communist who had in his youth entertained ambitions to be a writer, is a reverse image of the author, who in his youth had thought he might have a full career in the PCI but was now mainly a writer. Amerigo's first name also hints at Calvino's own 'nationalistic' first name. Chapter V is given over to Amerigo's thoughts on Beauty, since like the author he is always inclined to think of the opposite of what his immediate surroundings suggest. In particular he thinks of the body of his girlfriend Lia (her name too is significant, being traditionally contrasted with her biblical sister Rachel, and associated with fertility and the active life – in fact at one point it emerges that Lia is pregnant). But he appears to reconcile the potential clash of loyalties between sex and commitment by concluding that even his desire to spend that Sunday making love to Lia was not incompatible with his sense of civic responsibility: 'to make sure that the world's beauty doesn't pass in vain, he thought, is also History, civic action' (II, 25; *The Watcher*, 21). These very words underline Amerigo's proximity to Kim and his ability to subsume *amore* under *storia*, and it is not surprising to learn that this novel was actually begun as early as 1953. But Amerigo is also close to the other protagonists we have been examining in this chapter, especially in his problematic dealings with sexual desire and political commitment: although his adherence to communism is the most important aspect of the protagonist's existence, in reality he never discusses politics with Lia (II, 51; *The Watcher*, 46).

When Amerigo goes home for lunch Calvino makes it explicit, in a crucial paragraph describing his books, that there is a link between the protagonist's attitudes to literature and sex:

> His library was limited. As time went by, he had realized it was best to concentrate on a few books. His youth had been full of random, insatiable reading. Now maturity led him to reflect, to avoid the superfluous. With women it had been the opposite: maturity made him impatient; he had had a succession of brief, absurd affairs, all of them, as he could tell from the beginning, mistakes. He was one of those bachelors who, from habit, like to make love in the afternoon and, at night, to sleep alone. (II, 48; *The Watcher*, 43–4)

Like Quinto and Amedeo, Ormea is another of Calvino's lazy lovers. The contrast between Amerigo's and Lia's tastes in literature is also by now a familiar one: he reads Marx and scientific writers while she devours women's magazines especially for the horoscopes, in the same way that Amedeo loved the classics of the European novel while the sunbathing woman enjoyed *Annabella*, and the protagonist of *Smog* read Communist papers and committed journals as opposed to glossy magazines with pictures of Claudia on the front. By 1963 Calvino had still not progressed much beyond the stereotypical female characters which he had already noted as a limiting factor in his fiction back in 1950 – indeed his fictional women were to remain rather one-dimensional even after the 1960s (Bonsaver, 1995c, 240–51; De Lauretis, 1989).

The link between literature and sex is developed when we are told that Amerigo always liked to be reading something when Lia phoned him so that he could resume his train of thought when she hung up (II, 48–9; *The Watcher*, 44). But if Amerigo resembles Quinto and Amedeo in his lazy attitude to sex, in his approach to literature he is much closer to Cosimo: he does not like literature about people partly because he had in his youth nourished ambitions to become a writer himself, and partly because he was now looking for something more profound in literature: 'the wisdom of the ages, or simply something that helped to understand something' (II, 49; *The Watcher*, 44). Like Cosimo, then, he has progressed from novels about people to encyclopedic and utopian works, but he also reflects Calvino's own new poetics since after this novel Calvino too abandons 'literature about people', pursuing instead 'the wisdom of the ages'. In the course of this short work Amerigo develops from someone reluctant to discuss the most important thing in his life – politics – with the woman he loves, into a person who at the end wants to tell her everything – about the election, the Cottolengo, the people he had met there and the conclusions he had reached: 'humanity reaches as far as love reaches; it has no frontiers except those we give it' (II, 69; *The Watcher*, 64). This resolution of the tensions between sex, literature and political commitment, at the end of the cycle of Calvino's realist phase, brings us back full circle: superficially it appears as if Amerigo has reached the same synthesis of Desire and History as Kim.

However, there are differences. The main one is that unlike Kim Amerigo has no foils except within his own psyche: he progresses from being someone interested in realist fiction to someone who finds the answers to his questions in Marx's early *Economic and Philosophical Manuscripts*, in a famous passage about the alienation of man (II, 49–50; *The Watcher*, 45). The quote that he finds there, which emphasises the dual importance of nature as the source of both man's sustenance and of the raw materials for human industry, reflects Calvino's own dissatisfaction with anthropocentric realism, which can be documented in a number of important theoretical writings of this time. Already in 'Il midollo del leone (The Lion's Marrow)' (*S*, 9–27) and in 'Dialogo di due scrittori in crisi (Dialogue Between Two Writers in Crisis)' (1961, in *S*, 83–9), Calvino pointed out the inadequacy of the novel for providing a documentary mimesis of reality, and in a later essay, 'Per chi si scrive (Lo scaffale ipotetico) (Whom Do We Write For or The Hypothetical Bookcase)' (1967), he argues that novels should only now be written for those who have realised that they should no longer read novels (*S*, 201; *LM*, 84). In 'La sfida al labirinto (The Challenge to the Labyrinth)' (1962) he concluded that if literature cannot provide us with a way out of the labyrinth in which we live, it must at least supply us with its most accurate map, and this involves moving from a human to a cosmic perspective: 'We require from literature a cosmic image, . . . in other words one that is on a par with the levels of knowledge that historical progress has made possible' (*S*, 123). Calvino responds to this demand for cosmic, non-anthropocentric literature in the works which follow, particularly in *Cosmicomics* (1965) and *Time and the Hunter* (1967). It was presumably with these books in mind that in an essay of 1967 he underlined how his own interests diverged from Vittorini's anthropocentrism, moving instead towards

> a knowledge in which any anthropocentric investment is abolished, in which the history of man can at last go beyond its limits, and be seen as a link, allowing itself to merge at the two ends of the history of the organization of matter, at one end forming a continuous link with the animal world . . . and at the other extending to machines which process information. (*S*, 164–5)

Calvino's new poetics clearly articulate that rejection of anthropocentric realism and echo the quote from Marx in *The Watcher* with its emphasis on man's position between nature and technology.

Calvino's early fiction, then, revolves around these three terms of sex, literature and political commitment, which the author manipulates in a series of dialectical oppositions. In the earliest realist works and the fantasy trilogy we find a facile contrast between on the one hand the reality of a love which can be reconciled with political engagement, and on the other the escapism of literature. In the later 1950s Calvino writes more about sex than about love, and now sexual adventure is depicted as an escape from socio-political responsibilities. Throughout this period the status of the literary text is discussed not only in theoretical essays but also in Calvino's creative oeuvre (Bonsaver, 1994), and remains an ambivalent element, being viewed as an obstacle to reality and commitment on some occasions, and on others being considered as a positive adjunct to *impegno*.

Although the thematics of the later fictions still centre around sexual desire and the status of the literary text, the emphasis on political engagement wanes: the dynamics of desire are explored in an original way in many of the cosmicomic stories, particularly the 'Priscilla' sequence, which deals with 'the loves of molluscs or unicellular organisms' (*S*, 265; LM, 69). It has been argued that works such as *Time and the Hunter* (1967) and *Invisible Cities* (1972) are as committed as the earlier works, but if they are, it is certainly a vaguer, more generic type of commitment. The concluding paragraph of 'The Count of Monte Cristo', the final tale in *Time and the Hunter*, in which Edmond Dantès seeks a way out of his labyrinthine prison not by action but by deductive reasoning certainly seems to point to at least a cautiously optimistic humanism on Calvino's part. Indeed Calvino quotes it as an optimistic finale in an essay written in the same year ('Cibernetica e fantasmi (Cybernetics and Ghosts)', *S*, 225; LM, 27), and more specifically, in a 1974 interview, he interprets this conclusion as an allegory of the possibility of loopholes in all the great deterministic systems, from Darwinism and Marxism to contemporary science (*S*, 2780–1).

A similar case for a committed conclusion has been made for the finale of *Invisible Cities* (Bernardini Napoletano, 1977, 199–201). There Marco Polo warns the Grand Khan that there are only two ways not to suffer in the inferno in which we live:

> The first is easy for many: accept the inferno and become such a part of it that you no longer see it. The second is risky and demands constant vigilance and instruction [*apprendimento*, wrongly translated as 'apprehension']: seek and learn to recognize who and what, in the midst of this inferno, are not inferno, then make them endure, give them space. (II, 498; *Invisible Cities*, 165)

Though the first of these alternatives recalls the warning in an an earlier essay about surrendering to 'The Sea of Objects' (1959), and the second one echoes 'The Challenge to the Labyrinth' (1962), there is a difference in Calvino's terms of opposition: in the later work it is a generically humanist rather than a specifically Marxist commitment. There is no longer any reference in these later works to major aspects of *impegno* highlighted in earlier works such as History or class consciousness. The conclusions to *Time and the Hunter* and *Invisible Cities* certainly seem linked to that strand of Marxism which is, in Calvino's own words, 'purely and simply the awareness of the hell we live in, and anyone who tries to suggest ways out is sapping this awareness of its vital force' (*S*, 192; LM, 43). However, the conclusions are the only points in these texts at which such committed notions surface, and the *engagement* they promote remains at a very general level. The other two works of the 1970s, *The Castle of Crossed Destinies* (1973) and *If on a Winter's Night a Traveller* (1979) are remote from such concerns, and more preoccupied with the status of different sign systems and that of the literary text.

Only in *Mr Palomar* does an explicit concern with society reappear in Calvino's work, and even then some of that engagement resides almost invisible, like a palimpsest below the surface of the text (see chapter 9). Calvino's abandonment of his earlier Marxist convictions was determined partly by his disillusionment with the Italian Communist Party, but also by his growing awareness in the 1960s that History is no longer something positive that can be harnessed and directed by man for his own progress. In his retrospective preface to his first collection of essays, *Una pietra sopra* (1980), he notes that the essays in the volume chart the decline of his identification with the role of 'committed intellectual' as man's faith in directing a historical process becomes no longer tenable. What replaces that faith in his own case is an element that had informed his work right from the start: 'a sense of the complex, multiple, multi-faceted and yet ultimately relative nature of everything, which elicits an attitude of systematic perplexity' (*S*, 8). These last two words encapsulate Calvino's new outlook in the works written after 1963: the increasing sense of perplexity at the revolutionary changes taking place in technology and society is concomitant with a heightened desire to elaborate patterns and symmetries in the literary mimesis of that reality.

The sense of perplexity, which we saw emerging as a theme in *The Watcher*, also leads to the less totalising, more particulate approach of the later creative works and theoretical pronouncements (Patrizi, 1989). His pursuit of the cosmic and the comic are also both aspects of a strategy to circumvent the inadequacy of the written word in traditional realist narrative: 'What I look for', he says in a 1967 article, 'in the comic or ironic or grotesque or absurd transformation of things is a way to escape from the limitations and one-sidedness of every representation and every judgment' (*S*, 197; LM, 63). This aspiration towards a more universal discourse lies at the root of Calvino's rejection of the limited and temporary nature of contemporary class analysis. It is also for these literary reasons that the key concepts of *Storia* and *coscienza di classe* disappear from his work after *The Watcher* and *Marcovaldo*.

The second aspect of his 'perplessità sistematica' is reflected in the growing importance of numerical systems and symmetries in structuring his fictions. This can be documented from the relatively simple cycle of the five years of four seasons containing the twenty Marcovaldo stories (1963), through the elaborate eleven groups of five cities in the fifty-five *Invisible Cities* and the complex interweaving of the twelve chapters and ten micronovels in *If on a Winter's Night*, to the series of triads in *Palomar* and the five senses which would have acted as the structural framework for the posthumous, unfinished *Under the Jaguar Sun* (1986). His interest in literary texts that somehow embrace the universe and are subject to mathematical constraints certainly derives from his involvement with the French writers of the Ouvroir de Littérature Potentielle (OULIPO), such as Raymond Queneau and Georges Perec, but it is also prompted by a specifically Italian influence which he alluded to in a 1968 interview: 'This is a deep-rooted vocation in Italian literature, handed on from Dante to Galileo: the notion of the literary work as a map of the world and of the knowable' (*S*, 232–33; LM, 32). Yet although works such as *Invisible Cities* and *Mr Palomar* are clearly premised on this illusion of the work of art as map of the universe or summa of knowledge, the author is aware at the outset of the inadequacy of even this new form of writing. In a crucial essay of 1967 on 'Philosophy and Literature', he regards Borges' work as one of the exemplars of an ideal synthesis between philosophy and literature, but points out that although when reading Borges we expect at any moment to see 'the secret watermark of the universe', this never quite happens, as is right (*S*, 195; LM, 48). The important point is not that literature should explain the universe, science or philosophy, but that there should be a fertile interaction between these three elements: 'We will not have a culture equal to the challenge until we compare against one another the basic problematics of science, philosophy, and literature, in order to call them all into question' (*S*, 193–4; LM, 45–6). Calvino's later works clearly respond to this challenge and are informed by the two related disciplines of science and philosophy.

What has been outlined hitherto in this chapter is the extent to which the 'svolta' in Calvino's output was determined by socio-political change and by developments in science and technology. But in that 1976 essay quoted at the start of this chapter, the author also pointed to a third factor which came into play in the early 1960s: namely the new interests of the literary avant-garde. Although the fictions of the 1950s had adumbrated the problems of the reader's role in the literary process, it was only in the next decade that Calvino articulated these fully in theoretical terms. In the 1967 essay, 'Per chi si scrive (Lo scaffale ipotetico) (Whom Do We Write For or The Hypothetical Bookshelf)', he concludes that since even the most revolutionary works may be read by reactionaries and vice versa (one thinks of the character Kim reading Kipling's *Kim*), it is not the text but the reader who is crucial (*S*, 204; LM, 87–8). These new perceptions undermine the outmoded Marxist model whereby the writer and the text were the crucial agents effecting change in the reader, and the essays of this period stress instead the precarious status of the text and the primacy of the role of the reader, all of which help to explain the course taken by Calvino's fiction in the 1970s, with its new stress on the reader. But despite the clear change of direction after 1963, one of Calvino's major constants remains that of expanding the confines of fiction and allowing literature to embrace in a fertile union even the disciplines that seem furthest from it: history, science, philosophy.

One key text acts as link between early and late Calvino, between his realist and postmodernist phases. In June 1964 before abandoning realism altogether, when he was just starting to write his first cosmicomic stories, he went back to his beginnings and reissued his first novel in a definitive third edition (the second had been published in 1954). To accompany the novel he composed the substantial preface (discussed above in Chapter 2) which ends on the feelings of anxiety aroused by writing a first novel. This realisation that writing one's first novel means losing forever the infinite potential of beginning (I, 1202–4; *The Path*, 28–9), is something that Calvino also found confirmed by Borges's *Garden of Forking Paths* with its insistence that one plot solution automatically excludes all others. From 1964 onwards Calvino will be haunted by this univocal nature of all writing, and will adopt textual strategies to circumvent that limiting factor, seeking to endow the text with the potential to contain the other words that could have been written, the discarded plots, the text itself in negative. Reviewing Calvino's last work, *Mr Palomar*, the poet Seamus Heaney wrote of the author's fondness for 'binary blarney' and observed that 'symmetries and arithmetic have always tempted Italo Calvino's imagination to grow flirtatious and to begin its fantastic display' (Heaney, 1985, 1). Something of that love of binary systems and symmetries pervades, as we have seen, even the pre-1964 works, but it will more obviously inform those written after 1964, when Calvino is, again in Heaney's words, 'on the high wire, on lines of thought strung out above the big international circus' (Heaney, 1985, 60).

Chapter 6

Experimental Space

The Cosmicomic Stories

Just as the brief creative crisis of 1949–51 had been resolved by the originality of the first story of Calvino's fantasy trilogy, so the more protracted literary silence of 1959–63 was broken by an even more radical narrative solution. There were few clues in what Calvino had written up until 1963 that would point to his invention of an entirely new genre, the cosmicomic tale. This was to prove a fertile space for literary experiment for Calvino, as he continued to use the form for the next two decades, publishing a total of thirty-three cosmicomic stories: twelve in *Le cosmicomiche* (*Cosmicomics*) (1965), another eleven in *Ti con zero* (*Time and the Hunter*) (1967), including eight more new tales in the twenty that make up *La memoria del mondo e altre storie cosmicomiche* (*The Memory of the World and Other Cosmicomic Stories*) (1968) and two more in the definitive collection *Cosmicomiche vecchie e nuove* (*Cosmicomics Old and New*) (1984). Yet intimations there were. Milanini (II, 1320) drew attention to the precedents in the close of 'Dialogo sul satellite (Dialogue on the Satellite)', written as far back as November 1957 and inspired by the first satellite in space. But the rest of the 'Dialogo sul satellite' is also worth examining. The main topic is the then incipient space rivalry between the USA and USSR, concerning which the sceptical speaker argues that the presence of the satellite should not diminish but rather enhance other human enterprises which should reflect the fact that the interplanetary era has begun (III, 232–3). This sense of challenge and the aspiration that other areas of our activity, including literature, should match the progress made in science is the first articulation of the keynotes of Calvino's poetics in the 1960s ('The Challenge to the Labyrinth', *S*, 105–23; 'Philosophy and Literature', *S*, 188–96; *LM*, 39–49).

Alongside these scientific thematics, this early dialogue also evinces Calvino's admiration for the two Italian writers for whom the moon and space had a special resonance, and who would become key literary models for the new cosmicomic genre, Galileo and Leopardi. Galileo is mentioned explicitly as having radically altered our view of the relationship between the earth and the heavens (III, 231), while the reference to Leopardi is implicit in the sceptical speaker's question about what 'pastori dell'Asia centrale' will think about the satellite (echoing the title of one of Leopardi's most famous 'lunar' poems, 'Canto notturno di un pastore errante dell'Asia'). Calvino would continue to devote substantial attention to both authors in the 1960s, even going so far as to claim in 1967 that Galileo was the greatest Italian prose writer, and that his language when describing the moon was the model for Leopardi's (*S*, 228, 231–2; LM, 31–2), and both authors are cited as favourite models in *Six Memos* (*S*, 651–2, 653, 665–6; *Six Memos*, 24–5, 26, 41–3). This confirms that one of the constants of Calvino's creative method is an intertextual strategy which is based on the juxtaposition of literary opposites: just as for his first novel he had explicitly tried to mingle *For Whom the Bell Tolls* with *Treasure Island* (I, 1196), so in the 1960s he attempts to combine the world of science and astronomy (his reading matter in 1964) with the most literary of Italian scientific writers and the most pessimistic of Italian poets. Another intertextual model for the cosmicomic tales was Leopardi's *Operette morali*, a work Calvino regards without equal in other literatures (*S*, 671; *Six Memos*, 49). However, it would be pointless to list all the possible intertexts for the cosmicomic tales, since Calvino's literary eclecticism knows no bounds. His own lengthy list is both serious and ludic: '*Cosmicomics* are indebted particularly to Leopardi, the Popeye comics, Samuel Beckett, Giordano Bruno, Lewis Carroll, the paintings of Matta and in some cases the works of Landolfi, Immanuel Kant, Borges, and Grandville's engravings' (II, 1322).

An important non-literary source for these fictions, according to the author himself, was the work of the philosopher Giorgio de Santillana (II, 1320). Though a number of critics acknowledge this source, few investigate it in any detail. Calvino, who had met de Santillana in Boston during his trip to the United States in 1959–60, was on the committee of the Associazione Culturale Italiana that invited the philosopher to give a lecture in Turin in March 1963, entitled 'Fato antico e fato moderno (Ancient and Modern Ideas of Fate)'. At least four major points of the lecture would be important for the cosmicomic stories: first the idea that 'the great cosmological myths both preceded and had been the equivalent of modern science' (De Santillana, 1963, 39); second that the coldness of those early astronomical calculations is similar to the neutrality of contemporary physics (De Santillana, 1963, 41); third, the idea that Dante's poem is a kind of literary ziggurat, a summa or tower of Babel, with its astronomical, mathematical and musical intervals (De Santillana, 1963, 47); and fourth, de Santillana first quotes from Galileo the passage about the mutability of the earth being superior to its immobility (De Santillana, 1963, 55–6), a passage quoted by Calvino as epigraph to one of the most important cosmicomic tales, 'Priscilla' (II, 273; *Time and the Hunter*, 58). The fact that cosmogony, the study of the earth's origins, begins in the twentieth century was one of the points that validated the modernity of Calvino's new fictions, but at the same time the author, obeying his contrastive poetics, was keen to link these modern 'myths' with their ancient counterparts (II, 1305–6), as de Santillana had done.

As for chronology of composition, the earliest stories were begun as far back as November 1963, the first four being published in November 1964 (in the journal *Il Caffè*): 'La distanza della Luna (The Distance of the Moon)', 'Sul far del giorno (At Daybreak)', 'Un segno nello spazio (A Sign in Space)', 'Tutto in un punto (All at One Point)'. A collection of twelve tales was published as *Le cosmicomiche* in November 1965. Although for a long time the date of publication of the volume suggested to many critics a neat chronological divide between the works of the first two decades (1945–64) and those of the second twenty years (1965–85), the chronology of these first tales proves that such a division is too clear-cut: we now know that Calvino's activity as a writer goes back at least as far as 1943; in addition it is clear that even as early as the 1960s Calvino relished working on opposing genres at the same time, initiating the cosmicomic genre at the same time as writing the last Marcovaldo tales and composing an important preface to his first neorealistic novel, many echoes of which are found in 'Un segno nello spazio (A Sign in Space)' (Benedetti, 1993). To Benedetti's analysis it is worth adding that Qfwfq's sense of 'remorse' and 'shame' about his first sign in space are the dominant sentiments felt by the author about his first novel – 'rimorso' is mentioned six times in the preface, and at one stage was to have been its starting point (I, 1190). Other textual echoes confirm her argument: Qfwfq's phrase 'me lo portavo dietro . . . s'intrometteva tra me e ogni cosa' (II, 110) is similar to the key phrases in the preface 'un rimorso che mi sarei portato dietro per anni' (I, 1190) and 'il primo libro diventa subito un diaframma tra te e l'esperienza' (I, 1203). The precise date of composition of both the story and the preface clinches her hypothesis: the story, begun in November 1963, was mostly drafted in May 1964, while the *prefazione* was completed in June 1964. Another important chronological detail is the fact that for the first time ever Calvino does not place the date of composition at the end of the book (Milanini, 1990), again confirming the irrelevance of contemporary history to a narrative that occupies itself with larger and more important swathes of time.

Once more it is illuminating to begin by examining the architecture of each volume. In *Cosmicomics* the first two tales close on the motif of the lost female love (Signora Vhd Vhd, and Qfwfq's sister $G'd(w)^n$), while the third one concerns the rivalry between two males (Qfwfq and Kgwgk) with no female present. The next three tales follow this pattern: two stories of lost females (Signora $Ph(i)Nk_o$, Ayl), then a tale of male rivalry (Pfwfp). The seventh tale once more is of a lost female (Lll), while the eighth is of two males competing (Decano (k)yK); the next two contain love triangles (in 'La forma dello spazio (The Form of Space)', the desired female, Ursula H'x, is a cosmicomic version of Ursula Andress, star of the 1960s film *She*), the eleventh concentrates on a sole protagonist versus the universe, and the final tale comes down to earth to focus on the opposite end of the life spectrum, the first mollusc to secrete matter to form a spiral shell, but again in order to attract an unnamed female Other. The collection is thus framed by desire as the key motive force of the universe, and is not a univocal work about science and evolution. In fact, literature plays as important a role as science here: the love stories are often reworkings of ancient myths (Eurydice, Endymion), suggesting that fiction now can but repeat in a combinatory way the elements of all mythic stories, and there are, as we shall see, more literary than scientific intertexts.

The endings to the tales in the first collection are significant. Though many stories close with the motif of the lost female Other, the second tale 'Sul far del giorno', about the dawn of light, finishes paradoxically with the most important beginning of all, the Big Bang, this time in brief understated sentences rather than the long final sentences of the first, third and fourth tales: 'It was night. Everything was just beginning' (II, 107; *Cosmicomics*, 28). Indeed the last words of all twelve tales embody appropriate motifs of closure or infinity: the first story ends with the howling of dogs at the moon; the second, as we have seen, with the beginning of light; the third with the coexistence of signs and space; and so on, down to the last tale about the mollusc's spiral shell which ends on a proleptic view of an infinite future 'without shores, without boundaries' (II, 221; *Cosmicomics*, 153). Perhaps the most elegant conclusion is that of 'La forma dello spazio': the virtuoso penultimate sentence, almost a page long, replete with alliterations ('fare la furba infilandosi dentro i fiocchi della <<effe>> che si affinano finché diventano filiformi (trying to act sly, slipping behind the tails of the *f* which trail off until they become wisps)': II, 192; *Cosmicomics*, 123) is then followed by the final sentence which imagines a cartoon-like unravelling of all the words on the page, so that the ink forms the three parallel lines of the three characters in the love-triangle, which self-referentially signifies nothing other than itself (Bonsaver, 1995c).

Despite the many innovations in content, there are also links with other works. In 'Giochi senza fine' the motif of the chaser being chased is present, as in the later story 'L'inseguimento', but already the confusion between the two roles of pursued and pursuer had appeared in one of the first stories Calvino wrote, as early as 1943, 'Solidarietà' (III, 807–9). The clumsy Qfwfq trying to follow the talented Lll (II, 145) recycles the earlier motif of the inadequate boy skier trying to emulate the natural skill of the female skier in 'Avventura di uno sciatore' (1959) (Guj, 1988), the great uncle of 'Lo zio acquatico', who loves explaining about plants, is yet another version of Calvino's own father, while the motif of the tadpoles here (II, 146) had already emerged at the epiphanic close of another early fiction, 'Fiume asciutto' (III, 800), of 1943. 'Quanto scommettiamo' includes a reference to the fate of Lucien de Rubempré at the end of Balzac's *Les Illusions perdues* (II, 161), already a favourite passage of the reader in 'Avventura di un lettore' (II, 1127), while the image of the black words on the white page submerging all reasoning (II, 163) has many precedents (Bernardini Napolitano, 1977, 42, n. 41), but it is particularly close to the finale of 'Avventura di un poeta' (II, 1172). In 'I Dinosauri', the name Fior di felce hints at the fairy tale elements in this tale, as does the closing scene in which Qfwfq sees his own offspring clearly betraying dinosauric characteristics as they play at chasing butterflies or battering pine cones to extract the kernels: these hints of Pin and the child protagonist of 'Ultimo viene il corvo' confirm the thesis that these evolutionary tales are as much about Calvino's own development as an author as about evolution in general (Capozzi, 1989; Benedetti, 1993).

Before turning to the later cosmicomic collections, one should examine the stories which Calvino did not consider immediately suitable for publication. When putting together the first volume, *Cosmicomics*, he excluded from it 'Fino a che dura il Sole (While the Sun Lasts)' written in September 1964, 'La Luna come un fungo (The Moon as Mushroom)' written November–December 1964 and 'I meteoriti (The Meteorites)' written September 1965, all of which were reserved for the third collection of cosmicomic tales, *La memoria del mondo e altre storie cosmicomiche* (1968). The first of these concerns Colonel Eggg and his wife of diametrically opposed character, Ggge. When the retired colonel tries to reassure his wife that the sun will still last at least five million millennia, she starts to feel time is running out, and pulls out the suitcases to prepare for removal; he too realises that 'all that surrounds is merely temporary' (II, 1230), a pessimistic motif that will sound more insistently in Calvino's oeuvre in the 1970s and 1980s, especially in *Palomar.* Perhaps these more elderly thematics lack the propulsion of desire and rivalry that informs the twelve tales in *Cosmicomics* and the story was consequently omitted, since it would thus have made the collection less of a uniform macrotext (Bernardini Napoletano, 1977, 59–62).

'La Luna come un fungo' was also deselected, even though it did contain a love triangle between Qfwfq, the evil pirate Bm Bn and the girl Flw. At least one of the reasons why this was not included in the 1965 collection was probably because it rehearsed too closely some of the themes and characters of *The Cloven Viscount.* Inspector Oo, with his flawed calculations on how the earth would separate into continents, is clearly an updated version of Pietrochiodo and Dr Trelawney, since he is a scientific specialist who is explicitly said to be incapable of taking sides in the moral debate (II, 1189). As the moon starts to form like a mushroom on the earth's surface, the fisherman Qfwfq, perched atop the rising ball of granite, resists the temptation to steal other fishermen's fish, trying only 'to carry out good actions to help the victims' (II, 1460). This altruistic sentiment, which is articulated in the version of the story which first appeared in *Il Giorno* in May 1965, echoes the Good Half's actions in the first part of the trilogy, and is suppressed when the tale is rewritten for the 1968 collection, *La memoria del mondo,* thus adding weight to the idea that this repeated motif was one reason for the story's exclusion from the 1965 *Cosmicomics.*

'I meteoriti' was written in September 1965 and therefore at the same time as 'The dinosaurs', so theoretically it could have been included in the first collection since 'The dinosaurs' was in fact inserted in *Le cosmicomiche* at proof stage.

One reason for excluding it is that for the first time the love triangle in a cosmicomic story concerns Qfwfq caught between two women: his first wife Xha, obsessed with keeping the cosmos clean, and the disorganised Wha, who in the midst of chaos still manages to produce successful products, whether they be minestrone, the Sphinxes or the River Po, and who eventually becomes the reason why he leaves Xha. In the end, however, he loses both women, Xha in the increasingly untidy, pulviscular universe, Wha hidden in chaos. This theme of order and disorder has already been well explored (Hume, 1989), but it is worth adding that the obsession with rubbish and pollution looks both backwards to *Smog* (1958) and forwards to 'La poubelle agréée' (1974–76).

Also written by 1965 was 'La molle Luna' (1965), but it was left out of *Cosmicomics* to become the first item in the second cosmicomic collection *Time and the Hunter*, published in 1967. One reason for the story's omission from the earlier volume is that unlike all the tales in the 1965 *Cosmicomics* which are firmly set in the remote past (before the Big Bang, before the beginning of space and light etc.), this one is about a past that is also a present and a future – Calvino often stressed that his cosmicomic stories differed from traditional science fiction by being set in the remote past not in a dystopic future (II, 1300, 1305). In a glistening New York made out of nylon, plastic, and chrome steel, Qfwfq and Sybil discuss the alarming proximity of the moon to the earth. The idea of the moon falling to earth owes something to Leopardi's poetic fragment 'Odi, Melisso', in which the moon lands on a field and turns black like spent coals – a favourite passage actually quoted by Calvino in a 1984 lecture (*S*, 1675–6). The weak ending with Sybil now the opposite of her precise scientific self and simply gorging herself into obesity may also account for the story's omission from the 1965 collection.

'L'origine degli Uccelli (The Origin of the Birds)', the second story in *Time and the Hunter*, was begun in 1964 but not completed until 1967. As in *The Non-Existent Knight* Teodora claims to be drawing a map of Agilulfo's travels, so here the narrator maintains that he is using a semiotic medium, the comic strip, which is superior to words on a page (II, 236–7), though these cartoons are not visible, they are merely described verbally. Not long into the story the narrator decides that it is better to vary the kind of comic pictures used, alternating action frames with discursive ideological ones (II, 238), a pattern of contrast which we observed at work in alternate chapters of Calvino's first novel and throughout his oeuvre. The plot questions the criteria by which we define what is monstrous and what is not by suggesting that the appearance of birds long after all the other reptiles had developed underlines the arbitrariness of the categories of monster and non-monster. As the earth bangs into the continent of the birds Qfwfq leaps onto the latter: there he sees fishes with spiders' legs, worms with wings, all the potential but discarded forms that the animal kingdom could have developed but did not, in other words the natural world in negative. This is one of the key ideas of *Time and the Hunter*: it appears in this second tale, resurfaces in 'Meiosis' in the centre of the collection, and is prominent at the end when the definitive text of Dumas' *Count of Monte Cristo* is seen to exclude all the other possible developments the plot could have had – there too the metaphor used for these discarded alternatives is of a 'novel in negative'. Qfwfq's attempt to find beauty in the midst of these 'monsters' (II, 240; *Time and the Hunter*, 20) also links with the contrasting topics of beauty and deformation which had been central to *The Watcher.* The tale ends with both the motif of the lost female Other and with the note of infinity, this time a verbal equivalent of a series of photographic enlargements of a bird: first its head, then a detail of its head, finally its eye (II, 247; *Time and the Hunter*, 27).

'I cristalli' (1967) is set in today's New York, which is described as an agglomeration of imperfect prisms where right-angled streets encourage belief in a symmetrical crystal city, but Qfwfq knows these smooth surfaces of glass are rather a haphazard accumulation of molecules enclosing the original magma. He remembers the first springtime that he and Vug saw when beautiful symmetrical crystals and prisms emerged from the magma and he kissed her. This reversal of traditional associations is sustained when Qfwfq admits to being a lover of order, but not because he wants to repress his own instincts, rather because he associates passion and love with symmetry and pattern, not with disorder and excess (II, 250–1; *Time and the Hunter*, 31). He hopes that the irregularities of today are merely part of a giant symmetry that will eventually be visible – a motif that will be developed more fully in *Invisible Cities*. But in the meantime all he can do is go home, put whisky and ice in a glass, and in this flawed world listen to a record of Thelonious Monk, played by a diamond stylus.

The next story in the collection closes the first section of tales, but 'Il sangue, il mare (Blood, Sea)' was in fact written in 1966, before 'I cristalli', so Calvino must have felt it possessed more effective elements of closure. In fact, being about cells rather than about beings, this story does effect a better transition to the tales of the second section which are all about cellular organisms. Qfwfq is here a cell inside a passenger of a car on an Italian motorway: he is flirting in the back with Zylphia, with whom he remembers swimming in the primeval ocean eons ago. Page-length sentence-paragraphs (II, 259–63) which border on 'prosa d'arte' (Bernardini Napoletano, 1977, 74–80) convey Qfwfq's attempts to record with precision the differences that have taken place in the world since that time. The idea that the outside world is insignificant compared to the flowing of blood cells inside (II, 261) reflects Calvino's new poetics in the 1960s, abandoning the earlier project to inscribe within literature areas such as history, politics and society. The final description of the car crash that ends the tale is given in another enormous sentence, but ending on a predictable note of closure, that of death (as well as as constituting a verbal homage to the contemporary Goddard film *Weekend*).

The second section of *Time and the Hunter*, entitled 'Priscilla', consists of three tales, 'Mitosis', 'Meiosis' and 'Death'. 'Mitosis', the term for the ordinary division of cells as opposed to their mature division (meiosis), is also mostly written in half-page paragraph-length sentences. It opens with Qfwfq expressing his sense of 'pienezza' (II, 274) when he was a single cell, a distant echo of the pursuit of 'fullness of life' in Calvino's early works, *I giovani del Po* and *The Cloven Viscount*. Since he can only talk of the period before the cell's division, the real love story only happens when his memory fails as the cell splits, but he still has time to play with words when describing the feelings of the single cell: 'questo goloso geloso dolore'(II, 285), 'quel po' di plasma strozzato o strizzato lí' (II, 286). The tale ends with perhaps the longest sentence in Calvino's entire oeuvre describing the moment when one cell becomes two (II, 286–8), and Qfwfq anticipates his future down to the moment when he encounters Pr*iscílla* L*ang*-wood who lives at 193 Rue Vaugirard, Paris quinzième (a cipher, as the vowels and consonants suggest, for the name of the woman Calvino met in Paris in the 1960s and subsequently married, Ch*i*ch*ita* Si*ng*er). All three tales of this second section are in a sense one tale, since they have one overall title, 'Priscilla', and instead of having three individual epigraphs, the whole section begins with three pages of quotations from embryologists, computer experts, philosophers and Galileo. This structural ambivalence between the one story and the three reflects the thematics of the tales themselves, which deal with the development between monocellular and pluricellular beings.

'Meiosis' is a love story about two pluricellular entities, Qfwfq and Priscilla, though only at the end do we discover that they are in fact camels. The story explores the physical composition of the narrating subject, who notes that of the forty-six chromosomes in each cell, twenty-three derive from each parent, so 'I continue carrying my parents with me in all my cells, and I'll never be able to free myself of this burden' (II, 293; *Time and the Hunter*, 80). While this links with the quote from Sartre cited in the epigraph about the various Anchises that sit on their sons' backs, it also hints at how in writing in this scientific mode Calvino too is expressing his own DNA, the inheritance of his scientific parents. There is also the theme of forking paths: at one point Qfwfq is afraid he is not the sum of all the dominant features in his ancestors' heredity, but rather the product of all the elements that have been suffocated and excluded in his family tree – again the motif of elements in negative (II, 295; *Time and the Hunter*, 82). The tale ends with the male camel making love to Priscilla remembering moments of leisure.

'Death', which was the last narrative to be written for the volume, was composed in September 1967 after Calvino had written 'The Count of Monte Cristo'. It amounts almost to a history of the world in five pages, since it begins with the first drops of life on earth and ends stressing the links that extend from the nucleic acids to man's technological achievements in machines and computers, almost a narrative counterpart to the key passage from the essay on Vittorini (cited above in Chapter 5) about man's links at one end with the animal world and at the other with machines and matter (*S*, 164–5). Here the emphasis is on the discontinuity of sexual beings compared to the immortality of asexual organisms.

The image of the primitive, continuous mangrove forest leads to a glimpse of the sky, but above the forest is another roof suffocating us, the roof of words and signs that threaten to submerge us, again expressed in *enumeraciòn caotica*, beginning with the primordial matter of life and ending with the napalm bombs (which in 1967 the Americans were dropping on Vietnam).

The four stories that constitute the last section in *Time and the Hunter*, entitled 't zero', are not really cosmicomic tales but rather fictions inspired by mathematics and deductive logic. It has already been pointed out (Milanini, 1990) that the narrator of the first of these, the title story 't zero', is called simply Q, who thus acts as a transition from the earlier Qfwfq tales to the last three stories in which the narrator is not named at all. The formula t_0 (in Italian 'Ti con zero') expresses the point of time which marks the beginning of Q's speculations about whether his arrow A will hit the lion L leaping on him before t_0 becomes t_1, t_2, t_3, etc. The idea derives from one of Zeno's famous paradoxes, that an arrow in flight is actually stationary, since if space is divisible, then the arrow is always above just one piece of ground. But t_0 is also a mathematical formula to express the age of the universe. The story recounts Q's speculations as to whether the arrow will hit or miss its target, thereby saving or ending Q's life. Each point in time is so rich, however, that Q decides to inhabit only t_0, and the tale amply describes the richness of that infinitesimal moment, which extends from the savanna in which he is hunting all the way to today's cities with their red, yellow, green traffic lights. The story ends, predictably, as the instant t_0 slides into t_1 but we never learn the vital truth about the trajectories of the arrow and the lion.

Again there are links with contemporary essays by Calvino. At the start Q speculates that the sequel to his encounter with the lion will be 'either the tribe's festivities for the hunter who returns with the lion's remains or the funeral of the hunter as through the savannah spreads the terror of the prowling murderous lion' (II, 316; *Time and the Hunter*, 106). The idea that all tales originate from when the first hunter-gatherers returned from an expedition with the first ever narrative was the one which opened a famous essay written in the same year, 1967, 'Cybernetics and Ghosts' (*S*, 205–28; *LM*, 3–27). Yet this story, like all the stories of this section, is very different from the earlier cosmicomic tales in having no dialogue, only the deductive speculations of the protagonist.

If 't zero' was largely concerned with time, 'L'inseguimento (The Chase)' concentrates more on space; and if that first deductive tale alluded to the elementary nature of all narrative, this one is written in the vein of a thriller, an evolved but stereotyped genre which had long attracted Calvino, surfacing at least twice in his very first novel (in Zena's *Supergiallo*, and in the account of Pelle's death). The first-person narrator is trying to escape from his would-be killer by driving into the gridlocked city centre, where at a busy junction all traffic stops. But if all movement stops, he deduces, there can be no chase, the only room for manoeuvre is a theoretical space (II, 330; *Time and the Hunter*,

121). Consequently, he reasons, since all the cars are part of an interchangeable system, each car could contain a killer pursuing the driver of the vehicle in front. Following this line to its logical conclusion, he finds a pistol in the glove compartment and realises that he too must be a killer, and that the only way to survive is to break the chain by killing the driver in front (II, 334–5; *Time and the Hunter*, 126–7). What surfaces here is that motif of the flaws in great deterministic theories that lie at the root of the cosmicomic tales (*S*, 2780–1), though there had already been humorous deployment of the same notion in one of the author's earliest stories, 'La pecora nera (The Black Sheep)' (1944, III, 821–2), in which the chain of burglaries is broken because of one man who refuses to rob his neighbour. 'L'inseguimento' ends with the protagonist killing the man in front, but the infinite stalemate resumes since as he turns into the street at right angles he is in turn immediately deprived of movement by another traffic jam.

'Il guidatore notturno (The Night Driver)' continues the driving theme and that of the abolition of time and space, but in this tale the narrative situation is reversed: instead of heading into the congested daytime city centre, the driver here heads away from it along a motorway at night. Again mathematics informs this story: the first-person protagonist is presumably called X, since he tells us he is driving from A to B where he hopes to meet his lover Y with whom he wants to be reconciled after a quarrel, but he is afraid that his rival Z may reach Y in B first. The shift to the nocturnal setting means that the story dispenses with landcape details and 'requires a different method of reading, more precise but also simplified, since the darkness erases all the picture's details which might be distracting and underlines only the indispensable elements' (II, 336; *Time and the Hunter*, 129). This metaliterary mention of 'a different . . . reading' implies that we too have to read this tale differently, more as a neutral but accurate semiosis as opposed to traditional, referential mimesis (Gronda, 1983). X fears that every overtaking car may be that of his rival Z, and that any car coming in the opposite direction may be Y's, so that that crucial message might be drowned in all the other messages transmitted by the motorway and its traffic. The only solution is in fact an impasse: both X and Y must continue to travel along this motorway, avoiding arrivals and departures that would be so full of univocal sensations, 'freed finally from the awkward thickness of our persons and voices and moods, reduced to luminous signals' (II, 343; *Time and the Hunter*, 136).

The story is innovative in its attempt to integrate the clarity of mathematics with the ambiguity of literature (one of the ideals of the OULIPO, Ouvroir de Littérature Potentielle), and in its allusions to information theory, semiotics and a degree zero of writing. The structure of the tale is also mathematically symmetrical: the opening paragraph describes X's journey, the second paragraph recounts the quarrel with Y, the third describes the rival Z, while the middle paragraphs reverse the movement of travel and hypothesise all three characters travelling in the opposite direction. The aspirations to abolish the self of both the writer and fictional characters do indeed correspond to Roland Barthes' idea of a 'degree zero of writing' as has been suggested (Gronda, 1983), and the attempt to isolate a 'pure' communication amidst superfluous noise derives from information theory while the mathematical elements confirm Calvino's closeness to Queneau and other members of OULIPO. However, the attempt to eliminate 'lo spessore ingombrante delle nostre persone' is a constant literary ideal in Calvino, first adumbrated as early as the 1940s (in the article 'Saremo come Omero', *S*, 1483–7): there he identified the writer's main problem as 'how to deal with that cumbersome character [quell'ingombrantissimo personaggio] for the modern writer, the self' (*S*, 1484), and this aspiration to uncluttered writing remains a Calvinian ideal right till the end of his life, as we shall see in the crucial eighth chapter of *If on a Winter's Night a Traveller* (II, 779), and in his advocacy of 'lightness' as one of his own literary ideals (*S*, 631–55).

The concluding tale of *Time and the Hunter*, 'The Count of Monte Cristo', owes its position to its embracing of the many other themes in the rest of the collection as well as to its greater length and complexity. Divided into nine numbered sections, it opens with Edmund Dantès in his cell speculating on the labyrinthine structure of the Château d'If (II, 344–5; *Time and the Hunter*, 137–9). In section 2 a fundamental contrast is established between the Abate Faria's empirical approach in attempting to escape and Dantès' preference, in the light of the unreliability of sensory perceptions, for theory and deductive logic: he concludes that the only way to escape the condition of prisoner is to understand mentally how the prison is structured (II, 347; *Time and the Hunter*, 140), and this knowledge derives from Faria's mistakes. Gradually he realizes that apart from If, three other islands are involved, since with the money from the island of Monte Cristo Faria wants to release Napoleon from Elba, and later from St Elena, so perhaps the two prisoners Dantès and Napoleon are identical. The points of the past and future converge only at the time and space of If, but radiate out towards the past of Dantès' arrest and the future of Waterloo, as in 'L'inseguimento'. The Borgesian line of forking paths is specifically mentioned here: 'there are points where the line that one of us is following bifurcates, ramifies, fans out' (II, 353; *Time and the Hunter*, 148). These various lines are like the possible alternative plots of Dumas' novel, *The Count of Monte Cristo*, which Dumas' two assistants are working on, handing to him possible plot alternatives. Here is that anguish, first articulated in the preface to *The Path*, that once something is written in print it destroys not only all the plot alternatives but also the memories and experiences attached to it (I, 1202–4; *The Path*, 28–9). Faria and Dantès now struggle in the midst of the paper on Dumas' desk, covered in ink, trying to find out whether there is an escape route or not: the variants number 'miliardi di miliardi' (II, 355; *Time and the Hunter*, 150), an allusion to Queneau's combinatory text *Cent mille milliards de poèmes* (1961). The plot alternatives discarded by Dumas amount to a novel in negative (II, 355; *Time and the Hunter*, 151), and the consequence of this is an elegant paradox which will haunt Calvino's remaining works: 'To plan a book – or an escape – the first thing to know is what to exclude' (II, 356; *Time and the Hunter*, 151). This narrative too ends on the motif of infinity, Faria continuing to try to escape by trial and error, Dantès by deduction and hypothesis. The final sentence suggests but does not guarantee an exit from the labyrinth, but it was a conclusion that Calvino found optimistic ('Cybernetics and Ghosts', *S*, 224–5; LM, 27) and was also consistent with the views in 'The Challenge to the Labyrinth', in which no facile escape from the labyrinth is offered:

> If I succeed in mentally constructing a fortress from which it is impossible to escape, this conceived fortress either will be the same as the real one – and in this case it is certain we shall never escape from here, but at least we will achieve the serenity of one who knows he is here because he could be nowhere else – or it will be a fortress from which escape is even more impossible than from here – and this, then, is a sign that here an opportunity of escape exists: we have only to identify the point where the imagined fortress does not coincide with the real one and then find it. (II, 356; *Time and the Hunter*, 151–2)

Calvino's 'Count of Monte Cristo', like the other cosmicomic stories, is very much about not surrendering to the labyrinth, and suggests that rewriting is one of the escape routes (Bernardini Napoletano, 1977, 54–7; Musarra, 1996).

After the publication of *Time and the Hunter* Calvino issued in the following year a third, but less well known, volume of cosmicomic tales, *La memoria del mondo e altre storie cosmicomiche* (1968). It consisted of twenty tales, six from *Le cosmicomiche*, six from *Ti con zero* and eight 'new' ones. In fact five of the latter had already appeared in newspapers or periodicals, so the only three genuinely unpublished stories in this collection were: 'Le conchiglie e il tempo (Shells and Time)', 'Tempesta solare (Solar Storm)' and 'Il cielo di pietra (The Sky of Stone)' (II, 1457). The structure of this new volume was also important in that it was divided, like *Marcovaldo*, into five sections of four stories each, and the title of each section articulates the ambitious, global scope of the work: Four Stories on the Moon; Four Stories on the Earth; Four Stories on the Sun, the Stars, the Galaxies; Four Stories on Evolution; Four Stories on Time and Space. In a later statement the author claimed that this was the cosmicomic volume that he had wanted to write from the start, since it was a more 'organic' volume than the previous two (II, 1458) – presumably alluding to the comprehensive coverage suggested by the sections' titles.

We have already examined above the three tales that had been written by 1965, so now let us look at the other five. 'Le conchiglie e il tempo (Shells and Time)' began life as a continuation of 'La spirale', and was composed largely in October 1966, yet it and 'La memoria del mondo (The Memory of the World)' (1967) were the only two excluded from both *Time and the Hunter* and the 1984 volume *Cosmicomiche vecchie e nuove*. In fact even the version of 'Le conchiglie e il tempo' published in 1968 is a severely slimmed down story compared with its manuscript form. The epigraph claims that the first fossil shells go back to 520 million years ago, so Qfwfq, who had formed the first shell in 'La spirale', grandly claims at the outset that he created the dimension of time, since his desire to create a shell was an attempt to secrete one part of his present from the corrosive influence of time. However, shells are ultimately superseded by the sand which eventually settles on them, since sand-time deposits layers of other shells on them (II, 1245) – a phrase reminiscent of the close of 'La formica argentina (The Argentine Ant)' (I, 482; *Adam, One Afternoon*, 190). Paradoxically, the huge shell-cemetery in which fossils would later be found would turn out to be their ultimate monument to time, a vertical cross-section of history that would aid humanity in escaping from the eternal cycle of the seasons; but the only reason men know how to read the fossils is because the molluscs decided to write with them. The final paradox is that man has knit together from these discontinuous fragments the continuity of time and human history. Yet man's history is the opposite of the mollusc's: what has been lost to man is the hand of the potter who made the vase, the bookcases of the library at Alexandria, the pronunciation of the scribe who wrote the manuscript, the flesh of the mollusc that secreted the shell (II, 1247; see Hume, 1989)

'La memoria del mondo' is the counterpart to 'Le conchiglie e il tempo', but also its opposite. Set in an unspecified future, the tale is narrated by the outgoing director of an institute which is cataloguing for posterity information about every human, plant and animal in the world, but for the information to be manageable it has to be reduced to a meaningful minimum. The director is informing his successor, Müller, of the inside details of the project: excessive information may be confusing, therefore some details need to be eliminated, so one can, paradoxically, provide more information by supplying less! He recognises that since the really important information is what is omitted, perhaps then the catalogue project is not the record of the world but its negative. Hence he has falsified the picture of his late wife, Angela, by eliminating from the record the details of any of his male colleagues since one might have been her lover: the logical consequence of this is that he also has to eliminate Müller. The phrase in the centre of the tale used to define humanity at the moment of its extinction is significant: 'What will the human race be at the moment of its extinction? A certain amount of information on itself and on the world, a finite amount, since it will no longer be able to renew itself or increase' (II, 1250). This is strikingly similar to Calvino's own words about humanity in an interview from the same year (1967): 'man is only an opportunity which the world has to collect some information about itself. Consequently, literature is for me just a series of attempts to gain knowledge of and classify information on the world' (II, xxiii).

Why were these two tales excluded from the 1967 and 1984 collections? 'La memoria del mondo' was omitted because it departs from the cosmicomic

Qfwfq tales: it is cosmic without being comic, it borders more closely on realism, or at least on dystopian realism, with its institute, and its traditionally named characters (Dr Müller, Angelica), whereas the characters in *Cosmicomics* and *Time and the Hunter* either had defamiliarising names (Qfwfq, Vug, N'ba N'ga, etc.), mathematical names (Q, X, Y, Z), no names at all ('L'inseguimento'), or names from world literature (Dantès). It remains more difficult to understand why 'Le conchiglie e il tempo' was excluded, except when we remember that Calvino was unhappy with its length in manuscript form in 1966 and eventually cut it drastically for publication in *La memoria del mondo*. But like 'La memoria del mondo', it lacks a comic component, and it is also unusual in that it is a serious monologue on time and history, addressed to humanity with no mention of any other characters and therefore without dialogue or a comic dimension.

We can now turn to the remaining three tales, all written in 1968, of the eight new ones included in *La memoria del mondo*. 'Le figlie della Luna' is a modern variation on the myth of Diana, set in a futuristic New York and again indebted to Leopardi's 'Odi, Melisso'. The moon eventually becomes so old and worn that it is lured to earth by naked devotees of Diana and dumped on a scrap heap of old cars. It is dropped off Brooklyn Bridge with all the Dianas jumping in after it, but it finally resurfaces and floats up to the sky totally renewed, and inhabited by its virginal devotees. The tale ends with a reversal of the close of 'The dinosaurs': here time zips backward and the young mammoths go trumpeting through the savannah, as they always do when they realise that life is only just beginning and they will never have everything they want (II, 1205).

'Tempesta solare' is one of the most interesting of these late stories for although it may have been partly inspired by Leopardi's 'Dialogo della natura e un islandese' (Milanini, 1990, 107–8), it is even more indebted to English literature in general and to Conrad in particular. There had been a brief Conradian cameo in the very first cosmicomic story, 'La distanza della Luna', when Captain Vhd Vhd's features were described in terms that recall those of Captain MacWhirr at the start of *Typhoon*, one of Calvino's favourite Conrad texts (*S*, 39, 808–9, 817): 'There was never a trace of any expression on that face of his, eaten by brine, marked with tarry wrinkles' (II, 88; *Cosmicomics*, 10). In 'Tempesta solare' Conrad's presence, in particular three famous texts, informs the whole tale. Here Qfwfq is the captain of the steamer *Halley*, returning towards Liverpool, when it is caught in a magnetic storm occasioned by Rah, daughter of the sun and the captain's aerial lover, who wraps herself round the main mast invisible to the rest of the crew. Although the *Halley* obviously alludes to Halley's comet, the name is also determined by that of the protagonist of Conrad's *The End of the Tether*, Captain Whalley, whose wife used to live on board with him, and who makes one last voyage on a Liverpool-built ship, trying to conceal his increasing blindness from the crew, in order to provide money for his only daughter. Whalley's ship encounters an electric storm and eventually founders, partly through the captain's failing vision and partly because one of the crew uses iron filings to deflect the ship's compass from its true course. This was one of Calvino's favourite Conrad stories, being discussed on more than one occasion both in his university thesis (pp. 37, 131–2) and in reviews (*S*, 808–10, 811–13).

In addition to this text, there are also clear echoes of two other Conrad tales. The opening movement from calm sea to electric storm obviously owes something to a similar shift in the crucial third chapter of *Lord Jim*, and the whole idea of a story about a sun storm may have derived from a key simile there:

> The ship moved so smoothly that her onward motion was imperceptible to the senses of men, as though she had been a crowded planet speeding through the dark spaces of ether behind the swarm of suns, in the appalling and calm solitudes awaiting the breath of future creations. (*Lord Jim*, 22–3)

Certainly the description of the ominous calm preceding the storm is indebted to Conrad's depiction there of the tranquil sea and of Lord Jim's feelings of serenity just before the accident in the eponymous novel. The names of the other officers are also Conradian: the mate is Mr Evans (a Mr Evans appears in Chapter 4 of *The End of the Tether*), the helmsman is Adams, and the radio operator is called Simmons (Mr Symons is the helmsman of the training ship in the opening chapter of *Lord Jim*). Even the allegation that Adams is drunk, made by Evans as the storm breaks, recalls the same accusation directed by the captain to the engineer in that same third chapter of *Lord Jim* (pp. 23–5), while Qfwfq's instructions to the crew – 'There's nothing for it but to commend your souls to whatever it is you believe in, and keep calm' (II, 1234) – echoes Conrad's agnostic detachment in describing the faith of the Muslems on board the *Patna*. Similarly the description of the *Halley* as 'a heap of scrap iron, which all the arts and ingenuity of man are powerless to steer' (II, 1234) parallels the engineer of the *Patna*'s complaints about that ship being 'a rotten scrapheap . . . the refuse of a breaking-up yard flying round at fifty-seven revolutions' (*Lord Jim*, p. 23). One reason why we can be sure of these precise echoes of the early part of *Lord Jim* is that in the late 1940s Calvino had translated into Italian the first ten chapters of the novel, though he never completed his version (*Enciclopedia*, 69).

As if reference to these two intertexts were not enough, the description of Rah gripping the main mast, with 'her hair flying in the wind, and . . . the folds of her drapery blending with the smoke of the funnel and beyond it with the sky itself', and the mention of 'her exotic hair, her jewels, her shimmering raiment' (II, 1234–5) are obvious echoes of Conrad's *effictio* of the beautiful African woman who appears at the climax of *Heart of Darkness*, a passage commented upon more than once by Calvino in his thesis (pp. 35–6, 96–7) and quoted there almost in its entirety (pp. 35–6):

> She walked with measured steps, draped in striped and fringed cloths, treading the earth proudly, with a slight jingle and flash of barbarous ornaments. She

> carried her head high; her hair was done in the shape of a helmet . . . Suddenly she opened her bare arms and threw them up rigid above her head, as though in an uncontrollable desire to touch the sky, and at the same time the swift shadows darted out on the earth, swept around on the river, gathering the steamer in a shadowy embrace. A formidable silence hung over the scene. (*Heart of Darkness*, p. 99)

But this rewriting is also a reversal of the Conradian original, for if the African woman is a reflection of 'the dark continent', Rah is instead the daughter of the sun, who in the end comes to reclaim her. Similarly Qfwfq is also the antithesis of Captain Whalley, since unlike the blind captain, he can actually stare directly into the sun and perceive the stormy activity on its surface (II, 1233). There are also hints here of Conrad's *Chance*, in which the presence of the captain's wife on board ship arouses the suspicions of the crew, and of *Typhoon* in which MacWhirr calmly communicates with his wife (by letter) as the storm rages, just as Qfwfq does with Rah (II, 1235).

Apart from these precise intertextual echoes, the main themes of the story are also Conradian: Captain Qfwfq's admiration for boats, with their compasses, radio and maps epitomising rationality and control (II, 1235), derives from a major area of Conrad symbolism explicitly mentioned in the thesis: 'Ships, these instruments of human reason, these weapons against the power of nature and the irrational, are a perfect symbol of this idea of Conrad's' (thesis, 125). Like many Conradian heroes, Qfwfq is deprived of command of his ship and retires to live in Lancashire, where Rah's presence on the roof occasions a permanent aurora borealis and constant electric storms in the area. All these motifs are worked into a story written a full twenty years after Calvino completed his university studies on the English author. One explanation of why this 'Carsic' Conradian vein should resurface at this point (1968) is that in 1967 Mursia began publishing Conrad's entire Opera Omnia in accurate Italian translations. These enthused Calvino, who subsequently published two of Conrad's tales in the Centopagine series he launched with Einaudi in the 1970s: *The Shadow Line* in 1971, and *Heart of Darkness* in 1973 (Cadioli, 150–161), this latter text, as we have seen, being one of the major intertexts for 'Tempesta solare'. Once again it is clear that the cosmicomic stories are inspired as much by literature as by science.

The second half of the tale contains more generic allusions to other classic texts in English. The chaos caused by Rah is so great that migrating birds lose direction and albatrosses land on the wild heath in a passage in which *The Ancient Mariner* seems to meet *Wuthering Heights* (II, 1238 – the Italian title of Brontë's novel, *Cime tempestose*, is echoed in 'Tempesta solare'). The description of the country house lit up by candles is pure Gothic, and the Revd Collins who comes to relay the neighbours' complaints is modelled on the homonymous character from *Pride and Prejudice*, but is probably also a nod to Wilkie Collins, another admired English author. However, as one would expect from someone as concerned for for structure as Calvino, the Conradian echoes of the opening reappear at the end of the narrative when Qfwfq tells his neighbours that he would not have them believe that 'I ever departed from the line of conduct that I had set myself, that I ever surrendered' (II, 1241) – a distinctly Conradian ethic, mentioned in several Calvino essays (*S*, 808–9, 812, 816–18). When Rah departs, all the electrical equipment can work again, normal life can resume in the area, and again Conradian words are used to express this: 'everyone will return to their ration of daily rationality' (II, 1241). 'Tempesta solare', then, begins as a reversal of the many cosmicomic stories about lost females, for here Rah comes looking for her lost man Qfwfq not vice versa, but it ends up as a minimalist rewriting of archetypal Conrad narratives and a mini-pastiche of nineteenth-century English classics.

'Il cielo di pietra' is another piece of Calvinian reversal. It is the obverse of 'Senza colori (Without Colours)' from *Cosmicomics*, for instead of Qfwfq/Orpheus failing to persuade Ayl/Eurydice to come into the upper world of colour as in that earlier tale, here Qfwfq/Pluto is the one who is reluctant to follow Rdix (whose name both suggests Eurydice, and Radix or root) up the volcano into the world of air and sound, where Orpheus is playing to her with his lyre. Calvino defamiliarises our notions of 'extraterrestrial' (II, 1216) and 'superficial' (II, 1218), for Qfwfq uses both adjectives to describe the miserable creatures who merely inhabit the earth's surface not its core. In fact for him the surface was the negative of the earth, the locus of what the earth rejected, its refuse; the real sky was the 'cielo di pietra' that he could see looking at the earth's plates above him. His project is, then, 'to force the portals of the Outerworld' (an elegant reversal of the Orphic forcing of the gates of Hell) and to save Eurydice from that Hell of sound. From the bottom of the volcano he can see that at the top the earth ends and the void begins. He waits for Vesuvius to erupt, then swims out with the lava flow to find Rdix listening to Orpheus's sounds, the sounds of the city of Herculaneum, which then become the sounds of any city: guitars, loudspeakers, car engines and horns, sirens. The tale ends with a dystopian audio-picture of the stressful sounds of the anti-city, which is described as 'your endless slaughter' (II, 1222), one of the first hints of Calvino's later pessimism about city life in the 1970s and 1980s.

Before examining the final two cosmicomic tales of 1984, it is worth glancing briefly at a rewriting of 'Il cielo di pietra' which Calvino completed twelve years later in 1980: 'L'altra Euridice'. A comparison of the two versions provides a brief measure of how his writing evolved in that crucial phase. Milanini outlined three main differences in the later version: a paragraph added to the introduction, a central passage and the final sentence with its allusion to the gods of Olympus (II, 1465–6). Barenghi adds that the replacement of Qfwfq by the character explicitly called Pluto and his more antagonistic address to the readers on earth confer a much more serious tone on the fable (III, 1347–8). There is now no scientific epigraph; instead the opening paragraph contains Pluto's address to humanity, whom he accuses of falsifing history in claiming that Eurydice was human. The new central passage describes the plutonic cities that the god of the underworld planned to build in the earth's core, each one a living body-city-machine, a world of silence and earth music, that would accomplish in a second what it has taken centuries of sweat for man to achieve. The tale still ends on the same note of defeat for man, but now there is a greater contrast between the inner gods who inhabit the dense thickness of things and the outer gods of Olympus and the rarefied air who have given man everything but it is still not enough. The sense of a world of objects which are inhabited by different gods is one of the new elements in Calvino's phenomenological view of the material world in the 1970s and 1980s (Barenghi, 1996).

For the final authorised collection of cosmicomic stories, *Cosmicomiche vecchie e nuove* (1984) Calvino collected thirty-one of the thirty-three published fictions, but replaced 'Le conchiglie e il tempo' and 'La memoria del mondo' with two tales written for this new volume. 'Il niente e il poco (Nothing and Not Much)', written in 1984, opens with a cutting from the *Washington Post* declaring that the universe came into existence in an infinitesimal fraction of a second. Qfwfq of course remembers both the nothing that preceded the Big Bang and the relatively little (the universe, time, space, memory) that emerged from it. There are hints even at this late date of the 1964 preface to *The Path to the Spiders' Nests*, notably in that recollection of having lived through exciting times and the subsequent 'sense of invincibility, of power, of pride, and at the same time of conceit' (II, 1261; *Numbers in the Dark*, 267). The phrase 'we had come up from nothing (*Numbers*, 267; 'c'eravamo appena sollevati dalla nullatenenza assoluta': II, 1261) is identical, in the original Italian, to the words used to describe the world which produced his first novel: '*The Path to the Spiders' Nests* was born from this sense of absolute lack of belonging' (*The Path*, 26; '*Il sentiero dei nidi di ragno* è nato da questo senso di nullatenenza assoluta': I, 1200). Eventually Qfwfq comes round to the point of view of his female antagonist, Nugkta, and sees the universe as flawed, a system in collapse, therefore gravely inferior to the perfection of nothing. That description of the universe as 'a bungled, cluttered construction crumbling away on every side' (II, 1265; *Numbers*, 270) reminds us of Calvino's 1980s pessimism articulated in the preface to *Una pietra sopra* (1980), in which he sees society in terms of collapse and gangrene. The tale ends, as with many cosmicomic fictions, on an extended sentence, but once again suffused with pessimism: 'and the continents throng with masses whether jubilant or suffering or slaughtering each other' (II, 1267; *Numbers*, 272).

'L'implosione', written in September 1984, one year before his death, was one of the last fictions that Calvino wrote, though it was developed from a Palomar article, 'I buchi neri', which he had written for the *Corriere della sera* nine years previously (7 September 1975), and which he had then worked into a dialogue between Palomar and his opposite Mohole (III, 1171–3 – see below Chapter 9). Exploiting his favourite poetics of contrast, Qfwfq initiates his musings on 'black holes' parodying Hamlet's great soliloquy: 'To explode or to implode – *said Qfwfq* – that is the question' (II, 1268; *Numbers*, 260). He argues that humanity wrongly celebrates explosion as a metaphor for energy just because of the Big Bang, or because of the energy symbolised by Napoleon's artillery; instead the mushroom cloud of August 1945 should remind us that explosion is as much an image of the negation of energy and life. The laws of thermodynamics also confirm this, since all things will disappear 'in a blaze of heat' (II, 1270; *Numbers*, 262), an identical phrase ('una vampa di calore') to the one used at the end of *Palomar* (II, 979) to describe the end of time. The conclusion of the central paragraph, 'time is a catastrophe, perpetual and irreversible' (II, 1270; *Numbers*, 262) and of the whole tale – 'Any way time runs it leads to disaster, whether in one direction or its opposite and the intersecting of those directions does not form a network of rails governed by points and exits, but a tangle, a knot . . .' (II, 1272; *Numbers*, 264) – both echo key phrases from *If on a Winter's Night* and are typical of Calvino's dystopic vision of the early 1980s, and like the last section of *Palomar*, seem an uncanny prediction of his own death.

Despite the ludic and experimental dimension of many of the cosmicomic stories, Calvino is still concerned with 'the destiny of humanity and the meaning of individual existence' (II, xii). He is still dealing with the large themes that concern mankind, indeed the largest of themes, the very nature of the cosmos and the place of humanity in it. The author's aim in these tales is to raise the stakes of fiction, to put fiction on a par with science. He expands the frontiers of fiction in the 1960s by making his own literary discourse in these cosmicomic tales embrace not only science (physics, embryology, DNA, computing theory), mathematics and philosophy, but also the visual arts (paintings, cinema, architecture). He challenges literature to describe the indescribable, from the Big Bang to the division of cells, but he also still believes in the existence of the world, and not just language, as he says in a 1967 interview:

> I believe that a reality does exist and that there is a relationship between reality and the signs that we use to represent it . . . I believe that the world exists independently of man and will exist after him, and that man is simply an opportunity for the world to collect some information about itself. Consequently, literature in my view represents a series of attempts to get to know and classify some information on the world. (II, xxiii)

But despite the innovations in form and content, the cosmicomic tales continually allude to the author's own past works, as well as to other literary intertexts: they are, as we have seen, as much indebted to literature and autobiography as they are to science.

One final point is worth making. Scientific and other frames emerge in

Calvino's fiction in the 1960s partly for the biographical reason suggested above (in the introduction), but also because with the end of realism, fiction can no longer pretend to aspire to the modernist condition of pure mimesis of reality, but rather must proclaim in a postmodern fashion the artificial status of the text. This artificiality will be even more pronounced in the trilogy of works produced by Calvino in the 1970s. In the preface to the 1968 volume, *La memoria del mondo*, Calvino stated that his cosmicomic experience was at an end, and that another one was beginning, which would offer him 'a surprise, a different landscape, and also a new difficulty, a new obstacle to overcome' (II, 1302–3). By the time of writing this preface he had already begun investigating the potential of Tarot cards as an alternative semiotic system in an experiment which would in the end pose some narratological difficulties which, as we shall see in the next chapter, would never be overcome.

Chapter 7

Experimental Signs

Invisible Cities and *The Castle of Crossed Destinies*

Calvino never termed his three major publications of the 1970s a trilogy, but there are a number of elements that they have in common that justify considering them as such. Some critics see a unifying structural element of all three works in Borges' notion of a multiplied, ramified time. But there are other common factors. If the cosmicomic phase of the 1960s was characterised by an attempt to update literature by inscribing within it a scientific perspective, one common trait of each work of the next decade is its aspiration to incorporate within it other literary texts, in other words to be that typically postmodern genre, a rewriting of a canonical text or texts: *Invisible Cities* (1972) rewrites Marco Polo's travels recounted in *Il milione* as well as More's *Utopia*; *The Castle of Crossed Destinies* (1973) reworks Ariosto's *Orlando furioso* along with major myths of Western literature (Oedipus, the Grail, Lear, Hamlet, etc.); *If on a Winter's Night a Traveller* (1979) recycles the structure of *The Thousand and One Nights* as well as parodying in its ten *incipits* many contemporary novels or genres. This chapter will be concerned with the two works which were composed first and whose periods of composition overlap, *Invisible Cities* and *The Castle of Crossed Destinies*.

Calvino had been attracted to the legend of Marco Polo as early as 1960 (III, 1263–7), in that period of crisis in which he was searching for material with which to follow up the earlier trilogy (there are certainly similarities between the elderly Charlemagne and Kublai Khan, and between the young Rambaldo and Polo). He was asked to supply a screenplay for a film about Polo, but the text he wrote was unsuitable (II, 1364) and was only published after his death (III, 509–86). Around the same time his friends at Einaudi, Daniele Ponchiroli and Sergio Solmi collaborated on an edition of *Il milione* which appeared in 1962. But *Invisible Cities* was not begun until the summer of 1970 and was published in 1972. As was by now his custom, Calvino first wrote the individual, serial units, descriptions of cities, in a desultory fashion before grouping these microtexts into one overarching macrotext. But, as the author himself said, it was only by providing the serial descriptions with a frame, and thus with a beginning, middle and end, that they could be turned into a book (II, 1361).

This is one of the texts of which Calvino was most satisfied, for in it he had managed to say the maximum number of things in the smallest number of words (*S*, 689–90; *Six Memos*, 71). It is also his only creative work in which the complex index outlining the structure of the text appears at the beginning of the book and not, as is more usual in Italian fiction, at the end: this contents page is not simply a list of chapters, but an integral part of the work's structure and meaning, the index and the individual sections of the book interacting on a number of different levels with the text. Of course, Calvino's interests in complex structures go back at least to his division of the 1958 collection of *Racconti* into four books, and to the five cycles of four seasons in *Marcovaldo* (1963). But we have noted his growing preoccupation with mathematical problems in the final section of *Time and the Hunter*, and by 1972 he was even more familiar with the mathematical obsessions of his fellow members of the OULIPO, particularly Raymond Queneau and Georges Perec, who were engrossed in attempts to make mathematical devices structure literary texts by acting as *contraintes*. It is these more complex mathematical constraints that subtend the intricate structure of *Invisible Cities*.

Invisible Cities consists of nine chapters each of which is framed by two brief italicised dialogues between Marco Polo and Kublai Khan, dialogues whose theme is reflected in the cities that are described in between these conversations: the dialogue has here replaced the scientific epigraph which opened the cosmicomic tales, but in *Invisible Cities* the frame is more tightly wound, in that there is a concluding italic section to each chapter as well. The first and ninth chapters each contain descriptions of ten different cities, the intervening seven chapters describe five cities each; the fifty-five cities and nine chapters amount to sixty-four, the number of squares on a chessboard, a favourite symbol in structuralist theories of the time and one which is actually discussed in the text. The number 55 is also chosen because there are fifty-five cities in the archetypal utopian text, Thomas More's *Utopia* (Milanini, 1990, 144), but where More limits himself to describing the capital, Calvino rewrites More, or fills in the void in More's text by describing all fifty-five cities. However, the structural complexity does not stop here: not only do all the cities in each chapter have something in common, which is reflected in the enclosing dialogues, but Calvino assigns the cities to eleven different categories of five cities each, such as Cities and Memory, Cities and Desire, Cities and Signs, and so on, arranged in such a way as to provide a pattern which has usually been represented by critics in one of the two following ways:

I:	1	a
	21	ab
	321	abc
	4321	abcd
II:	54321	abcde
III:	54321	bcdef
IV:	54321	cdefg
V:	54321	defgh
VI:	54321	efghi
VII:	54321	fghij
VIII:	54321	ghijk
IX:	5432	hijk
	543	ijk
	54	jk
	5	k

In each case, reading the diagram from top to bottom and from left to right corresponds to the order in which the cities are described in the text. The numerical pattern on the left above, where the digits refer to the first, second, third etc. appearance of a particular category of city, is the one first advocated by Milanini (1990, 130–1) and identical to that found amongst the author's own papers (II, 1360). The use of letters, where a stands for all the cities of memory, b for all the cities of desire, c for all the cities of signs, etc., makes a similar pattern but in negative: the letters have a progressive sequence (abcde), the numbers a regressive sequence (54321).

There have of course been other interpretations suggested for the architecture of the book (Mengaldo 1975, 410, n. 6; Briganti, 1982, 218–19), but whether one uses numbers or letters to signify the cities, it is always a symmetrical lozenge or diamond-shape structure which emerges, and which suggests that the top triangle of Chapter I, and the bottom triangle of Chapter IX represent complementary, regular patterns which omit the irregularities of reality – this being one of the themes of the work. As in 'I cristalli' Qfwfq strove to regard each irregularity of the world around him as actually forming part of a perfect regular crystal that he could not quite discern, so here in the very first dialogue the Khan sees in Polo's accounts of the cities of his empire 'the tracery of a pattern ('filigrana') so subtle that it could escape the termites' gnawing' (II, 361; *Invisible Cities*, 6), a phrase which recalls the evocative metaphor used by Calvino himself, in a 1967 essay, when he says that in Borges' fictions the secret watermark ('filigrana') of the universe always seems to be about to appear (*S*, 195; *LM*, 48). Later in the fourth chapter the Khan claims that his cities form a regular diamond, as indeed they do in Calvino's ordering of the cities, and he upbraids Polo for dwelling on their melancholy aspects. The whole book plays on this ambivalence between symmetry and irregularity, between the neatness of numerical structures and the messiness of the real world, hovering between utopian dream and dystopic pessimism. There are plenty of negative elements: in that first dialogue, the sense of the void and 'sfacelo (collapse)' encroaching on the Khan's empire is mentioned, phrases which Calvino himself used to describe the world of the 1970s in his preface to *Una pietra sopra* (*S*, 7), and which therefore establish a link with contemporary events, in a text which has usually been considered to be at the furthest remove from reality.

The cities of that first chapter are all described, as in *Il milione* and other medieval travelogues, with a stress on the precision of external statistics: cities with sixty cupolas, or four aluminium towers, or a thousand wells; but the chapter's closing dialogue hints that the Khan almost prefers the gestures and emblems Polo initially used to portray the cities when the visitor knew no oriental language. Marco's original emblems shed light on the factual statistics and vice versa, we are told, a statement that recalls exactly the way in which the emblematic index–grid interacts with the textual descriptions of the cities.

The cities in Chapter II are all concerned with their own past, and they also illustrate the theme of the framing dialogues. Polo realises that the farther he travels the more he understands his past, so the more he travels in space the further he proceeds in time, and therefore each person he sees in a city could have been himself had he taken a different track at various crossroads: 'Futures not realised are only branches of the past, dead branches' (II, 378; *Invisible Cities*, 29), a statement that echoes the Borgesian idea of forking paths, that every decision taken excludes a whole range of other potential choices and destinies. The closing dialogue here is one of the most elegant and characteristic of the entire book. Marco, unable to speak the Khan's language, begins to describe his cities using emblems, then progresses to words which are good at conjuring up monuments and markets but imprecise at describing life in that city, so in the end to convey the reality of existence there he resorts to gestures once more, and as he and the Khan come to know each other more, their gestures lose their unfamiliarity and vivacity, until at the end 'most of the time, they remained silent and immobile' (II, 387; *Invisible Cities*, 39). The key sentence – 'The descriptions of cities Marco Polo visited had this virtue: you could wander through them in thought, become lost, stop and enjoy the cool air, or run off' (II, 386; *Invisible Cities*, 38) – is remarkably close to Calvino's own statement about this work:

> A book, I believe, is something with a beginning and an end (even if it is not a novel in the strict sense of the word); it is a space into which the reader must enter, roam around, maybe even lose direction, but at a certain point will find a way out, or even several ways out, or just the possibility of opening up a road to come out. (II, 1361)

Since the third chapter opens with the Khan complaining that all of the cities described by Polo are similar, the Venetian describes cities that are the opposite of what they seem. In the city of Armilla all that is visible are waterpipes and basins and nymphs washing (the motif of the water being summoned into the city is also the theme of 'Il richiamo dell'acqua (The Call of the Water)', written a few years later in 1976 (III, 277–81; *Numbers in the Dark*, 206–10)). Ipazia is the city of opposite signs, where love is found in the stables, music in the cemetery and so on: 'Signs form a language, but not the one you think you know' (II, 394; *Invisible Cities*, 48) is the gnomic warning, and the conclusion is that 'there is no language without deceit' (II, 395; *Invisible Cities*, 48).

In the fourth chapter the Khan complains that Polo's descriptions are simply 'consolatory fables' (II, 405; *Invisible Cities*, 59) which disguise the rottenness of his empire, but the traveller replies that it is only by measuring the few glimmers of happiness in the empire that one can assess its real poverty. This idea is then neatly reversed when Kublai says he knows that his cities form a regular diamond and reproaches the Venetian for dealing with melancholies. Polo answers that we have to know the measure of unhappiness to work out the worth of any diamond. Cities like Olivia are then described as beautiful but Polo knows it is covered in smog: to describe it truly to the emperor he would need to resort to metaphors of soot and pollution (II, 408; *Invisible Cities*, 61) – the motif of *Smog* and 'Adventure of a poet' are clearly still present in this text.

Chapter V is the central arch of this carefully architectured nine-chapter work. In the opening dialogue the Khan, sensing that his empire is now dying under its own weight, dreams of cities of filigree lightness ('città filigrana', II, 419; *Invisible Cities*, 73). He recounts his dream of the city of Lalage, a city so light that the moon dances on its pinnacles and it grows only in lightness. This evocative Greek name introduces the classical core of the work in the five cities that are then described. The first city has a name from Roman history, Ottavia; the second, Ersilia, exhibits a series of Ariadne-like threads through the labyrinth of its streets, signifying the various relations between the houses; the central city Baucis recalls the myth of Baucis and Philemon, which is also the central tale of Ovid's *Metamorphoses*, but instead of being a city of hospitality and love like its classical model, this city above the clouds resting on thin stilts is a city of absence, hovering over the void. The concluding description of Baucis is one of Calvino's most poetic prose passages – in fact the author considered this whole chapter 'la zona piú luminosa del libro' (Martignoni, 1997, 18):

> There are three hypotheses about the inhabitants of Baucis: that they hate the earth; that they respect it so much that they avoid all contact; that they love it as it was before they existed, and with spyglasses and telescopes aimed downward they never tire of examining it, tirelessly observing it, leaf by leaf, stone by stone, ant by ant, contemplating with fascination their own absence. (II, 423; *Invisible Cities*, 77)

Calvino was haunted by the Baucis myth, which had been present in his very first novel (when Pin visits the old rural couple in Chapter XI), and it receives particular attention from the author in his introductory essay to an Italian edition of the *Metamorphoses*, written a few years after *Invisible Cities* (1979). There he describes the story as a pearl that emerges from the layered shell of stories in that central eighth book of Ovid's fifteen-book poem, calling it 'the humble idyll of Philemon and Baucis, which embraces a whole minutely delineated world and moves at a totally different pace' (*S*, 910; LM, 154). For Calvino Ovid's poem is an epic of 'rapidità', which occasionally requires a slower pace, as in the Baucis story where the poet fixes on tiny details such as the tile that is placed under the leg of the table to make it even and the particulars of the whole meal offered to the visiting gods (*S*, 911–12). The other point of the story is that the city the old couple inhabit is destroyed and replaced by an uninhabited marsh because the gods were unable to find any hospitality elsewhere – hence Calvino's Baucis is also a locus of absence. The myth is an oriental one analogous to the tale of God's search for ten just men in the Old Testament. This motif of justice, in both the pagan and Christian traditions, links with the final cities of Calvino's book which, as we shall see, are cities of the just which at the same time contain the unjust within them. The fourth city, Leandra, is inhabited by the ancient Roman household gods, both Lares and Penates, a classical motif which becomes more insistent in the works of the 1970s (Barenghi, 1996), while the last city, Melania, contains stock characters from ancient comedy: the boastful soldier, the parasite, the prostitute. The concluding dialogue is one of the briefest, most gnomic and most quoted: in it Kublai criticises Marco for describing a bridge stone by stone when it is the arch that supports the bridge, but Polo replies that without the stones there is no arch (Mengaldo, 1975). In a metatextual sense this fifth chapter is also the central arch which supports the bridge of this carefully wrought work, and with its classical core it demonstrates that this text, like many written in this period, strives to embrace not just contemporary ideas but also medieval and ancient aesthetics as well. This Ovidian centrepiece to *Invisible Cities* is no accident, and Calvino's interest in the ancient world and classical texts is a feature which also characterises his later writings: apart from the substantial essays on Xenophon (*S*, 936–41) and Ovid (*S*, 904–16; LM, 146–61), both written in 1979, there is also the seminal article 'Perché leggere i classici?' (1981: *S*, 1816–24; LM, 125–34), the preface to *The Odyssey* (also 1981, but whose origins go back to the mid-1970s: *S*, 888–96; LM, 135–45), the introduction to Pliny the Elder (1982: *S*, 917–29; LM, 315–30) and the central importance of Lucretius and Ovid in Calvino's literary testament to the next millennium (*S*, 633–38).

In Chapter VI, Marco tells Kublai that although he never mentions Venice, la Serenissima is in every city he describes, and to the Khan's request for a description of Venice Polo replies: 'Memory's images, once they are fixed in words, are erased' (II, 432; *Invisible Cities*, 87). It has been argued that in every city described resides the San Remo of Calvino's youth (Nocentini 1987, 1989), and this is confirmed by the fact that exactly the same idea about the violence done to memory by words is found at the conclusion of the 1964 preface to *The Path*, where he discusses the destruction of his war memories through the writing of the novel (I, 1203–4; *The Path*, 28–9). The cities of this chapter are all canal cities, like Venice, and in the closing section, Polo watches the smoke from his and Kublai's pipes, thinking either of the mist that clears to reveal cities or of the smog hanging over them in a passage that echoes the central description in the story *Smog* (I, 926; DL, 139).

The seventh chapter introduces the theme of refuse and rubbish that begins to obsess Calvino in the 1970s, and which is most fully articulated in the short work written immediately after *Invisible Cities*, 'La poubelle agréée' (1974–76: III, 59–79). Both men speculate, in the opening and closing dialogues, that perhaps the cities and the garden in which they are sitting only exist in their imagination and that in reality both are beggars sitting amidst detritus, in which case, concludes Polo, only their eyelids separate the two worlds. The cities that follow are all analysed both in their gleaming facades and in their filthy interiors: Leonia, for instance, wakes up each morning to the latest consumer goods, while on the pavement the rubbish sacks containing the refuse of yesterday await the garbage collectors, who are described as angels of purification (II, 456) in terms very similar to those used in 'La poubelle' (III, 68). The closing dialogue plays with the Berkeleian notion that perhaps the warriors and merchants described exist only because the Khan and Polo are thinking of them; this is then reversed to produce the Borgesian paradox, that perhaps only the warriors and merchants exist, not Kublai and Marco.

Chapter VIII develops the then fashionable metaphor of chess and its rules, used by structuralists, particularly Saussure, to describe the arbitrariness of the signifier in its relation to the signified (Cannon, 1981). The Khan decides that since all his cities are like a game of chess, then if he knew the rules of chess he would be able to possess his entire empire, so he asks Polo to describe them using chess pieces, but at checkmate Kublai is left staring at the empty void ('il nulla') of the chess square. This theme of the void that lurks beneath the sameness of cities informs the descriptions that follow. Of these Trude is the most contemporary: its airport and suburbs look identical to the city from which Marco has just left, as the only sign that signifies to the traveller that he is in a different city is the name of the airport. The opening paragraph of the final dialogue of Chapter VIII repeats verbatim the closing paragraph of the opening dialogue but without the final phrase 'il nulla', and in a brilliant reversal Polo manages to show the Khan that in the empty chess square there is no void, instead the wood of the square reveals the ebony woods from which the tree that made the board was carved, the rafts thundering downstream, the women at the windows above the city harbour. Again there is an important echo in Polo's words to describe the wood: 'vedi *come si dispongono le fibre*? Qui si scorge *un nodo* appena accennato (you see how its fibres are arranged? Here a barely hinted knot can be made out)' (II, 469; *Invisible Cities*, 131; emphasis mine). The metaphor of wood confirms, if confirmation were needed, that again Calvino is also discussing here the medium of language. The words used recall the important passage in the 1963 letter to Mario Boselli about his own style, which was cited as an epigraph in the introduction: 'La pagina . . . è uno spaccato di un legno, in cui si possono seguire *come corrono le fibre*, dove fanno *nodo*, dove si diparte un ramo (The written page . . . is like a cross-section of a piece of wood, in which one can follow the lines of the fibres, see where they form a knot, where a branch goes off)' ('Lettera a Mario Boselli', 106; also cited in I, 1355; emphasis mine).

The opening dialogue of the final chapter describes the Khan's atlas which contains all the cities of his empire. Polo warns Kublai that although he may repeat in the West the same descriptions of cities, his audience will only hear what they want to hear: 'It is not the voice that commands the story: it is the ear' (II, 473; *Invisible Cities*, 135), a phrase that echoes the many theoretical statements of these years about the pre-eminence of the act of reading over that of writing. There is also a hint of despair about the nadir which the urban existence has reached and the difficulty of imagining the cities of the future. The atlas contains both past and future cities: Jericho, Ur, Carthage, Troy, Byzantium, San Francisco, New York. Naturally the ten cities that are then described in the chapter are all mixtures of utopias and dystopias: the last city, Berenice, a city of unjust men, does however contain within it the future polity of just citizens, which in turn contains another future city of unjust inhabitants, and so on. This supports Calvino's own view (*S*, 2790–2) that the famous ending to the book, with its mention of the inferno in which we now live, is not to be seen as unequivocally pessimistic; instead the passage is, predictably, more nuanced: the present and future will, like the past, contain a mixture of good and evil, justice and injustice. Polo's final words in fact offer two alternatives: either to surrender to the inferno to the point of no longer being able to notice it, or to identify whatever within the inferno does not belong to it and to give that both time and space (II, 498; *Invisible Cities*, 165). And it is only the latter approach that conserves that spirit of challenge to the labyrinth, the sea of objects, the inferno (Bernardini Napoletano, 1977, 182–4).

Despite the intricacy of the structural pattern of the book, and consequently the multiplicity of ways of reading this 'open text' (Martignoni, 1997), there is a clear progression in the cities described from visible to invisible elements. As has been observed, there are a number of intertextual links between *Il Milione* and Calvino's work (Bernardini Napoletano, 1977, 171–6), the adjective in the title of the later book deriving from the first sentence of the medieval text which alludes to the cities that Polo has seen and will describe for the benefit of those who have not seen them (Weiss 1993, 150). There is also a move from simplicity to complexity: we move from the lists of external features in the first chapter, to the past lurking beneath cities, to cities of opposite signs, cities containing happiness or poverty, suspended cities, canal cities, cities of rubbish, identical cities and lastly labyrinthine cities within cities – the very motif of enclosure and complexity on which *The Watcher* had closed.

Stylistically *Invisible Cities* is a tour de force. Calvino has pared down his style from the lengthy sentences that characterised so much of his output in the 1960s, from *The Watcher* to *Time and the Hunter.* Instead there is a cult of Borgesian *brevitas* in his clipped descriptions of cities and in the minimalist dialogues. There are still some lists (II, 421, 456), but now the sentences are on the whole much shorter and always in the present, while the dialogues emanate an almost authentic whiff of oriental, gnomic wisdom. Calvino called it a 'poema d'amore', an epic love poem to the city, paradoxically written just when cities are becoming almost uninhabitable, and his prose here reaches its most poetic heights – for just one example among many see the concluding description of the central city, Baucis (quoted above). It was the work of which the author himself was most satisfied because he was able to concentrate all his meditations on a single symbol, and because its multifaceted structure allowed multiple, non-hierarchical readings, both sequential (page after page) and ramified (following any of the different patterns – see *S*, 689–90; *Six Memos*, 71). Its appeal is enormous, particularly in the USA, where it is Calvino's most popular and most famous work, and part of that appeal must lie in its conciliation of opposites: the brevity that encompasses infinity (a lesson learnt from Borges), the prose that borders on poetry (*S*, 671; *Six Memos*, 49), the descriptions that abound with substantives rather than adjectives (Bonsaver, 1995c), and the single work that embraces all his own previous works, as well as alluding to many other canonical texts (The Bible, classical literature, medieval texts, oriental literature and utopian/dystopian literature from More to Huxley).

Invisible Cities presents a less experimental, more completed structure than the cosmicomic stories. Nevertheless, it is not just a postmodernist game, but a serious, and beautiful, prose-poem about real problems in urban existence. The author's own words confirm this:

> I think that I have written something that resembles a final, lengthy love poem to the city, just at the time when it is becoming more and more difficult to live in them as cities. Perhaps we are nearing a moment of crisis in urban living, and *Invisible Cities* is a dream which arises out of the heart of uninhabitable cities . . . My book opens and closes with images of happy cities which continually emerge and disappear, hidden inside unhappy cities. (II, 1362)

Invisible Cities and *The Castle of Crossed Destinies* may be hailed by postmodern critics as exemplary texts about the art of telling stories which also include an essentially ludic element as well an attempt at rewriting famous texts, but they also articulate 'clear value judgments on the world which surrounds [the author]' (Milanini 1990, 137). The same critic also notes that in these experimental works of the 1970s, Calvino is on the one hand innovatively exploiting new technical and literary knowledge to generate sophisticated metaliterary texts, but he is also committed to considering what is going on both within and outside the individual subject (II, xxviii–xxix). In fact some of his most autobiographical writings ('La poubelle agréée', *Eremita a Parigi*, 'Ricordo di una battaglia') fall in the mid-1970s, the middle of this experimental period, and we have seen that echoes of autobiography resound even in *Invisible Cities*. As Barenghi observes (II, 1363), no univocal interpretation of the work is possible, since the most important section of the work is not in the utopian conclusion but in the centre, in the void of Baucis; in any case the dialogues between Marco and Kublai, which are the generative nucleus of the book, propose several different ways of reading the cities, just as seven different ways of reading are proposed in the penultimate chapter of *If on a Winter's Night a Traveller* (see Chapter 8).

The volume, *The Castle of Crossed Destinies*, consists of two texts, 'The Castle of Crossed Destinies' and 'The Tavern of Crossed Destinies'. The former contains a frame story and seven other tales written in 1969 to serve as narrative accompaniment to Franco Maria Ricci's de luxe edition of the fifteenth-century Visconti Tarot cards, designed by Bonifazio Bembo and reproduced in the margin. 'The Tavern of Crossed Destinies' also consists of a frame story and seven other tales written between 1969 and 1973, and illustrate the traditional Tarot cards which again are reproduced in the margins. The volume ends with an author's note (II, 1275–81; *The Castle of Crossed Destinies*, 123–9), penned in October 1973, which explains the troubled genesis of 'The Tavern', particularly Calvino's vain attempts at finding an all-embracing pattern for the cards which would allow him to tell the stories in order, as he had managed to do in 'The Castle'. The note also informs us that at one stage he thought of adding a third text to the volume, 'The Motel of Crossed Destinies', in which characters – survivors of some apocalyptic catastrophe – would find themselves in a ruined motel, having lost the power of speech and possessing only the comic-strips of a half-burnt newspaper to allow them to recount their stories. But this project never came to fruition.

The idea for constructing narratives based on Tarot cards derived from a seminar held by Paolo Fabbri in Urbino in 1968 and attended by Calvino (II, 1276), but it is worth recalling that in *The Castle of Crossed Destinies* Calvino also realises the narrative aspirations already expressed both in *The Non-Existent Knight* and in 'The Origin of the Birds' in *Time and the Hunter*, in each of which the narrator wanted to recount the story more effectively by using a visual or pictorial medium, though in fact no pictorial representations appeared in the text or its margins.

In the first chapter of 'The Castle', the narrator, lost in a forest on a stormy night, seeks refuge in a castle in which he and everyone else discovers that they are deprived of the power of speech. Only the Tarot cards which are brought out after the meal allow the guests to recount their adventures. 'The adventures we had undergone' (II, 505; *The Castle*, 4) recalls the phrase used in the 1964 preface to *The Path* to describe the populace's universal craving to recount their adventures after the war. Interestingly a number of other phrases recall that preface: one narrator, the grave-robber, is said to have 'provocatoria spavalderia (a provocative, bold manner)' (II, 524; *The Castle*, 25), a phrase all but identical to that used to describe the theme of his first novel, which possessed 'spavalderia quasi provocatoria' (I, 1192) – this young narrator is clearly in one sense the young Calvino himself. Apart from experimenting with visual forms of narration, Calvino is also here exemplifying something which he had discussed on several occasions in the previous years, the fact that all narrative can be reduced to a finite number of units or functions which can then be put together in a combinatory process that yields infinite solutions. He can also be ironic about various styles of narration here, claiming that one narrator is wasteful in his use of the Sun card if all he wants to say is 'it was a nice, sunny day' (II, 510; *The Castle*, 11), or that another was a poor communicator and probably more prone to abstract than to visual narration (II, 520; *The Castle*, 21). There are a number of poetic echoes, especially once Orlando begins to tell his tale, from the lengthy onomatopeic description of the battle (II, 527; *The Castle*, 29), to the single hendecasyllable: 'per la rovina delle armate franche (to ruin the French armies)' (II, 528; *The Castle*, 30). One of the main motifs of Calvino's memories of his own partisan experience is also present in this tale, the conflict between *natura* and *storia*: the world of battle is the discontinuous, distinct world, unlike the green, mucillaginous, continuous nature of the forest in which Orlando goes mad. Yet the two worlds could have a reciprocal relation, as Calvino himself discovered in the spring of 1945, when the partisans were waiting for the rhododendrons to flower and offer them and their weapons camouflage (*S*, 2778–9). In Astolfo's story there are a number of deliberately anachronistic allusions to Metro stops in contemporary Paris, the city in which the author was living when composing this work: Monte Martire, Mon Parnasso, Menilmontante, Monteroglio, Porta Delfini, Porta dei Lillà, all form a metro circle round Paris now, but they allude to the city encircled by its Saracen besiegers in Ariosto's poem (II, 534; *The Castle*, 37). The first six stories after the opening frame-chapter are all narrated by individuals, at first four nameless narrators, then in Chapter 6 Orlando tells his tale of love, jealousy and madness, and in Chapter 7 Astolfo recounts his fantastic journey to the moon. The last chapter of 'The Castle' contains 'all the other stories', the first one being told by Helen of Troy, the others by other narrators, and ending with the chatelaine reshuffling the pack.

'The Tavern of Crossed Destinies' follows a similar structural pattern, a *cornice* followed by seven more chapters, the first four of which have individual nameless narrators. The sixth chapter, as with Orlando's tale in 'The Castle', has a famous narrator, or rather narrators, Dr Faustus and Parsifal, in which Calvino elegantly suggests the unity of the two stories, the pursuit of the alchemist's formula and the pursuit of the Grail being two sides to the same coin. Symmetry would have demanded that the other named narrators, Hamlet, Macbeth and Lear, should have appeared in the next chapter, as Astolfo had followed Orlando in 'The Castle', but in fact the three Shakespearean tales are reserved for the last chapter. Probably the author also initially thought of what is now the sixth chapter, 'Anch'io cerco di dire la mia (I also try to tell my tale)', as the one corresponding to the last chapter of the first part in which all the stories are told; this is confirmed by the fact that in a later interview with Daniele Del Giudice, Calvino does say that 'in the last chapter of *The Castle of Crossed Destinies* I compare the figure of the Hermit with that of the knight who slays dragons' (III, 1212), whereas this comparison of St Jerome and St George in fact occurs in the penultimate chapter of 'The Tavern'. Presumably he inverted the order of these two concluding chapters of the book in order to disrupt an otherwise excessive symmetry, and to confirm the feeling expressed in the author's note about it being time to pass on to something else: Calvino himself here reshuffles his own 'carte', and would produce a radically different work in 1979.

Another major difference between the two sections is that in 'The Tavern' the cards are not laid down and read sequentially as in 'The Castle', but in a random order, and some are used more than once by the same narrator (Bernardini Napoletano, 1977, 135–42). The tone is also different: the Quattrocento cards had inspired Ariostesque and Homeric narrators and language, while the modern pack elicits in a less poetic style essential myths of Western literature from Parsifal and Faust to Shakespearean and Freudian archetypes. Nevertheless, as has been pointed out, the two texts embrace, in a kind of haiku-ising technique, the whole of Western literature from Homer to Eliot (Milanini 1990).

Already in the first story of 'The Tavern', the waverer's tale, there is an allusion to the fact that every choice has its obverse (II, 552; *The Castle*, 56), and the branches have bifurcations which constantly force the indecisive man to make anguished decisions: 'the branches . . . which with their succession of repeated forks, continue to inflict the torment of choice on him' (II, 553; *The Castle*, 57). Both of these passages allude to the title of Borges' *The Garden of Forking Paths* and its thematics of ramified time, in which each decision leaves suspended the alternatives to that choice. The story also brings in Madame Sosostris and the drowned Phoenician sailor, the intertextual allusion to Eliot's *The Waste Land* (lines 43–59) being made explicit by the reference to 'the distinguished Lloyds employee' (II, 558; *The Castle*, 62) as well as by a later allusion to 'Terre desolate (Waste Lands)' (II, 588; *The Castle*, 82). The contemporary city also reappears here even in what looks like a remote, semiotic text. At the end of the second chapter there is a dystopic vision of the machines which have, along with the animals of the forest, taken over the city: 'For the world to receive information from the world and enjoy it, now computers and butterflies suffice' (II, 564; *The Castle*, 69). The fourth chapter is the most poetic, containing a manneristic description of the city as 'traforata dalla grattugia di finestre dei grattacieli, saliscesa dagli ascensori, autoincoronata dalle altostrade, non parca di parcheggi (pierced by the cheesegrater of the skyscrapers' windows, the pulleys of the elevators, auto-crowned by the superhighways, with lots of parking space)' (II, 573; *The Castle*, 80), a baroque passage remarked upon by Mengaldo (1989), and later the chiastic play of 'Tesa all'altezza dell'alta tensione (At the height of the high tension' (II, 580; *The Castle*, 88). Elsewhere the city is described as being not made of crystal, but cancered and porous (II, 577; *The Castle*, 85), phraseology that recalls the words used to describe contemporary society in the preface to *Una pietra sopra*: 'collasso', 'frana', 'cancrena', 'crollo' (*S*, 7–8), and there is also the cosmicomic theme of the moon as celestial rubbish-bin (II, 579; *The Castle*, 87). The fifth chapter is reminiscent of *Invisible Cities* in its two conclusions: Faust says that the world does not exist, there is simply a finite number of elements whose combination, however, can reach 'miliardi di miliardi' (II, 589; *The Castle*, 97); Parsifal, on the other hand, believes that the hub of the world is the void, like the empty space at the centre of the Tarots. Presumably the phrase 'miliardi di miliardi' is another allusion to Queneau's *Cent mille milliards de poèmes*, his combinatory text for generating thousands of different sonnets, mentioned by Calvino in the important essay, 'Cibernetica e fantasmi (Cybernetics and Ghosts)' (*S*, 212; LM, 11–12), as well as to the whole combinatory narrative structure of this book. The emphasis on the void also links this work with *Invisible Cities*.

The sixth chapter, 'Anch'io cerco di dire la mia (I also try to tell my tale)', is the most important one of the entire volume. In it Calvino describes himself as now a 'sedentary character' (II, 591; *The Castle*, 99). The volutes of the Due di Denari card suggest the primitive exchange that lies behind each signifier in its attempt to stand in for the signified in this alliterative passage:

> Pur sempre avvolgendo nelle sue spire significanti il circolante del significato, la lettera Esse che serpeggia per significare che è lí pronta a significare significati. (Always enfolding in its significant coils the currency of significance, the letter Ess that twists to signify that it is there ready and waiting to signify signification.) (II, 592; *The Castle*, 100)

The ludic tone of this passage confirms the notion that this is a parody or at least an ironic portrayal of contemporary structuralist discussions. There is also a hint here that the successful writer has to make a Faustian pact with the devil, writing only about the darker side of man: *Les Fleurs du mal* and *Heart of Darkness* are cited (II, 592; *The Castle*, 100), as well as Sade's *Justine* and Freud's interpretation of the Oedipus myth (II, 593; *The Castle*, 101). Even here there are hints of poetry in the hendecasyllables describing Oedipus setting out: 'Lo si faccia partire alla ventura / su un *Carro* riccamente addobbato (You send him off at random in a richly adorned Chariot)' (II, 594; *The Castle*, 102). There are other poetic lines when the narrator alludes to Shakespearean tales in the final chapter. A minimalist account of *King Lear* even conveys some of the force of his famous speech in the storm: 'Cateratte, uragani, / traboccate a sommergere i campanili, / ad annegare i galli marcavento! (Blow, winds, and crack your cheeks! You cataracts and hurricanoes, spout till you have drenched our steeples, drown'd the cocks!)' (II, 605; *The Castle*, 115). The writer feels affinity with Stendhal in that he and his novels embody 'the provincial out to conquer the world' (II, 595; *The Castle*, 104); he read Stendhal when young as though he expected him to provide the romance 'to write (or live: there was confusion between the two verbs in him, or in the me of that time) (scrivere (o vivere: c'era una confusione tra i due verbi, in lui, o nel me di allora))' (II, 595; Weaver's translation actually reads: 'there was no confusion between the two verbs' (p. 104), but it must be an oversight). A similar confusion between the two meanings of *romanzo* and the two verbs 'vivere' and 'leggere' will be taken up in *If on a Winter's Night* (II, 641; *If on a Winter's Night*, 32). He sees his life as being represented first of all by three figures in the cards. The Cavaliere di Spade embodies his youthful militant spirit, his existential anguish and the energy expended in adventures. The Eremita is the 'topo di biblioteca' that he has become – the same phrase was used by the author to describe the change in his writing in the 1960s (*S*, 2784 and *Eremita a Parigi* in III, 106–7) – and his search for 'a knowledge forgotten (una sapienza dimenticata)' (II, 596; *The Castle*, 105) recalls Amerigo's rejection of realist fiction and pursuit of 'the wisdom of the ages (la sapienza delle epoche)' in *The Watcher* (II, 49). Finally he now sees himself as Il Bagatto: 'a juggler, or conjurer, who arranges on a stand at a fair a certain number of objects and, shifting them, connecting them, interchanging them, achieves a certain number of effects' (II, 596; *The Castle*, 105) – again an allusion to the limited narrative units (and their infinite combinatory potential) at the writer's disposal. But while the first two figures represent the author in successive chronological phases, the third one embraces his art throughout his career.

The last section of this chapter is the important one in which the author, without reproducing them, describes various famous representations of St Jerome and St George, embodying respectively the contemplative and active existences. St Jerome, the writer, is represented with the instruments of reading and writing forming part of the natural 'mineral–vegetable–animal continuum' (II, 597; *The Castle*, 106), which Calvino had first mentioned in the introduction to the *Fiabe* (p. 13). The skull represented there alludes to that elimination of the writer's personality which all writing entails. The presence of the city in the background is important for both Jerome and Calvino. Even closer to Calvino's frame of mind in these years is Botticelli's painting of St Augustine (in the Uffizi Gallery in Florence), in which the writer in crisis is depicted with many crumpled pieces of paper strewing the floor – a motif that recurs in a near contemporary text about refuse and cancellations, 'La poubelle agréée' (1974–76). Nevertheless Calvino also identifies certain aspects of St George as his own. In paintings of St George, the dragon is often a source of greater interest than the saint, therefore the dragon represents the saint's psychology, and his battle with it is his own interior struggle. Thus a typically Calvinian reversal manages to make St Jerome turn towards the city and St George turn inwards on himself: the contemplative becomes active and vice versa; the animal present in both cases, lion or dragon, is the beast we have to confront either outside or inside ourselves. In one of the last sentences of the volume we find another hint of the wrong and right ways of living in the city mentioned at the close of *Invisible Cities*:

> There is a guilty way of inhabiting solitude: believing we are serene because the fierce beast has been made harmless by a thorn in his paw. The hero of the story is he who in the city aims the point of his lance at the dragon's throat, and in solitude keeps the lion with him in all its strength. (II, 602; *The Castle*, 110–11)

The ideas of 'Il midollo del leone (The Lion's Marrow)' thus resurface even at this late stage in Calvino's career: the praise of the hero who faces up to his trials. The final two sentences of this chapter are too similar to the close of 'The Castle' for us to have any doubts that they were originally intended to be the last words of 'The Tavern': 'Thus I have set everything to rights. On the page, at least. Inside me all remains as before' (II, 602; *The Castle*, 111).

Despite this, Calvino reverses the order of the last two chapters so that the final one is 'Three stories of folly and destruction', those of Hamlet, Macbeth and Lear. The volume thus ends with Macbeth's words 'I 'gin to be a-weary of the sun, / and wish the estate o' the world were now undone!' (*Macbeth* V.5), followed by three phrases, the first recalling the reshuffling of the pack at the end of 'The Castle', the second alluding metatextually to the papers of the folios in which the play and this tale were written, the third mentioning mirror-fragments of disaster: 'I 'gin to be a-weary of The Sun, and wish the syntax o' The World were now undone, that the playing cards were shuffled, the folio's pages, the mirror-shards of the disaster' (II, 610; *The Castle*, 120). That final word, *disastro*, and the asymmetrical disruption of the last two chapters confirm that beneath the complex textual and pictorial surface of this elegant text lurks the gathering gloom of Calvino's 1970s pessimism. As the work had opened with the loss of speech, so this ending on a note of disaster maintains the dark tone of the volume. The general pessimism and the specific theme of 'mutismo' will continue in the silences of Palomar, who will make his first appearance just two years later in 1975 (see Chapter 9).

In the note at the end of *The Castle of Crossed Destinies*, the author explains that he had eventually reached an impasse both with the patterns of the cards in 'The Tavern' and with his unrealised project for 'The Motel of Crossed Destinies': now he feels, writing in October 1973, that his 'interest in the theory and the expressive potential of this kind of literary experiment is at an end. It is time (from all points of view) to move on to something else' (II, 1281). This understated promise to produce something else would take another six years to be realised, but it would be worth waiting for.

Chapter 8

A Borgesian Summa

If on a Winter's Night a Traveller

The six years that followed the publication of *The Castle of Crossed Destinies* (1973) represented the most prolonged creative crisis in Calvino's otherwise prolific writing career. All that he managed to publish in that time was a slim essay, 'La poubelle agréée (The Approved Dustbin)', which nevertheless took two years to write (1974–76), and which dealt, appropriately enough, with the contents of the writer's rubbish-bin, ending with a description of the sheet of paper containing the notes for this very essay but clearly also destined for the wastebin (III, 79). Both the topic in general and its metatextual conclusion were emblematic of a writer in crisis. Nevertheless, after this six-year silence Calvino finally resolved his problems in virtuoso, self-referential style by writing a hypernovel about a contemporary novelist with writer's block, whose fictions exhaust themselves after the first chapter. *Se una notte d'inverno un viaggiatore* (*If on a Winter's Night a Traveller*) (1979) uses the structure of frame and intercalated stories derived from archetypal story collections such as *The Thousand and One Nights* and Boccaccio's *Decameron*, but to this traditional framework Calvino adds avant-guarde elements to produce his homage to the novel in a work that is also a summa of contemporary fiction, and a resolution of his own particular creative difficulties.

The frame story, recounted in Chapters I to XII, narrates how a male and female reader try to read Calvino's latest novel, *If on a Winter's Night a Traveller*, only to discover that they can never read more than the first chapter of that or of any of the other substitute texts they are offered in its place. Each frame chapter takes place in a locus associated alternately with the consumption or production of literature: the reader's home in Chapters I, the bookshop in II, the university in III and IV, the publishing house in V and VI, the female reader's bedroom in VII, the writer's study in VIII, the censorship control room in IX and X, the library in XI and the bedroom again in XII. The symmetrical patterns are obvious: from the reader's sitting room in the first chapter the path leads back to the source of the text in the author's house in what is the thematic centre of this labyrinth in Chapter VIII – which the author acknowledged as 'the generative nucleus of the book' (II, 1382) – before travelling outwards again to where the text interfaces with the public, in libraries and that antithesis of a library, the censors' office, and then back symmetrically to the reader's (or rather now both readers') bedroom.

Intercalated after each of the first ten chapters of the frame are the ten *incipits* that are supplied to the fictional readers: these do not have chapter numbers but instead have the title of the novels of which they purport to be fragments. The title story finishes after its first chapter because, we are told, there has been a fault in binding, such that the fictional volume consists entirely of that chapter in pages 17–32 repeated perpetually (not an impossible occurrence: Calvino probably derived the idea from such incidents during his time at Einaudi, or from an earlier critical book about himself which did indeed contain a first chapter of twenty-six pages mistakenly reproduced twice at the beginning of the volume). In Chapter II the male reader takes the defective volume back to the bookshop where he meets a female reader who has encountered the same problem. The bookshop owner informs them that the binding error was even greater than at first thought, since the chapter they have read was not by Calvino at all but by a little known Polish author called Tazio Bazakbal: so gripped are the two readers by what they have read that they want a pristine copy not of Calvino's novel, but of Bazakbal's. The volume they are subsequently given of course turns out to be not by the Polish Bazakbal either, but by the Cimmerian poet Ukko Ahti, and after reading this, it is the sequel to Ahti's novel that the two readers naturally want to obtain next, and so on.

Similar contretemps disrupt their reading of all ten novels, but in the meantime their relationship blossoms in the frame story and becomes a 'romanzo da vivere' alongside the 'romanzo da leggere' (II, 641). In each frame chapter from II to X inclusive, the female reader, Ludmilla, frustrated by the fragment just finished announces the kind of novel she would like to read next, usually the antithesis of the one just read, and invariably the type of fiction that the two readers are then offered corresponds exactly to her desire. The fictional novel segments they obtain represent an astonishing tour de force on Calvino's part, because each of them belongs to a popular genre which he himself felt incapable of writing:

> That's what happened with my last novel, *If on a Winter's Night a Traveller*: I started imagining all the kinds of novels I would never write because I couldn't; then I tried to write them and for some time I felt in myself the energy of ten different imaginary novelists. ('The Written and Unwritten World', 39; *S*, 1874)

The genres he originally felt incapable of writing include spy-thrillers, Russian or East European revolutionary novels, Borgesian fables, Japanese erotica and Latin-American magic realism (specifically works by Márquez, Juan Rolfo, Vargas Llosa). The ten *incipits* also have exotic international settings, ranging from Russia and Eastern Europe, to Paris, the USA, South America and Japan. Given its ambitious, global scale and its successful aspiration to encompass world fiction within the bounds of a single volume, Calvino's *If on a Winter's Night* must be regarded as certainly his most ambitious work and arguably his masterpiece. Similar to his previous two books, *Invisible Cities* and *The Castle of Crossed Destinies*, in that it creates a literary work out of contemporary theories of reading and literature, this hypernovel is much more accessible than them in its narrative brio, its return to a comic dimension and in its virtuoso variety of styles (as well as in its ability to produce a masterpiece out of a personal creative crisis).

From the outset of the novel the affinity with Borges (to whom we shall return later in this chapter) is made explicit, in particular his rejection of the novel form. The narrator in the first chapter insists that 'the dimension of time has been shattered' (II, 618; *If on a Winter's Night*, 8), therefore traditional, lengthy novels are no longer viable: these were appropriate only in the nineteenth century when a more continuous notion of time prevailed. The first story takes up this theme, when the secret codeword 'Zeno of Elea' reminds us of the Greek philosopher's theoretical abolition of time and space in the stories of Achilles and the tortoise, and the arrow in flight, as in 't zero' (see Chapter 6). Each of the intercalated narrations, as well as the frame story, self-reflexively dwells on the nature of the text being read: in the station setting of the first *incipit* a cloud of steam is said to cover part of the first paragraph, at the start of the second one a smell of frying hovers over the first page, and so on. The second tale, set in Eastern Europe (and written in a style reminiscent of Günter Grass), even has a digression about the use of leitmotifs in literature, while the fourth tale describes itself as 'a bridge over the void'.

It has been claimed, though without much substantiation, that this hypernovel 'is as much a rewriting of Calvino's previous works as it is an "original" text' (Cannon, 1981, 97). Although all the micronovels contain echoes of the rest of his oeuvre, most obviously 'Adventure of a reader' and 'Adventure of a traveller' (De Lauretis, 1989), the third novel-fragment, 'Leaning from the steep slope' contains probably the highest number of allusions to earlier works by Calvino himself. The description of the prison by the harbour recalls the jail by the port in two of his earliest stories, 'Attesa della morte in un albergo' and 'Angoscia in caserma' (Calvino himself was incarcerated in the harbour jail which still exists in San Remo). The precise textual echoes are of 'Attesa':

> Today I saw a hand thrust out of a window of the prison, toward the sea. I was walking on the seawall of the port, as is my habit, until I was just below the old fortress. The fortress is entirely enclosed by its oblique walls; the windows, protected by double or triple grilles, seem blind . . . the prisoner must have performed an acrobat's feat – or, rather, a contorsionist's – to get his arm through grille after grille, to wave his hand in the free air. (*If on a Winter's Night*, 55)
> (Oggi ho visto una mano sporgersi da una finestra della prigione, verso mare.

> Camminavo sull'antemurale del porto, come è mia abitudine, arrivando fin dietro la vecchia fortezza. La fortezza è tutta chiusa nelle sue mura oblique; le finestre, difese da inferriate doppie o triple sembrano cieche . . . il carcerato deve aver compiuto uno sforzo da acrobata, anzi da contorsionista, per far passare il braccio tra inferriata e inferriata in modo da far svettare la sua mano nell'aria libera. (I, 663))

Later there is a description of the wives and families coming to visit the prisoners (II, 668; *If on a Winter's Night*, 60). Similarly the first two sentences of 'Attesa' describe the arrival of the prisoners' wives at the prison, and the hand-gestures of wives and internees:

> At a set hour every morning the prisoners' wives began to arrrive and would start making gestures, with their faces raised towards the windows. From the top floor the prisoners leaned out to ask and reply to questions; the women's hands down below and the men's hands up above seemed as if they wanted to join together across those few metres of empty air.
> (A una cert'ora del mattino cominciavano ad arrivare le mogli dei prigionieri e si mettevano a far gesti, con il viso alzato verso le finestre. Dall'ultimo piano loro si sporgevano a domandare, a rispondere; e le mani delle donne, a basso, e le mani degli uomini, lassú, sembrava volessero raggiungersi attraverso quei metri d'aria vuota. (I, 228))

Shortly after this we are told that 'The prison was an old fortress near the harbour . . . The grilles on the windows faced toward the sea-cliff . . .' ('Il carcere era una vecchia fortezza sul porto . . . L'inferriata dava sulla scogliera . . .' (I, 229–30)). These intertextual echoes thus link the thirty years that span the beginning and the peak of Calvino's writing career.

But there are many other allusions in this one story to images from his earlier works: the fortress-like bastions also recall the Château d'If at the end of *Time and the Hunter*; the empty deckchairs on the beach suggesting 'a world in which the human race has disappeared and things can do nothing but bespeak its absence' (II, 664; *If on a Winter's Night*, 56) are reminiscent of Baucis, the city of absence at the centre of *Invisible Cities*; the symmetrical spiral shell drawn by Zwida alludes to the final story of *Cosmicomics*, 'La spirale'; the pointlessness of dictionaries in reading between the lines of things (II, 669; *If on a Winter's Night*, 61) is redolent of the deceptive language of things emphasised in *Invisible Cities*, and the protagonist's lack of interest in representations of the human figure parallels the anti-anthropocentrism of the cosmicomic narratives. Even the protagonist's trust in barometers and anemometers symbolises a Conradian faith, embraced initially by Calvino, in rationality and measurements in the face of a disordered universe, a symbolism explicitly remarked upon in the young Calvino's university thesis (see Chapter 6). This micro-novel alone is almost a summa of Calvino's individual output.

The fourth fragment, 'Without fear of wind or vertigo', which is set during the Russian revolution, may owe something to *Dr Zhivago* and perhaps to Gogol with the mention of 'la Prospettiva' (Lucente 1987, 380), but the Banca Levinson mentioned (II, 685) derives its name from the hero of Fadeev's *The Rout* (singled out by Calvino in an important essay discussed above in Chapter 2: *S*, 1310), as do some of the details of the crowds and the woman railing against the 'signori'. We might then expect here an allusion to that first novel which Calvino claimed was inspired by Fadeev, and we find it when Irina stares into the void of the pistol barrel:

> 'Vertigo is everywhere.' And she takes the revolver . . . holds the weapon aimed at her eye, again spinning the chamber. 'It seems a bottomless pit.' (*If on a Winter's Night*, 86–7)
> (– Le vertigini sono dappertutto, – e prende la rivoltella . . . , tiene l'arma puntata contro l'occhio facendo girare il tamburo. – Sembra un pozzo senza fondo. (II, 694))

There is a similar moment in *The Path to the Spiders' Nests*:

> But then suddenly Pin cannot resist the temptation any more and points the pistol against his temple; it makes his head swim . . . Then, the most frightening thing of all, he puts it up to his eyes and looks right into it, down the dark barrel which seems deep as a well. (*The Path*, 47)
> (Ma a un certo punto Pin non resiste piú alla tentazione e si punta la pistola contro la tempia: è una cosa che dà le vertigini . . . Poi, cosa piú paurosa di tutte, portarla agli occhi e guardarci dentro, nella canna buia che sembra fonda come un pozzo. (I, 19))

Once again, the original Italian words of these two passages have an even closer correspondence than the English translations. Another proof that Calvino here is writing the kind of fiction he normally never would write is the fact that even within this short fragment, there is a flashback to the protagonist's first meeting with Irina, a technique which Calvino rarely used since it went against his cult of linear narration (*S*, xxvi–xxvii). But he also deploys an alliterative, poetic style, which recalls the more baroque passages of *Cosmicomics* and *The Castle of Crossed Destinies*, in describing Irina's writhings:

> I tried to escape, insinuating myself with crawling movements toward the center of the spirals, where the lines slithered like serpents following the writhing of Irina's limbs, supple and restless, in a slow dance where it is not the rhythm that counts but the knotting and loosening of serpentine lines. (*If on a Winter's Night*, 89)
> (Cercavo di *s*fuggire addentrandomi con movimenti *s*tri*s*cianti ver*s*o il centro della *s*pirale dove le linee *s*gu*s*ciavano come *s*erpenti *s*eguendo il contorcer*s*i delle membra d'Irina, *s*nodate e inquiete, in una lenta danza in cui non è il ritmo che importa ma l'annodar*s*i e lo *s*cioglier*s*i di linee *s*erpentine. (II, 696, italics mine))

In the fifth story there is an allusion to the end of *Invisible Cities*, when it is said that since Jojo was murdered while making love to Bernadette, he did not have time to notice the 'border between the hell of the living and the hell of the dead' (*If on a Winter's Night*, 108) ('passaggio di frontiera tra l'inferno dei vivi e l'inferno dei morti' (II, 715)), while the emphasis on plastic bags and the Arab streetsweeper are linked to the problematics of 'La poubelle agréée', also written in the mid-1970s. Even in Chapter VI the allusion to Silas Flannery's writing on commission for whisky firms presumably derives from Calvino's own experience of being commissioned to write in 1973 for a Japanese whisky firm the story that became 'La glaciazione' (III, 257–60; *Numbers in the Dark*, 203–5).

In Chapter VII Ludmilla's evident taste for reading more than one book at a time and for having a different book to read in every room also derives from the author's own habits. The five senses used in the lovers' reading of their partner's body (II, 762) in this central chapter (and towards the close of the final *incipit*, II, 860) link with the stories concerning the five senses written in the 1970s and 1980s: 'Il nome, il naso (The Name, the Nose)', later published in *Under the Jaguar Sun* (III, 113–26), was written in 1971–72, while from 1977 Calvino had worked both on *If on a Winter's Night* and on the libretto of Berio's opera, *Un re in ascolto* (*A King Listens*) (III, 1214–18), later to become the third of the three tales on the senses (III, 149–73). There are also allusions to earlier phases of his writing career in the seventh story, 'In a network of lines that intersect': in it the narrator claims that Athanasius Kircher's theatre of sixty mirrors was able to multiply a branch into a forest, a soldier into an army, a book into a library. These three emblems are not chosen at random since they represent three major themes of Calvino's writing from the outset: the forest, the army, and the library symbolise respectively nature, armed Resistance and *impegno* in general, and self-referential texts about texts.

The frame chapters VI, VII and VIII constitute what has been termed 'the doctrinal core' of the novel (Feinstein 1989). In it the two contrasting authors, the falsifier and mystifier Ermes Marana and the author in search of truth, Silas Flannery (even their first and second names have an identical number of syllables), emerge as the central contrasting pair – once again Stevensonian opposites lie at the heart of this novel's structure. But although Chapters VI and VII are important in that they give us respectively extracts from Marana's letters, and then the sexual encounter of the male and female reader, it is Chapter VIII, containing excerpts from the diary of the writer in crisis, Silas Flannery, that is the generative nucleus of the book, as Calvino himself admitted (II, 1382). Its centrality is confirmed by the fact that it describes the book's own complex structure in a *mise-en-abîme* (II, 785, 806; *If on a Winter's night*, 177, 197–98) reminiscent of the mythical 602nd night of *The Thousand and One Nights* mentioned by Borges. According to the Argentinian writer, on that night Scheherazade told the Sultan a story about Scheherazade who told the Sultan a story, and so on ad infinitum – an infinite regression that Calvino too had singled out in a key essay written in 1978, therefore during the composition of *If on a*

Winter's Night, 'I livelli della realtà in letteratura (Levels of Reality in Literature)' (*S*, 394–5; *LM*, 116–17).

The writer in crisis, Silas Flannery, decides that the only way out of his creative difficulties is to write a book consisting entirely of beginnings. But his ideal is also to write about atrocious crimes with the lightness of a butterfly (II, 780). It is certainly possible that this butterfly image came to Calvino from La Fontaine via Gide (Milanini, 1990, 152) or from Nabokov (Musarra, 1996, 172–5), but the strident contrast between 'un delitto atroce' and 'la farfalla' (II, 780) is a contrastive idea emblematic of Calvino's own poetics, as he says in the preface to *Our Ancestors*: virtuosity resides not in writing in a fairy-tale way about typical fairy-tale subjects such as castles and swans, but in writing fabulously when dealing with the condition of the proletariat and terrible crimes (I, 1209). Equally characteristic of Calvino is the desire, expressed by Flannery, to eliminate his own personality from his writing (II, 779), an aspiration that, as we have seen, goes back to the 1940s. But there are other echoes of Calvino's own ideas: 'memory is true as long as you do not set it, as long as it is not enclosed in a form' (II, 789; *If on a Winter's Night*, 181) is a reiteration of one of the cardinal concepts of the Preface to his first novel (I, 1202–4; *The Path*, 28–9). Flannery's conclusion in this crisis is that either he must write a single book that contains everything (but that would be a sacred text), or he must write all books. He thinks of inserting 'a cosmic truth' (II, 792–3) into his latest book, to satisfy the UFOlogists, and this phrase too echoes a key idea from 'La sfida al labirinto (The Challenge to the Labyrinth)' (*S*, 123).

Also in Chapter VIII Ludmilla's militant sister, Lotaria, confronts Flannery with a computer analysis of word-frequencies in three novels, and this computer study (Alinei, 1973) had in fact been carried out on Calvino's own first novel, the first one alluded to by Lotaria (the other two were novels by Carlo Cassola and Alberto Moravia). Since all Flannery's literary efforts now peter out after the first chapter, he decides to write about a reader's attempts to obtain the sequel to that chapter (which is of course yet another description of *If on a Winter's Night*). What he really longs to write about is 'the unwritten world', another key concept of the time, since it gave the title to one of Calvino's most famous essays of the early 1980s which actually discussed the genesis of this hypernovel.

In 'Intorno a una fossa vuota (Around an Empty Grave)', references to spicy food are similar to those in 'Sotto il sole giaguaro (Under the Jaguar Sun)', a story first written in 1981 with the title 'Sapore, sapere (Taste, Knowledge)' (III, 1218). In 'Quale storia laggiú attende la fine? (What Story Down There Awaits its End?)' the character Arkadian Porphyritch has a surname which has links, as has been shown (Usher 1996), with the Neoplatonic philosopher Porphyry mentioned in 'In una rete di linee che s'intersecano (In a Network of Lines that Intersect)', but his Arcadian first name must have been generated by a now familiar Calvinian dialectic, since the country in which Porphyritch resides is the literary opposite of

Arcadia, Hyrcania, the fabled land of origin of all things savage. Similarly the mythical countries of Cimmeria and Cimbria, the countries of origin of the third and fourth tales, are also of classical derivation. The paradoxical notion that only police states respect literature is another of Calvino's ideas expressed in 'Usi politici giusti e sbagliati della letteratura (Right and Wrong Political Uses of Literature)' (1976): 'Wherever writers are persecuted, it means that . . . fiction, poetry, and literary criticism in such countries acquire unusual political specific gravity, insofar as they give a voice to all those who are deprived of one' (*S*, 357; *LM*, 96). Both the frame and the mini-narratives thus contain a network of allusions to the author's own fictional and non-fictional works.

In Chapter XI, set in a library, we are offered seven different ways of reading: the first reader becomes so stimulated by the first phrases of any book that he immediately loses sight of the text and starts reflecting; the second is the opposite: he finds the typeface so 'puntiforme e pulviscolare (punctiform and pulviscolar)' (II, 864; *If on a Winter's Night*, 254) that he cannot extricate himself from any of the words in the text. For the third each book seems new to him even if it is not, while for the fourth reading simply absorbs each new work into his ideal library. The fifth is seeking the archetypal book he had read in childhood; the sixth loves all the preliminaries of any book: the title and everything that precedes it; while the seventh prefers all that comes after the end. The fifth reader intervenes again to recount an interrupted story from *The Thousand and One Nights*, thereby suggesting that that indeed was the archetypal text read in childhood that he was seeking and also the ultimate model for the book we have just read. These many different approaches to reading, like Ludmilla's demands for constantly varied kinds of books, endorse our right to read Calvino's text in any number of different ways and thus avoid univocal interpretations. This avoidance of closure is reaffirmed when the male reader notices that the ten titles of the fragments he has read themselves form an enticing opening sentence of a novel: 'If on a winter's night a traveller, outside the town of Malbork, leaning from the steep slope without fear of wind or vertigo, looks down in the gathering shadow in a network of lines that enlace, in a network of lines that intersect, on the carpet of leaves illuminated by the moon around an empty grave – What story down there awaits its end?' (II, 868; *If on a Winter's Night*, 258). Here again a kind of vertigo is hinted at, since if this process is reversed, the implication is that each opening sentence we read in any novel may contain ten other novels beneath it, and even the concluding words of Calvino's novel may contain further stories in the interstices. Once again Calvino forestalls closure.

The final brief chapter defeats our expectations since if it had followed the alternating pattern of the rest of the book, of frame chapter followed by micro-novel, it ought to have been an eleventh novel fragment. The end of Chapter XI also suggests this, since it points out that 'the ultimate meaning to which all stories refer has two faces: the continuity of life, the inevitability of death' (II, 869; *If on a Winter's Night*, 259), and we consequently expect a mini-novel that exemplifies one or both of these two 'faces'. But it appears to be a frame chapter, since it is entitled Chapter XII (rather than having the title of a mini-novel) and is about the male and female reader. However, there is a definite hint that this is also a micro-novel, since it consists of a parodistic closure of the 'Reader, I married him' type, the two readers putting out their lights having read Calvino's *If on a Winter's Night a Traveller.*

Like everything else in this hypernovel, even the overall architecture of the work is determined by several different factors. The structural interplay of the numbers 12 and 10 for the frame chapters and the micro-novels respectively is both an allusion to our two basic systems of measurement, in particular to the decimal measurement of space and the duodecimal units of time, and also a nod to Calvino's own use of such structures in previous works (the twelve chapters of *The Path to the Spiders' Nests*, of *The Non-Existent Knight*, of *Cosmicomics*; the ten chapters of *The Cloven Viscount*, the twenty stories in *Marcovaldo*, the thirty tales of *The Crow Comes Last*, the thirty chapters of *The Baron in the Trees*). There is also a famous Borges story which is a source for this idea: 'Tlön, Uqbar, Orbis Tertius' describes an imaginary planet where the decimal and duodecimal systems are compatible.

In fact Borges' presence haunts this entire text. We have already noted his presence in this 10/12 structure, in the remark at the beginning about the dimension of time being shattered and in that central Chapter VIII where there was the allusion to the mythical 602nd of *The Thousand and One Nights*, a night mentioned only by Borges. But the Argentinian writer's presence is all-pervasive in the central chapters. Even the key thematics of writer's block and the lightness of the butterfly in Chapter VIII also derive from him. In his most important essay on Borges, written in 1984, Calvino noted that the Argentinian resolved his own difficulties about writing fiction 'first by imagining that the book he wanted to write was already written, written by another author, a hypothetical, unknown writer, an author from another language and from another culture – and then by describing, summarising, reviewing this hypothetical book' (*S*, 1294–5). This accurate account of Borges' early works such as 'The Approach to Almotásim', provided Calvino with the inspiration for solving his own creative block in the 1970s, for he too imagined that the book or books he wanted to write were already written, and he simply describes, summarises or offers fragments of them in *If on a Winter's Night*. We have seen that Calvino had already been interested in the idea of *enchâssement* of stories, in the important essay written in 1978 during the composition of this text, 'I livelli della realtà'. There he cites Borges' allusion to the 602nd night of *The Thousand and One Nights* (*S*, 394–5; *LM*, 116–17), and Borges' discussion of this, in an essay 'Partial Magic of the *Quixote*' (Borges, 1989, II, 47), is relevant here because it points out that what disturbs us in the tale of Scheherazade within the tale of Scheherazade, or the play within the play of *Hamlet*, or Don Quixote reading *Don Quixote*, is that if fictional characters can become readers or spectators, then conversely we spectators or readers may in turn be merely fictional. This confusion of levels of real and fictional readers is at the root of Calvino's hypernovel.

The other main ideas of Chapter VIII are also Borgesian in origin: the notion of using the verbs *pensare, scrivere, leggere* as impersonal verbs recalls similar ideas in 'Tlön, Uqbar, Orbis Tertius' and 'A New Refutation of Time', while the allusion to the butterfly echoes the dream mentioned in the latter tale, of Chuang Tzu, who dreamt he himself was a butterfly. Immediately after this, Flannery sets out to obtain inspiration by transcribing the opening passage from a classic novel, such as Dostoevsky's *Crime and Punishment*, but he finds it extremely difficult to stop and nearly ends up transcribing the entire work, just as Borges' famous Pierre Menard copied out the whole of *Don Quixote*. Segre (1979) noted that the genres of the *incipits* in *If on a Winter's Night* correspond to the various novels contained in another phantomatic hypernovel mentioned by Borges, Herbert Quain's *April–March*. In 'An Examination of the Work of Herbert Quain', Borges claims that in *April–March*, a novel which contains a complex series of novels within it, 'one novel was symbolic in character, another a supernatural tale; another was a detective story, another a psychological thriller; another was a Communist work, another was anti–Communist, and so on' (Borges, 1989, I, 463). The contrasting styles of Calvino's intercalated fictions no doubt correspond to this idea, as Segre suggests. But other details of the fictional Quain's works are exploited by Calvino. Borges' summary of the first chapter of *April–March* ('The first chapter reports the ambiguous dialogue of unknown characters in a station') describes precisely the first micro-novel of *If on a Winter's Night*.

The overall structure of Calvino's hypernovel has been considered analogous to the complex organisation of Borges' *The Garden of Forking Paths*, though more symmetrical and classical than the Argentinian's 'baroque proliferation' (Milanini, 1990, 152). It is worth, once more, enquiring further into this Calvinian structure. The pattern of twelve chapters containing ten mini–novels is numerically closely indebted to Quain's 'ramified' text, *April–March*, in which thirteen chapters contain nine different novels. Borges' description of the eight stories contained in Quain's other work, *Statements*, also must have proven suggestive for the Italian author: 'Each one of the eight stories either sketches or promises an interesting topic, which is then deliberately cut short by the author' (Borges, 1989, I, 464).

It is also significant that these Borgesian allusions should cluster in this eighth chapter, for the micro-novel that precedes it, 'In una rete di linee che s'intersecano (In a Network of Lines which Intersect)', is an almost perfect copy of a Borges fiction. The title comes, as has been seen (Chapter 6), from a phrase in the last tale of *Time and the Hunter*, and also from the author's 1959 definition of what a novel is, a definition articulated a full twenty years before *If on a Winter's Night*: 'The novel today (and therefore always) is *a narrative work which can signify and be enjoyed on many different planes which intersect* (Il romanzo è: *un'opera narrativa fruibile e significante su molti piani che s'intersecano*)' (Calvino's italics, *S*, 1525). But if the title stems from the author's own writings, the atmosphere of the tale derives from the Argentinian writer's work: 'A thriller which includes another tale, in which the suspense is of a logical-metaphysical nature' (*S*, 1298) is how Calvino characterised the successful formula of *The Garden of Forking Paths*, and this description also fits Calvino's seventh story perfectly. The opening is classic Borges:

> Speculate, reflect: every thinking activity implies mirrors for me. According to Plotinus, the soul is a mirror that creates material things reflecting the ideals of the higher reason. (II, 769; *If on a Winter's Night* 161)

The first sentence contains an allusion to mirrors, another Borgesian theme par excellence, while the second refers to the Neoplatonic philosopher Plotinus, cited often by the Argentinian, notably in 'The Approach to Almotásim', one of the stories that Calvino openly admitted influenced him in this hypernovel (II, 1396). The erudite framework is sustained by a series of allusions to similarly arcane works: Sir David Brewster's *Treatise on New Philosophical Instruments*, Athanasius Kircher's *Ars Magna Lucis et Umbrae*, Giovanni Battista della Porta's *De Magia Naturali*, and Plotinus' disciple Porphyry. Borges' fondness for quoting Neoplatonic philosophers and writers on natural magic is too well known to need documenting here. But Calvino's sense of symmetry demands that, as at the opening so at the end of this seventh fiction, the two final sentences should recall his Argentinian model:

> In a fragment of Novalis, an adept who has managed to reach the secret dwelling of Isis lifts the veil of the goddess . . . Now it seems to me that everything that surrounds me is a part of me, that I have managed to become the whole, finally . . . (II, 776; *If on a Winter's Night* 168)

Of course it was another Novalis fragment, about total identification with a particular author, that inspired Pierre Menard to his absurd enterprise of transcribing *Don Quixote* (Borges, 1989, I, 446). The final sentence alludes to the Plotinus passage cited by Borges in the note at the end of 'The Approach to Almotásim', namely that each thing can become everything. Calvino admitted in a letter to Angelo Guglielmi that this story was meant to be a thriller of the kind typical of Borges (II, 1389), and he even cites 'Almotásim' as the text that made *If on a Winter's Night* seem a search for the real novel (II, 1396). For good reason, then, Calvino later described himself in a 1984 essay as 'a faithful follower of the sage of Buenos Aires' (*S*, 1037).

It has been argued whether this is more a novel about reading than about writing. It is certainly a manifestation of the powers of both author or text and reader. Its main thrust, it is claimed, is to subvert 'the notion of a text as a medium, but also the notion of the author as a privileged origin of a unified and univocal meaning "transmitted" through the text' (Cannon 1981, 98). However, it is also a playful extension and reversal of Barthes' sexual metaphor of 'the pleasures of the text' (Musarra, 1996, 147–8). If reading is a kind of intercourse, then this work moves backwards to celebrate both the literary foreplay that takes place before a text can be read as well as the central act of intercourse/reading itself (the sexual union of the male and female readers is described as a reading of each other's body by all five senses, not just by the eye as in the reading of a text). Throughout, of course, there is also a play on the ambiguity of climax in both its literary and sexual meanings, while the whole structure of the novel is a series of interrupted coitions. In this context it celebrates Western fiction's obsession with adultery, since each of the *incipit*s involves a triangular relationship, usually two men and a woman, as indeed happens in the frame where Ludmilla is contended by both the male reader and the writers Marana and Flannery. But the work is serious as well as playful: Milanini (1990, 153) noted that the two key strands in the book dealt with mirrors and with traps, and Usher's computer analysis of the text confirms this (Usher, 1996), while Hume has pointed out the insistence on the themes of the void and of flux (Hume, 1992a). Again the poetics of intertextual contrast is at play: inside the traditional, almost fairy-tale frame ending in marriage, there are a series of detective stories (Barenghi, 1984). Calvino is warning us to be aware of the slippery status of language, under which lurks the void, and to learn to decipher the various sign-systems in operation in the world.

Calvino's words to Guglielmi on the significance of the ten micro-novels are also worth quoting:

> Viewed in this light, the book came to represent (in my eyes) a kind of autobiography in negative: the novels I could have written but which I had rejected, and at the same time (in my eyes, and in the eyes of others) a significant catalogue of existential attitudes which lead only to so many blind alleys. (II, 1396)

This book is both a humorous homage to the novel as a genre and 'a serious essay on the triangular relationship between reader, writer, and text' (Usher, 1990, 81). Its serious and comic aspects are also closely bound up with the sombre and ludic essays written in the same years ('Right and Wrong Political Uses of Literature' of 1976, and 'Levels of Reality in Literature' of 1978). The author's diagram for the structure of the novel (II, 1394–5) confirms both these more solemn and more playful constraints that subtend the work. Most of all, the work represents a virtuoso resolution of a creative crisis, and constitutes Calvino's response to Borges and to the problem of writing fiction in the late twentieth century. It is both an autobiography in negative, as the author suggests, in that it contains all the genres that were absent from his previous fiction, but at the same time it contains allusions to many of the previous works he did write. Right to the very last chapter, in which the frame story becomes a micronovel with a 'genre' ending and thus both closes and fails to close, Calvino manages to have it both ways.

Calvino's attempt to expand the confines of literature continues to pervade the works he was planning to complete in the 1980s, such as *Under the Jaguar Sun* (1986) in which he hoped to compose five stories on the five senses despite the fact that, as he admitted with his usual self-deprecating irony, 'my sense of smell is not very sharp. I lack really keen hearing, I am not a gourmet, my sense of touch is unrefined, and I am nearsighted' ('The Written and Unwritten World', 39; *S*, 1874). These short pieces, of which only three were completed before the author's death, are paradoxically linked to an overarching ambition to change both literature and the author's life: 'I don't know if I shall succeed, but my efforts, in this case as in the others, are not merely aimed at making a book, but also at changing myself, the goal of all human endeavour' ('The Written and Unwritten World', 39; *S*, 1874). After the end of *impegno*, Calvino seemed continually to narrow the public to which he addressed ever more specialist works (from *Cosmicomics* to *Invisible Cities* to *The Castle of Crossed Destinies*) – the logical conclusion of this process should have been silence. Instead, with *If on a Winter's Night* he published his most accessible and successful volume for years. But at the same time, following the laws of his own inner creativity, he was also working on a totally antithetical project, a series of minute descriptions which do tend towards silence. The complex implications of that silence will be fully explored in the next chapter.

Chapter 9

Words and Silence

The Strange Genesis of *Mr Palomar*

Although *Palomar* was not published until 1983, the last book of fiction to be published in the author's lifetime (*Cosmicomiche vecchie e nuove* published in 1984 was substantially a reissue, containing only two new stories), it is essential to remember that its genesis actually precedes that of *If on a Winter's Night a Traveller*: the first Palomar pieces were published in the *Corriere della sera* in August 1975, while work on the hypernovel did not begin until 1977. Working on more than one project at a time was part of Calvino's contrastive creativity, and it is no surprise that the two works are specular opposites: where the hypernovel dealt largely with the realm of literature and language, the written world, *Palomar* explores the world of things, the unwritten world ('The Written and Unwritten World' is in fact the title of the important lecture, also written in 1983). The author himself articulates these poetics of alternation in the chapter on 'Exactitude' in *Six Memos*:

> In the last few years I have alternated my exercises in the structure of the story with other exercises in description, today a very neglected art. Like a schoolboy whose homework is 'Describe a giraffe' or 'Describe the starry sky', I applied myself to filling a notebook with such exercises and made a book out of the material. This is *Mr Palomar* . . . It is a kind of diary dealing with minimal problems of knowledge, ways of establishing relationships with the world, and gratifications and frustrations in the use of both silence and words. (*S*, 692; *Six Memos*, 75)

Calvino's own statement sums up best the book's tripartite thematics: minimalist attempts at solving epistemological problems, then the larger question of relating these to the wider world, and finally the themes of words and silence.

Paradoxically for a book which thematises silence, *Palomar* appears to have generated the largest number of critical studies of any of Calvino's works, outstripping even those on *Invisible Cities* and *If on a Winter's Night*. Part of the explanation for its appeal is the fact that its fragmentary structure and pulviscular poetics are considered emblematic of the contemporary postmodern condition. Some critics see the work as a continuation of Calvino's long-standing quest to confront with a rational consciousness the sea of objects, this time using the instruments of defamiliarisation and enumeration (Cannon 1985 and 1989). Others regard the protagonist as spokesman for contemporary philosophical and cognitive problems, and judge the work to be the final statement of Calvino's modest Stoicism in the protagonist's 'obstinate search for the tiny islands of the rational' (Biasin, 1989, 168). The fact that the eponymous, and closely autobiographical, protagonist dies in the final four-word sentence of the book in a way that seemed uncannily prophetic of the author's own death two years later has channelled the attention of most critics towards the thematics of silence and death. Benussi acutely observes that since according to *If on a Winter's Night* literature points to only two things, 'the continuity of life and the inevitability of death' (II, 869; *If on a Winter's Night*, 259), then the conclusion of the hypernovel clearly embodies the former and the final section of *Palomar* the latter. Roelens (1989) notes that the twenty-seven short pieces that compose the volume amount to a macrotext which is oriented in a clear direction, as Palomar abandons the various screens that he puts between himself and the world (glasses, telescope, TV screen etc.) and finally confronts his own mortality. But unlike the cosmicomic stories, here death is final, looking forward to no metamorphosis or renaissance (Hume, 1992a). Milanini (1990) stresses the work's epistemological pessimism and its unique lack of a frame (unlike his other works from *Cosmicomics* onwards) to expand its minimalist units, and sees it as no coincidence that the two most autobiographical works, *Palomar* and *The Watcher*, each took almost ten years to complete (II, xiv). However, it would be wrong to consider silence and death as exclusively pessimistic thematics in this book.

The intertexts and poetics of the work are also important. For Celati (1987) the 'vignetta' or cartoon strip informs much of Calvino's output, and it is certainly in evidence here, notably in the often slapstick endings to the individual units. Benussi (1989) discerns a contrasting pair of literary models for *Palomar* in both the comic strip and Leopardi's *Operette morali*, while Prete (1987) actually specifies the titles of two pieces from the latter which influence *Palomar*, though without analysing them. But even a cursory glance shows that the opening of Leopardi's 'Elogio degli uccelli (Eulogy of the Birds)', in which the solitary philosopher Aemilius sits reading one spring morning in the shade of his country house, listening to the birds singing in the open air, clearly inspires the beginning of 'Il fischio del merlo (The Blackbird's Whistle)'. Similarly, the mention of Saturn and Jupiter in Leopardi's 'Frammento apocrifo di Stratone da Lampsaco (Apocryphal Fragment of Strato of Lampsacus)', which is explicitly praised by the author in *Six Memos* (*S*, 686; *Six Memos*, 67), lies behind Palomar's observation of these two planets in 'L'occhio e i pianeti (The Eye and the Planets)', while the Romantic poet's mention of the destruction of the earth by fire in the same piece is echoed in the penultimate paragraph of the final section of *Palomar*. Hume (1992a, 180–3) sees *Palomar* as inspired by Valéry's *Monsieur*

Teste, particularly his notion of *civilisation intérieure*, though others consider the protagonist more M. Hulot than M. Teste (Roelens 1989). But there are clearly other aspects of Valéry's character that lie behind Calvino's protagonist. Teste is also obsessed by precision (Valéry, 1946, 7) and likes to designate objects merely by using abstract words and proper nouns (22), though it is unclear whether his eyes miss everything or whether the whole world is merely a small detail of everything they behold (38). Teste, like Palomar, is 'un *mystique sans Dieu*', who does not possess a single grain of hope (51–3), and Calvino in the Harvard lecture on 'Exactitude' cites the whole page (32–3) in which Teste talks of seeing into his body, counting grains of sand, and concentrating on a single object (*S*, 684–5; *Six Memos*, 65–7). Apart from these common character traits, there is a particular episode which caught Calvino's attention, the one in which Teste contemplates the huge leaves of a water-lily, which probably inspires the water-lily scene at the start of the eighth micro-novel of *If on a Winter's Night* (II, 809–10; *If on a Winter's Night*, 201–2). But Teste's conclusion on the botanical garden is closer to Palomar's idea of the Parisian fromagerie as a dictionary of cheeses – '*C'est un jardin d'épithètes*, dit-il l'autre jour, *jardin dictionnaire et cimetière* . . . (Valéry, 194, 55) – while his aspiration – '*Doctement mourir . . . Transiit classificando*' (55) – could obviously be Palomar's own epitaph. Even the title and thematics of the last fragment of Valéry's text – 'Fin de Monsieur Teste' (139–40) – closely resemble those of the final unit of *Palomar*, with the transition from life to death being defined as 'de zéro à zéro' and Teste being described as someone who is now out of this world, simply an 'oeil frontière entre l'être et le non-être' (140).

A few scholars have devoted attention to other aspects of the genesis of the volume. Here strict attention to chronological detail is crucial. Most acknowledge the fact that Palomar makes his first appearance in a number of pieces written for the *Corriere della sera* between 1975 and 1977. Barenghi (II, 1402–36) and Serra (1996, 13–73) provide the fullest details: of the twenty-seven units that comprise the volume ten had appeared in the *Corriere* between 1975 and 1977, four in *la Repubblica* between 1980 and 1982, and thirteen new pieces were written specifically for the forthcoming book between 1982 and 1983 (see Appendix), two of them appearing in *Repubblica* in summer 1983 ('La spada del sole', 29 July; 'La contemplazione delle stelle', 25 August 1983) as excerpts from a book which was more or less complete. Of the many journalistic pieces written in the 1970s and 1980s, with or without Palomar as protagonist, some ended up in the 1983 volume while others were included as first-person reportages in one of the two collections of essays, *Una pietra sopra* (1980) and *Collezione di sabbia* (1984). This breakdown between the confines of fiction and non-fiction, between *narrativa* and *saggistica*, was a Borgesian textual practice which Calvino consciously embraced in this period. We now know that originally Palomar was conceived of as having a double or opposite, Mohole, who looked inward rather than outward, and Palomar's 'Dialoghi col Mohole' was to have been the finale of the book (II, 1402–3). This Mohole sequence shows that Calvino considered the Jekyll and Hyde motif of the double as a useful narrative machine from his earliest stories about two brothers, such as 'La stessa cosa del sangue (In the Blood)', and the time of *The Cloven Viscount* right down to his last fictions. However, the author did not elaborate this project beyond a few brief dialogues since, he claims, he realised that Palomar contained that darker side to him within his own character (II, 1403). But in what follows I hope to show that there is another important reason for the absence of the dialogues with Mohole from the finished volume.

Barenghi (II, 1411) and Serra (1996, 63–5) also inform us that initially the author conceived of a much more substantial volume of 125 pieces (divided into five groups of five units each containing five pieces), but that subsequently he narrowed this down to thirty-nine sequences, before opting for the twenty-seven–unit formula (three groups of nine pieces, which in turn are subdivided into three units of three). This ternary structure is emphasised by the author in the book's index, which numbers the units in a sequence that suggests a half-serious, half-playful analogy with contemporary semiotic studies: 1.1.1, 1.1.2, 1.1.3, 1.2.1, 1.2.2, and so on until 3.3.3. The note in the index claims that pieces designated by the number 1 in any position are generally visual and descriptive in character, those with the number 2 are usually cultural in content and in narrative mode, while the number 3 indicates speculations on topics such as time and the cosmos, usually written in a meditative style. However, the fact that this index appears at the end of the text rather than at the beginning as happened with *Invisible Cities* suggests that the grid does not enmesh integrally with the text, but rather is there as a premise to future rereadings (Musarra 1996, 196–7). As for the preference here for a ternary rather than quintuple structure, this was determined, as usual, by more than one motive: Calvino had already used a unit of five to structure the fifty-five *Invisible Cities*, and the original 125–unit structure obviously had 'totalising ambitions' (II, 1411) since the five major categories were 'The World', 'Man', 'The Cosmos', 'Eros', and 'Other People'. This slimmer twenty-seven–unit format suited better the minimalist poetics of the book and, most importantly, the tripartite structure implies that the volume constitutes a modern, secular, equivalent of Dante's three-part summa of his world in the *Divine Comedy.* This last idea is developed interestingly by Guj (1987), who pushes the correspondences even further: Dante's *Inferno*, like the first sections in *Palomar*, is largely visual; similar to the second sections in Calvino's text, *Purgatorio* contains many cultural, artistic and poetic reflections; and parallel to the third sections of the 1983 work, *Paradiso* is also replete with metaphysical speculation. We have seen in previous chapters that intertextual echoes of Dante occur throughout his oeuvre, but it is his view of the *Comedy* as epitomising one of the key trends in Italian literature that explains the significance of the Dantesque echoes in *Palomar*: 'This is a deep-rooted vocation in Italian literature, handed on from Dante to Galileo: the notion of the literary work as a map of the world and of the knowable' (*S*, 232–3; LM, 32). Again the poetics of paradox are present here: this is a consciously slim book which is at the same time a kind of encyclopedia.

A few critics have noted the implications of this complicated genesis. Ferretti (1989) stressed that the thematics of violence in 'La pancia del geco (The Gecko's Belly)' gained added significance from the more precise allusion to violence in Calvino's accompanying article which was not included in the book ('La diplomazia e la mimica', now in *Enciclopedia*, 32–3). Milanini (1990, 177) observed that the author omitted in the book any calls to action which had been present in the original journalistic pieces, thus rendering the protagonist even more neutral and contemplative. Both critics and Serra (1996) remind us that the same journalistic material was often rewritten, items composed originally in the third-person about Palomar shifting to first-person accounts or vice versa, depending on whether the ultimate destination of the piece was to be in *Palomar, Collezione di sabbia* (1984), *Una pietra sopra* (in the case of the homage to Groucho Marx – see *S*, 369–71), or even *Cosmicomiche vecchie e nuove* of 1984 (in which 'I buchi neri (Black Holes)' of 1975 (*Enciclopedia*, 48–51) became 'L'implosione'). Barenghi pointed out that a substantial passage from 'Un chilo e mezzo di grasso d'oca (Two Pounds of Goose Fat)', which observed that the affluence of one half of the world depended on the malnutrition of the other half, was rejected because it dealt with global themes that went far beyond the minimalist problematics which this book explores (II, 1425–8). The same was true of the first redaction of 'Il gorilla albino (The Albino Gorilla)', which included a contrast with the bestial conditions in which political prisoners were held in Uruguay (II, 1429–31). Perrella (1990) drew attention to the importance of Pier Paolo Pasolini's review of *Invisible Cities* in 1973 and of Calvino's subsequent letter to him, which emphasised the twin topics of reading and silence or death, topics which adumbrate respectively the thematics of *If on a Winter's Night* and *Palomar*. This diachronic approach seems the most illuminating way of approaching this last book published in Calvino's lifetime, particularly in view of its complicated evolution. It is essential to study the genesis of Palomar as a character and his relation to Pasolini, as well as the considerable amount of Palomar material omitted from the volume, what amounts almost to *Palomar* in negative, in order to understand what is included: as Calvino himself said, 'to plan a book . . . the first thing to know is what to exclude' ('Il conte di Montecristo', II, 356; *Time and the Hunter*, 151). Even the author's own initial presentation of *Palomar* dwelt largely on the parts he had rejected and he justified this approach by underlining the importance of discussing a book '"in negative", that is discussing the various projects for a book which have been discarded in order to arrive at the final version' (II, 1403).

It is vital, therefore, to consider all the Palomar sequences excluded from the 1983 volume. If we examine those which had already appeared as newspaper articles (listed in II, 1407–9), we shall see that they all have a number of aspects in common: they deal with ephemeral political events ('Le brave persone (Good People'), works of literature such as *The Odysssey* ('I Lotofagi (The Lotus-Eaters)') or Holanda's dialogues on painting ('L'uomo di fronte a disegni segreti (Man Confronted with Secret Patterns)'), books on science ('Un maremoto nel Pacifico (A Seaquake in the Pacific)', 'Al centro della ruota (At the Centre of the Wheel)', 'Ultime notizie sul tempo (Latest News on Time)'), reviews of or references to other books ('La foresta genealogica (The Genealogical Forest)', 'L'uovo enciclopedico (The Encyclopedic Egg)', 'L'origine degli elefanti (The Origin of Elephants)', 'La donna fantasma (The Phantom Woman)'), replies to socio-political criticisms by Fortini ('La seconda natura (Second Nature)') or Forcella ('Non ditemi che è inutile (Don't Tell Me It's Pointless)'), specific television programmes ('I buchi neri (Black Holes)'), precise historical incidents ('Nei boschi degli Indiani (In the Indians' Woods)', 'La forma dell'albero' (The Shape of the Tree), 'Il tempo e i rami (Time and Branches)') and straight pieces of travelogue/reportage – the latter are mostly about Japan and are also excluded because they contain allusions to Japanese literature or culture ('Due donne, due volti del Giappone (Two Women, Two Faces of Japan)', 'L'amara ricchezza delle ville di Kyoto (The Bitter Riches of the Villas of Kyoto)', 'I gentili miracoli del Giappone (The Kind Miracles of Japan)', 'La luna in tasca (The Moon in a Pocket)', 'Una pietra, un sasso (A Stone, a Rock)'). Explicit allusion to other texts, then, whether literary or scientific, is consistently excised since *Palomar* is to be a work that embraces the unwritten world, not the literary and metaliterary topics of *If on a Winter's Night* nor the cultural explorations of *Collezione di sabbia*.

All the items that would date precisely the individual units are also dropped: *Palomar* aspires to the quality of timeless reflections. No precise historical or political events are alluded to except for those in the distant past (the fall of Rome, or the end of Toltech civilisation). There are merely imprecise allusions, in 'Del mordersi la lingua (On Biting the Tongue)' (3.2.1) to the current epoch being one in which people are too quick to sound off opinions (II, 960–1; *Mr Palomar*, 93–4), and in the next piece (3.2.2), 'Del prendersela coi giovani (On Becoming Angry with the Young)', to it being an age in which the gap between old and young has become almost insurmountable (II, 962–3); and since those two pieces open with a reference to 'un'epoca', so the third unit of this section, 'Il modello dei modelli (The Model of Models)' (3.2.3), begins with a vague reference to 'un'epoca', an epoch in his life in which Palomar started with an ideal model to which he tried to make the world correspond (II, 964; *Mr Palomar*, 97).

As with time, so with space it is instructive to analyse the travelogues which are included or excluded. Serra (1996, 90, n. 17) rightly reminds us that from the time of his early abortive attempt at a major effort in the genre (*Un ottimista in America*), Calvino was very sceptical of the literary worth of travel writing. The only three travelogues retained in this book are those which deal with the Zen temple at Kyoto, the Toltech temple in Mexico, and an unnamed Middle Eastern country (probably Iran) in which Palomar bought an unmatching pair of slippers. Excluded from this book and destined for *Collezione di sabbia* are those reportages on Japan which contained, as we have seen, references to works of literature or culture (books, museums, architecture, etc.) and a diptych about Mexico that would have been difficult to split up. In any case, the first of these Mexican pieces, 'La forma dell'albero (The Shape of the Tree)', contained precise historical allusions to the Conquistadors, and the second, 'Il tempo e i rami (Time and the Branches)', to the history of the French kings; as we have observed, Calvino excluded from the volume pieces with historical references. Most indicative of all is the fact that the one account of Palomar's stay in the USA ('Nel bosco degli Indiani (In the Indian Wood)') is omitted – presumably not only for its specific historical allusion to the American wars of independence, but particularly because one of the key points of this travelogue section in *Palomar* was to contrast Western traditions of rationality with the very different epistemological heritage of the Orient, the Middle East and Latin America.

Palomar's name derives, of course, from the enormous telescope on Mount Palomar in California, but names are polysemous in Calvino's works: the protagonist is not only an observer of the world around him (ironically, being short-sighted his vision is the opposite of telescopic), his name's link with the Spanish *paloma* suggests his observations of birds in several stories here, while the association with *palombaro* (meaning deep-sea diver in Italian), an association acknowledged by the author (II, 1405–6), points to his constant delving into the exterior of the universe, and his despairing conclusion that even the surface of things is inexhaustible (II, 920; *Mr Palomar*, 51).

As was the case with *Invisible Cities*, the structure of this book is integral to its meaning, both in its tripartite numbering and in the order in which the material is presented. The first three units, 'Palomar on the beach' (1.1.1–1.1.3), are unified by the element of water; the second three, 'Palomar in the garden' (1.2.1–1.2.3), by earth (the tortoises and blackbirds on the lawn); the third three, 'Palomar observes the sky' (1.3.1–1.3.3), by air. There then follows a descending sequence as we move from 'Palomar on the terrace', observing birds (2.1.1–2.1.3), to 'Palomar goes shopping' amongst his fellow-humans (2.2.1–2.2.3) and 'Palomar at the zoo' amidst earth-bound animals (2.3.1–2.3.3) – even within this last section the three micro-units are in descending order, moving from the giraffe to the gorilla to the iguana. The final nine stories move at first outwards in 'Palomar's travels' (3.1.1–3.1.3), then inwards in 'Palomar in society' (3.2.1–3.2.3), before shifting inside the protagonist himself in 'Palomar's meditations' (3.3.1–3.3.3). The opening tension between the ternary divisions and the four elements may owe something to a similar clash of ternary and quadruple systems in Borges' famous detective story, 'Death and the Compass', but whether Borges is the source or not, in *Palomar* the tension between these elements, of which only three are initially prominent, is resolved at the end when the fourth element, fire, appears in the apocalyptic vision of the end of the world in the penultimate paragraph of the book: 'when the last material record of the memory of existence will disintegrate in a flash of heat, or will crystallize its atoms in the ice of a motionless order' (II, 979; *Mr Palomar*, 112).

It is also illuminating to examine the mixture of old and new material within individual units, for even in pieces originally published in the 1970s Calvino often inserts or deletes material. Serra (1996, 68) has shown that there is a consistent narrowing down of the titles of the individual units, moving from colloquial journalistic headlines in the originally published pieces to laconic statements of general content in the book: 'Un uomo e un seno nudo all'orizzonte (A Man and a Naked Breast on the Horizon)' becomes 'Il seno nudo (The Naked Bosom)', 'L'ansia annullata nei giardini giapponesi (Anxiety Eliminated in Japanese Gardens)' becomes 'L'aiuola di sabbia (The Sand Garden)', and so on. But there is more to be discovered by examining the texture of the individual units. In the first piece, 'Lettura di un'onda (Reading a wave)', originally written in 1975, Calvino adds another third to its substance, mostly fleshing out Palomar's character, his unsuitability for contemplation (II, 875; *Mr Palomar*, 3), his general irritability (II, 876; *Mr Palomar*, 4) and his desire to advance to phase two of his cerebrations: to extend his knowledge of a limited area of the world, the wave, to an understanding of the whole universe (II, 879; *Mr Palomar*, 7). In 'Il fischio del merlo (The Blackbird's Whistle)', also initially published in 1975, most of the central section (II, 893–5; *Mr Palomar*, 22–4) was added for the 1983 edition, notably the idea that the blackbird's communication may reside as much in the silent pauses as in its whistles (II, 893; *Mr Palomar*, 24), and the elegant contrast between the laconic conversation of Mr and Mrs Palomar and the whistles and silences of the blackbird (II, 894–9; *Mr Palomar*, 24). Exactly the same two elements are added to 'La pancia del geco (The Gecko's Belly)': namely, the mention of both Mr and Mrs Palomar turning from the television to watch the gecko on the window (II, 921; *Mr Palomar*, 52), and the powerful contrast between the slaughter visible on TV screens and that in which the gecko naturally indulges (II, 924; *Mr Palomar*, 55). Calvino also expands a number of descriptive details of the gecko, as well as detailing the haphazard items that surround the window: a collection of *Art-Nouveau* vases, a 75–watt bulb, a plumbago plant (II, 921; *Mr Palomar*, 52). New in 'L'invasione degli storni (The Invasion of the Starlings)' is the telephone discussion at the end between Palomar and his friends about the starlings' behaviour (II, 928–9; *Mr Palomar*, 59–60). Even in 'La corsa delle giraffe (The Giraffe Race)' he inserts a little phrase to explain the symbolic link between the asymmetrical spots on the giraffe and its inelegant gait: 'an unevenness that preannounces the unevenness of the movements' (II, 941; *Mr Palomar*, 72). The entire first two paragraphs of the 1983 version of 'Del prendersela coi giovani (On Becoming Angry with the Young)' (II, 962; *Mr Palomar*, 95) were prefixed to the item originally published in 1975, passages which link with the previous unit about Palomar biting his tongue before speaking, but I shall return to the significance of these two early pieces later.

'Il seno nudo (The Naked Bosom)' began life as an article about topless bathing in 1977 and was transformed into a Palomar narrative for the book. In the course of rewriting, Calvino adopts an alternating and symmetrical dialectical structure that we have witnessed often elsewhere. Palomar walks past a topless sunbather on the beach and instinctively averts his gaze. This simple piece of narrative is immediately followed by the protagonist's reflection that perhaps to refuse to look is to maintain a prudish taboo about breasts, so on his way back he decides to look as much at the woman's chest as at the other elements of the marine landscape. But after this second walk he reflects again that perhaps this last attitude represents a typical male reduction of what is specifically feminine to the level of all other objects. So when he walks past again, he allows his eye to dwell slightly longer on her bosom. But even this he feels is to underestimate the significance of breasts and to misrepresent his own complex feelings about topless sunbathing. His fourth walk past the same woman and his even more intense gaze of course finally cause her to cover herself and walk away as if escaping 'the tiresome insistence of a satyr' (II, 882; *Mr Palomar*, 10). This alternation of narrative and reflection is a technique similar to that contrast between description and dialogue which was the basic structural device of early stories such as 'Andato al comando (Gone to Headquarters)' (see Chapter 1). The slapstick ending also becomes a closing formula for many of the Palomar pieces.

'L'occhio e i pianeti (The Eye and the Planets)', as mentioned earlier, is partly inspired by Leopardi's 'Apocryphal Fragment of Strato of Lampsacus', and it is therefore no surprise that the description of the sky takes on poetic overtones. The opening sentence of the second paragraph is a pure Leopardian hendecasyllable: 'Il cielo è chiaro per la luna piena (Because of the full moon the sky is light)' (II, 904; *Mr Palomar*, 34 – for Calvino's admiration of Leopardi's 'lunar' poetry see *S*, 651–2; *Six Memos*, 24–5). The reference to Mars in the same paragraph also has intertextual resonances, this time from the description of Mars burning red at the beginning of *Purgatorio* II (13–15), while hendecasyllabic rhythms close the third paragraph: 'Le stelle intorno sono tutte impallidite, / tranne Arturo che brilla con aria di sfida / un po' piú in alto verso oriente (The stars all around have paled, except Arcturus, which shines with a defiant air, a bit higher to the east)' (II, 904; *Mr Palomar*, 34). There are further echoes of the opening of *Purgatorio* in 'La contemplazione delle stelle (The Contemplation of the Stars)', set as it is on 'a lonely beach on a very low coast' (II, 909; *Mr Palomar,* 39), while a Dantesque hendecasyllable in 'Dal terrazzo (From the Terrace)', describing the seagulls flying – 'remando l'aria con le lunghe ali (rowing the air with their long wings)' (II, 919; *Mr Palomar,* 49) – recalls the three famous bird similes of *Inferno* V.40–84, which describe starlings, cranes and doves. There is also effective assonance in this piece, reproducing the gulls' cries: '*i*l loro gr*i*do mar*i*no str*i*de tra *i* rumor*i* c*i*ttad*i*n*i* (their marine cry shrieks among the city noises)' (II, 919; *Mr Palomar,* 49). The other bird section, 'L'invasione degli storni (The Invasion of the Starlings)', is also haunted by Dantesque memories: it deals with migrating starlings in winter, as does the first of Dante's similes (*Inferno,* V.40–2), it contains deliberate alliteration – '*v*olatili in *v*olo: . . . tra pennuto e pennuto si spalancano *v*oragini di *v*uoto (birds in flight: . . . between one winged animal and the next, chasms of emptiness yawn)' (II, 926; *Mr Palomar,* 57) – and it has recourse to its own elaborate series of similes: the birds are compared to grains of powder in liquid, to a cloud, a column of smoke or spray, an explosion, iron-filings patterned by a magnet, a sphere, a bubble or cartoon thought-bubble, a swift-flowing current, sand in an hour-glass, a zig-zagging ribbon, a swarm of bees. But since *Palomar* is a modern, prosaic equivalent of Dante's poetic summa, the piece ends with the new sequence of banal telephone conversations about the birds. The final words are again alliterative, though here the Dantesque doves have become, in an effective, alliterative conclusion, squalid city pigeons: 'la *s*o*s*pen*s*ione d'ali nere degli inva*s*ori *c*ele*s*ti pre*c*ipita fino a confonder*s*i col greve volo degli *s*tolidi *s*cacazzanti pi*cc*ioni *c*ittadini (the suspension of the black wings of the celestial invaders precipitates until it is confused with the grievous flight of the stupid, spattering city pigeons)' (II, 929; *Mr Palomar,* 60). The echoes of *Inferno,* V conclude in 'L'universo come specchio (The Universe as Mirror)', where the protagonist's wish – 'A chi è amico dell'universo, l'universo è amico. Potessi mai, – sospira Palomar, – essere anch'io cosí! (To the man who is a friend of the universe, the universe is a friend. "If only," Palomar sighs, "I could be like that!")' (II, 971; *Mr Palomar,* 104) – seems a secular equivalent of Francesca da Rimini's: 'Se fosse amico il re dell'universo, / noi pregheremmo lui della tua pace (If the king of the universe were our friend, we would pray to Him for your peace)' (*Inferno,* V.91–2).

'Un chilo e mezzo di grasso d'oca (Two Pounds of Goose Fat)' also has a high incidence of similes in its first half when the delights of a Parisian charcuterie are described: the salamis hang from the ceiling like fruits dangling from the branches of trees in the land of Cockaigne, the birds' claws atop the pheasant pâté resemble those in a coat-of-arms, the truffles are like the buttons on Pierrot's coat, or like notes on a score, or like black evening dress at a masked ball (II, 931; *Mr Palomar,* 62). The pleasurable associations of these referents are immediately contrasted by the first words of the second half of the piece: 'Grigia e opaca e arcigna è invece la gente (Gray and opaque and sullen, on the contrary, are the people)' (II, 931; *Mr Palomar,* 62). Those three adjectives, however, not only enforce the thematic and colour contrast but remind us that what stylistically unites the whole piece are the series of triads used throughout: 'il nome, la visione, l'idea (the name, the sight, the idea)' at the beginning (II, 930; *Mr Palomar,* 61), 'montagne di vol-au-vent, di budini bianchi, di salsicce cervellate (mountains of vol-au-vents, white puddings, cervelats)' (II, 931; *Mr Palomar,* 62) in the middle paragraph, and in the closing words 'lui il profano, l'estraneo, lui l'escluso (he the profane one, the alien, the outsider)' (II, 932; *Mr Palomar,* 63). These tricola are a prose equivalent of Dante's terza rima, as they reflect the triadic structure upon which the whole work is constructed.

If 'Lettura di un'onda (The Reading of a Wave)' (1.1.1) – an almost manifesto piece exemplifying the text's poetics (Serra, 1996, 32) – was the most visual and descriptive piece, according to Calvino's note, then the central tale, 'Il museo dei formaggi (The Cheese Museum)' (2.2.2), should in theory be the most cultural and narrative sequence: here Palomar sees the cheese shop as embodying 'the knowledge accumulated by a civilisation' (II, 933; *Mr Palomar,* 64). The shop's name contains the rare French adjective 'froumagères', a signifier appropriate to the recherché cheeses on offer: names such as 'bouton de coulotte' hint at excesses of other kinds – indeed the cheeses seem to 'proffer themselves as though on the divans of a brothel' (II, 934; *Mr Palomar,* 65). The shop, then, is a kind of cheese encyclopedia, or dictionary, or an olfactory-gustatory equivalent of the Louvre. The narrative ends again in slapstick fashion with Palomar being disturbed from his reverie and being able to remember only the most banal cheese to buy.

The third and final section of *Palomar* opens with the protagonist's efforts in the Zen garden at Kyoto to follow the advice of the tourist brochure and shed the relativity of his own self, an aspiration which, as we have observed, goes back to the outset of his literary career. 'Serpenti e teschi (Serpents and Skulls)' shows Palomar caught between two ways of viewing the world: either to interpret everything, even to interpret interpretations, as his Mexican friend does when he allegorically explains the meaning of the reliefs on the Toltech temple, or to profess a hermeneutic agnosticism, like that of the Mexican schoolteacher, whose constant refrain to his pupils is: 'No se sabe lo quiere decír' (II, 955; *Mr Palomar,* 87). This piece seems emblematic of the whole volume: the protagonist recognises the virtues in two opposing philosophical standpoints but is still in the process of deciding which, if any, he should adopt. This is consonant with the two-sentence summary the author himself gave of the book: 'A man sets out to reach understanding, one step at a time. He has not yet arrived' (II, 1405). For that reason, as well as others, I would not interpret the book as pessimistically as most other critics have done: it is certainly a critique of the limits of Western reason (II, xv–xxii), but Palomar never quite reaches a nadir in his epistemological quest.

The last four pieces of *Palomar* were written rather late in the evolution of the volume (July 1982–August 1983); indeed the final three units were composed especially for this book, one after the other, between late August and mid-September 1983 (see Appendix). Although the two pieces which precede these four, 'Del mordersi la lingua (On Biting the Tongue)' (3.2.1) and 'Del prendersela coi giovani (On Becoming Angry with the Young)' (3.2.2), were, respectively, the first and second Palomar articles ever written, all six pieces are consistent in tone, continuing Palomar's *askesis* as the subject-matter becomes ever more abstract. 'Il modello dei modelli (The Model of Models)' (3.2.3) is a discourse about the failure of utopian models, especially Marxism (II, 1435), though in accordance with the universal poetics of the work there is no such explicit historical reference. The final unit, 'Come imparare ad essere morto (How to Learn to be Dead)' (3.3.3), though mostly abstract, does have a deliberately unifying echo of the opening wave-watching sequence of the whole book, when the impassibility of the waves beating against the rock is described (II 976; *Mr Palomar*, 109), but on the whole these last six pieces are informed by a deliberately increasing abstraction. Here the protagonist makes the ultimate attempt to transcend the limitations of the self by aspiring to be dead. His thoughts run forward to the end of time when the universe will end in a final burst of heat or of frozen immobility. But if this happens, then time must be finite, therefore each instant of it can be described so that the end of time recedes into infinity again. Palomar consequently decides to describe every instant of his own life, but at that very moment he dies. This gradual rarefaction of the text, as it moves away from the observation of nature, the animal world, and other societies towards abstract ratiocination, as well as the evidence that the last three pieces were written together, confirm that despite its composite origins, *Palomar* is not simply a sequence of interchangeable microtexts like the early *Marcovaldo* stories (Corti, 1975), but is clearly a macrotext in which the order of the units is deliberate, inalterable and meaningful.

The early genesis of Palomar sheds light in one final, crucial way. Perrella (1990) brilliantly pointed to the relevance of the public and private debates between Calvino and Pasolini in the first half of the 1970s: the critic imagines Pasolini on Friday, 1 August 1975 buying his copy of the *Corriere della sera*, in which he had written a front-page article, 'A che serve capire i figli (What is the point of understanding the young)?', which expresses his disgust for contemporary Italian youth, and then noticing that on page 3 a new character, invented by Calvino, is making his first appearance. The first two Palomar passages on page 3 were 'La corsa delle giraffe (The Giraffe Race)' and 'Del mordersi la lingua (On Biting the Tongue)' (not 'Del prendersela coi giovani' as Perrella claims), that is to say a brief descriptive exercise and a piece about the virtues of silence rather than speech. As Perrella says, Pasolini would attack both Calvino's 'descrittività' and his cult of silence in the coming months, but it is worth examining the whole context of this debate between the two writers in even greater detail. 'Del mordersi la lingua' (as much as 'Del prendersela coi giovani (On Becoming Angry with the Young)') was partially directed at Pasolini, who had criticised Calvino's growing silence in his review of *Invisible Cities* (Pasolini 1979, 34–5). The opening paragraph of the Palomar piece certainly seems aimed at the film-director:

> In a time and in a country in which everyone goes out of his way to announce opinions or hand down judgements, Mr Palomar has made a habit of biting his tongue three times before asserting anything. After the bite, if he is still convinced of what he was going to say, he says it. If not, he keeps his mouth shut. In fact, he spends whole weeks, months in silence. (II, 960; *Mr Palomar*, 93)

Pasolini read Calvino's contribution that day, but equally Calvino must also have noticed Pasolini's front-page attack on the youth of the day, and his more measured response ('Del prendersela coi giovani') came in the second Palomar piece which appeared on Sunday, 10 August. In fact Perrella's analysis is worth extending even further, as he hoped to do (Perrella, 1990, 71–2, n. 16): the whole chronology of this fascinating period, which extends from the first appearance of Palomar in August to Pasolini's death in November 1975, is crucial for the light it sheds on the genesis and meaning of Calvino's last work.

On 22 August Franco Fortini also intervened in the *Corriere* in the debate about the young generation with an article entitled 'Calvino e i giovani (Calvino and the young)'. He began by calling 'Del prendersela coi giovani' a kind of 'lay Sunday sermon' (it had been published on a Sunday), criticising both its style (its 'dry eloquence') and its content (its 'silent acceptance of reality'). Unlike Calvino/Palomar, Fortini promises he will continue to preach to the young, 'even although Calvino pretends to stand mute before them, like Parsifal hearing the song of the birds' (Fortini, 1985, 124) – this last barb alludes of course to the other Palomar piece which had appeared on 10 August, 'Il fischio del merlo (The Blackbird's Whistle)'. Calvino responded immediately, since his reply to Fortini, the third Palomar piece, 'La seconda natura', was published two days later along with 'Lettura di un'onda' (Sunday, 24 August). 'La seconda natura' is an eloquent defence of Calvino's non-anthropocentrism of the time, and a risposte to Fortini's criticism that Palomar (or Calvino) paid too much attention to 'natura' and not enough to 'storia':

> Reading Franco Fortini's *Tribuna Aperta* in the *Corriere* on the 22 August [1975], Mr Palomar more than identifies with the target of this attack, who observes human affairs, according to Fortini, 'from a standpoint that is so elementary as to warrant the adjective "human" only with great difficulty'. Mr Palomar would genuinely like all observations on human history not to lose sight of the horizon which embraces not just *homo sapiens*, but also beyond that the animal realm, the totality of living things, and beyond that again every cluster of molecules or force field or planetary or galactic system. (*Corriere della sera*, 24 August 1975)

As *Smog* contained beneath its narrative surface a partially visible palimpsest essay on pollution, so here beneath the *brevitas* and silence of 'Lettura di un'onda' and 'Il fischio del merlo' lies the rumble of the theoretical polemics in 1970s Italy –

indeed the initial idea for the very first Palomar piece had been to have him discuss the serious contemporary problem of kidnappings with his doppelgänger Mohole (II, 1402), a dialogue which was written in early 1975 but never published by the author (now in III, 1164–7). Calvino wrote three other Palomar–Mohole dialogues (III, 1168–73) as late as August 1983, planning them as the climax of the book before changing his mind when he realised that the protagonist already contained within himself the antithetical psychology of Mohole (II, 1403). Leaving aside 'Dietro il retrovisore (Behind the Rear-View Mirror)' (III, 1159–63), which is simply a re-elaboration in Palomar form of a 1976 article on a famous Montale poem ('Forse un mattino andando in un'aria di vetro'), the only other Palomar item written but never published was 'Dialogo con una tartaruga (Dialogue with a Tortoise)' (III, 1155–8), written in 1977. What links this last item with the Mohole pieces and therefore explains all these omissions from the book is the fact that it is a dialogue: since silence is one of the themes of *Palomar*, the book in the end could contain no sustained discussions with any one other than the protagonist himself. This stylistic pursuit of silent monologue is surely as much a reason for the elimination of Mohole as the psychological motive cited by Calvino.

The debate about young people in Italy intensified when at the beginning of October a group of Roman middle-class, neo-fascist youths savagely murdered a young woman at Monte Circeo. Calvino wrote a front-page article in the first person denouncing the crime in the *Corriere* on 8 October ('Delitto in Europa (Crime in Europe)', now in *S*, 2270–4). A week later, on 16 October, Enzo Forcella criticised 'Lettura di un'onda' in an article in *Il Mondo* headlined 'Calvino si tuffa nel disimpegno', implying that wave-watching meant that Palomar/Calvino was 'guilty of deliberately underestimating the importance of human history' (*Enciclopedia*, 52). To this Calvino responded a fortnight afterwards with an important defence of Palomar's attitude in 'Un maremoto nel Pacifico' (*Corriere*, 29 October 1975):

> Might it not be that the concentration on a limited and precise field of observation, the attempt to define exactly the complexity of the most banal event that takes place before our eyes every day, might these not constitute a suitable exercise for testing skills . . . which are necessary in many other fields, first and foremost in socio-political activity? Could it not be that a way of looking at waves, which in itself as an activity can only be compared with other ways of looking at waves, might lead us also on to a comparison between different ways of facing up to the world, along with all the other matters of public, historical importance implied in the latter? (*Enciclopedia*, 54)

Again it is clear that underneath the smooth surface of the book's minimalist, non-specific eloquence there lurk the strident debates of the most violent decade in Italy's postwar history, as well as a last, tentative defence of *impegno* (Serra, 1996, 208; Paulicelli, 1996).

This same issue of the Milanese daily contained that Palomar piece on page 3 and an article by Pasolini on the front page, 'Le mie proposte su scuola e TV (My proposals for school and TV)', which despite its title was another attack on contemporary youth in the light of the Circeo murder. The divide between Pasolini and Calvino was made more explicit the very next day when Pasolini's last 'Lettera Luterana' was published, addressed to Calvino himself (*Il Mondo*, Friday, 30 October). This open letter attacks Calvino's 8 October article on the Circeo crime, criticising in particular his silence in the face of Pasolini's outbursts ('your silence in the face of so many of my letters is also a Catholic reaction': Pasolini 1976, 180) and his interest in mere 'descrittività' (182). The letter ends: 'But you know full well how you can become informed, if you want to write back to me, to discuss this, to make your response. In fact, I demand that you come clean and do this' (183). Calvino could not reply in time to this attack because, in an extraordinary conclusion to this turbulent period in recent Italian history, Pasolini was murdered the next evening, on the night of 1–2 November, a victim of that violent young generation which he had so loudly denounced in public. Calvino's response could only come post-mortem, in his front-page 'Ultima lettera a Pier Paolo Pasolini', in the *Corriere* of 4 November. There he points out that Pasolini's claim to be surrounded by silence was untrue since the film director's 'discorso ininterrotto' had never prompted more public discussion than in the last months. Calvino's defence against the personal attack on his own silence is worth quoting in full:

> And it was not even true that I had not replied with my own opinion; *it was just that I did so, by channelling my response into other discourses, without ever naming him* [*lo facevo entrare in altri discorsi, senza nominarlo mai*]; he understood perfectly well that I did so in order not to satisfy his craving for personal attacks, but instead of repaying me in kind, he attacked me head-on: that was his temperament. (*Corriere della sera*, 4 November 1975, p. 1; my italics)

These 'other discourses' which Calvino claims were responses to Pasolini but in which his name never appears clearly include pieces of *Palomar*. In fact the character Palomar is a kind of anti-Pasolini, as the protagonist's silence represents the antithesis of Pasolini's 'endless discourse'. Such an interpretation finds confirmation in one other event from that eventful period. On 24 October, exactly a week before Pasolini's murder, as Franco lay dying in Spain, the Italian poet Eugenio Montale was awarded the Nobel Prize for Literature. Calvino's reaction to his fellow-Ligurian's premiation came a few months later, in February 1976, in that important essay which has been cited before, 'Right and Wrong Political Uses of Literature' (*S*, 351–60; LM, 89–100). In it Calvino bemoans the pressure from newspapers to have writers express their opinion on everything happening in their country, and regards this pressure as explaining the increasingly provocative tone adopted by some writers. The writer who embodies this provocative sermonising is explicitly named: 'The life and death and posthumous life of Pasolini have consecrated the provocative role of the writer' (*S*, 356; LM, 95). But immediately afterwards Calvino adds: 'There is a fundamental flaw in all this', and goes on to remind us that the characteristic style of Montale, who had received the Nobel that year, was the opposite of Pasolini's shouting from the rooftops: 'the strength of his poetry has always lain in keeping his voice low, without emphasis of any kind, using modest and doubtful tones' (*S*, 356; LM, 95). Ligurian taciturnity clearly remained a preferable intellectual ideal for Calvino compared with Pasolini's loud loquacity.

One final proof should be mentioned of the relevance of the relations between Calvino and Pasolini to *Palomar*. Calvino's letter of 7 February 1973, replying to Pasolini's review of *Invisible Cities*, contains an interesting verbal anticipation of the thematics of the last section of *Palomar*, 'Come imparare ad essere morto', written a full ten years later. One sentence in the letter claims that 'The dead, since they are no longer in a world in which too many things do not concern them, must feel a mixture of resentment and relief, not too different from my own present state of mind' (Naldini, 1989, 374). This mixture of relief and resentment felt by the dead are the two themes that dominate the first two-thirds of the final unit of *Palomar*. As in the letter, so here the protagonist, aspiring to the condition of the dead, feels 'a sensation of relief, no longer having to wonder what the world has in store for him' (II, 975; *Mr Palomar*, 108); meanwhile the dead look on the living with a look that is 'deprecatory', and their attitude to them is one of 'reluctance, almost of embarrassment, but at the same time of smugness' (II, 976–7; *Mr Palomar*, 109–10): in other words, that mixture of irresponsibility and happiness which corresponds to the 'relief and resentment' mentioned in the earlier letter. Ten years later Calvino is still haunted by the same feeling of being cut off from the world.

The thematics of silence and death are, of course, not new in Calvino (Roelens, 1989), but the work's polished poetics of *brevitas*, laconicism and non-specificity are now seen to have precise but paradoxical roots in the noisy and violent reality of the mid-1970s in Italy. The links between Palomar and Calvino's relations with his most outspoken antagonist at the time, Pasolini, are closer than even Perrella suggests: Palomar's name is not singly determined, by the famous telescope on Mt Palomar, but is, like most things in Calvino, polysemous. Even as far as back as 1952 Calvino felt that the names of his fictional characters should act as 'a kind of phonetic definition of their temperaments, [becoming] one with their characters' (*S*, 1746). Palomar is of course a telescope, a bird, a diver beneath surfaces, an observer, even a near anagram of *parola* (Serra, 1996, 92), but he is also, as the similar but different letters of their names suggest, the antithesis of Pasolini, the symbol of tongue-biting silence in the face of 'endless discourse'.

Chapter 10

Calvino's Style

Abstract Aspirations for the Next Millennium

Amidst the welter of studies on Calvino, few are devoted to the writer's style. Most critics restrict themselves to an assessment which recycles adjectives that formed an integral part of his poetics, such as 'preciso', 'leggero', 'limpido', 'lineare'. It is worth stressing here that Calvino's cult of precision is an ideal from the outset, deriving from his praise of Conrad's 'lingua molto pulita e precisa e limpida', particularly in lesser known works such as *The Mirror of the Sea* (thesis, p. 44; *S*, 815–16). Coletti (1988) was one of the first to offer, in a brief paper, useful examples of his 'concrete and precise Italian', this formula itself deriving from a statement of the author's linguistic ideal in an important 1965 essay on the Italian language (*S*, 153). He exemplified Calvino's lexical precision from *Palomar* and from the important tenth chapter of *The Baron in the Trees*, but pointed out that the counterpart of this almost technical exactness was an equally rich vein of fantastic wordplay, often involving onomatopoeia and a form of plurilingualism, again equally evident in *The Baron*. This capacity for embracing antithetical stylistic tendencies is on a par with Calvino's acceptance of opposing literary values, such as precision and vagueness, rapidity and delay, as articulated in the Harvard lectures, and reflects his 'forma mentis', in particular his desire never to be circumscribed by univocal, limiting definitions either in terms of content or in style.

More substantial and wide-ranging than Coletti was Mengaldo's contribution on 'La lingua dello scrittore' (1989). Mengaldo's initial paradoxical statement anticipates his conclusion: 'In fact, one could claim that Calvino is not a very Italian writer' (Mengaldo 1989, 9). He substantiates this claim by arguing that the author resists four tendencies which characterise modern Italian literature and which in turn are largely determined by the existence of the Italian 'questione della lingua':

1. *Dialect influences*: in his early fiction Calvino tends to explain in standard Italian any dialect words used, such as 'beudi', 'lingéra', etc.
2. *Linguistic expressionism*: he does have a fondness for sound-words such as 'scatenío', 'zoccolío', 'mastichío' – it is worth adding that Calvino

deliberately substituted this last, onomatopoeic form for the more neutral 'masticazione' in one of the *Marcovaldo* stories (I, 1378), while in 'Pesci grossi, pesci piccoli' (1950), 'come a un piovere di gocce' becomes 'come a un gocciolio di pioggia' (II, 1442). But although Calvino does occasionally indulge even in the Italian equivalent of a spoonerism, sandwiched between two puns – 'grattugia dei grattacieli, autoincoronata di altostrade, non parca di parcheggi', in *The Castle of Crossed Destinies* (II, 573) – such expressionism, according to Mengaldo, is usually in a parodic context.

3. *Figurative language*: the uniquely high proportion of metaphor and simile in 'Adventure of a Poet' is due, according to Mengaldo, to the low level of 'narratività' in that important story, but it is also due to the fact that the story refers, in a metaliterary fashion, to neorealism's reluctance to deal with positive elements like the beauty of nature, and its consequent rejection of metaphor and simile (McLaughlin, 1993a, 74–5).
4. *Hypotaxis and the periodic style*: the early works are of course characterised by short, staccato sentences (Mengaldo cites 'Uomo nei gerbidi', 'Il gatto e il poliziotto', *Il barone rampante*), but before *Cosmicomics*, the only works which break this rule are those with intellectual protagonists (*A Plunge into Real Estate*, *Smog*, 'Adventure of a Reader', *The Watcher*). However, we have seen that after the often lengthy periodic sentences in the complex cosmicomic works, there is a deliberate return, probably partly under the influence of Borges, to the *brevitas* that characterises late works such as *Invisible Cities* and *Mr Palomar*.

Mengaldo sees Calvino's elimination of these extreme, Italian-specific elements as an attempt to write a language other than Italian, as if the 'questione della lingua' did not exist. A recent, subtle analysis of the variety of Calvino's comic styles confirms Mengaldo's hypotheses, particularly about the author's avoidance of the extremes of dialectalisms and lyricism, and his cult of '[la] *medietà* linguistica' (Falcetto 1994, 53). Mengaldo's conclusion is that 'Calvino's . . . is on the whole the richest and most accomplished prose that the pen of any Italian writer in the last forty years has managed to compose' (1989, 55).

The most linguistically comprehensive analysis of the author's style was provided in the central second chapter of Bonsaver's monograph (Bonsaver, 1995c, 111–217). He too attempts to go beyond the clichés, noting that ideals such as 'linearità' and 'precisione' are potentially contradictory, as Calvino himself was aware, since the cumulative detail necessary for maximum precision militates against linear narration or description. Similarly Bonsaver backs up the mere impression of the author's clarity by studying the computerised statistics of the first novel (Alinei, 1973), which prove the directness of Calvino's style: he actually uses indefinites and qualified colour adjectives (such as 'azzurrino' or 'verdastro') considerably less than his contemporary Cassola. Like Falcetto (1994), Bonsaver shows that there is a tendency, particularly in the cosmicomic tales, for the technical, scientific lexis to be balanced by comic colloquialisms in pursuit of a classical restraint and a style that is both colloquial and dignified

(1995c, 122–4). In terms of syntax, he confirms that the parataxis of the early narratives, indebted as they are to models such as Hemingway, gives way to the complex, parenthetic style of the 'intellectual trilogy' (*A Plunge into Real Estate*, *Smog*, *The Watcher*) and the cosmicomic stories: again, he produces convincing statistics to demonstrate that there is a consistent increase in the number of clauses per sentence, and a concomitant decrease in total number of sentences per page, from *The Path* to the first cosmicomic story to the late 'Under the Jaguar Sun' (131–2).

There are just one or two elements missing from Bonsaver's analysis, but which have surfaced in previous chapters of this study. The short, clear, paratactic sentence which opens nearly all Calvino's narratives (and essays) receives little attention, yet it is the contrastive *raison d'être* for the many lengthy final sentences which, as we have seen, attempt to delay narrative closure – for instance, in several *Difficult Loves* stories ('Adventure of a Bather', 'Adventure of a Poet', 'Adventure of a Skier'), and many cosmicomic tales ('All at One Point', 'The Form of Space', 'Blood, Sea', 'Mitosis' 'Time and the Hunter'). On the first kind of sentence there is an illustrative piece of advice from Calvino to a fellow writer in 1961:

> When writing a sentence, it is best to put the central thematic idea to the fore, so that it is visible immediately, and to put subordinate clauses after this main idea not before it. In fact better not to put any subordinates at all: write a separate sentence beginning 'but', 'nevertheless', 'however'. (*ILDA*, 372)

Another element worth recalling is the rhythmical, often hendecasyllabic cadences, which recur not just in tales inspired by Ariostesque octaves such as *The Cloven Viscount* and *The Non-Existent Knight* (Bonsaver, 1995c, 126–7), but throughout the oeuvre, from an early tale such as 'Uno dei tre è ancora vivo' through to *Palomar*. Another significant stylistic feature to emerge in this study is Calvino's poetics of contrast and paradox (it is no surprise that he alludes to Zeno so frequently), whether in fictional or non-fictional works, and his penchant for contrasting intertexts, be it Dante, Stevenson, Leopardi or Conrad. However, rather than provide simply more examples of static features of the author's style, the aim of this chapter is to analyse his language diachronically, paying particular attention not so much to the way Calvino writes as to the way he rewrites.

In 1937 Gianfranco Contini wrote a famous article, 'Come lavorava l'Ariosto', in which he demonstrated that the variants and the alterations made by the poet to the *Orlando furioso* helped to explain how Ariosto achieved his famous qualities of 'harmony' and 'irony'. Contini was writing 400 years after Ariosto and was therefore able to rely on the scholarship of the previous centuries in studying the available redactions of the poem in manuscript and in print. In the case of Calvino, as we approach the millennium, we are already in almost as privileged a position barely a decade after the author's death. The three volumes of his collected *Romanzi e racconti*, even though they contain little manuscript evidence, nevertheless provide us with a rich field of variants from printed editions alone, which allow us to infer important clues about the stylistic development of this great enthusiast of Ariosto, also renowned for his harmony, lightness and irony. If, as Maria Corti says, 'the creative works of an author develop according to the laws of a system' (1974, xii), then an analysis of these variants can help make some general assessments about the laws governing Calvino's system of writing and rewriting – in short, about 'come lavorava Calvino'.

Contini pointed out that an author's alterations either concern subject matter, i.e. what the ancients called *inventio*, or formal aspects, style – in classical rhetorical theory *elocutio*. The changes observable in Calvino's writing embrace both form and content, but so far only Falaschi (1988b) has devoted considerable attention to the variants in Calvino's rewriting of some of his partisan tales. In an important contribution to the 1987 conference on Calvino, Falaschi analysed a number of stories from the late 1940s, comparing their initial publication in *l'Unità*, with their subsequent, definitive redaction in collections such as *Ultimo viene il corvo* (1949) or *I racconti* (1958). He discerned two constants in Calvino's rewriting of these tales:

1. in terms of content, the elimination of 'obscene situations' – for example, the details of the naked women reflected in the brothel mirrors in 'Uomo nei gerbidi' (I, 1290), details of the hand in between the woman's thighs in both 'Avventura di un soldato' (I, 1300), and 'Si dorme come cani' (I, 1302); and a hand on a woman's breast in 'Dollari e vecchie mondane' (I, 1297);
2. in terms of language, the suppression of 'inappropriate lexical units' – for instance, the passage from 'Paura sul sentiero' about Regina's 'grande, morbido sedere' (I, 1286).

The overall conclusion was that the unifying motive behind the more substantial alterations was 'the attenuation and excision of anything excessive [and] the elimination of strong tones and extreme situations' (Falaschi, 1988b, 118).

Falaschi's article, however, was limited to the early neorealist period, to a few short stories from 1946–50. The publication of the collected fiction now permits a more comprehensive, diachronic assessment of the import of both the substantive and formal changes Calvino made in his fictional works. In what follows I would like to consider first a number of changes, mostly concerning content, made by Calvino in the works of his 'first period', from 1945 to 1964. In a brief second section I broach some general conclusions about his rewriting in the last twenty years of his life. Lastly, I analyse a range of alterations made in the manuscript of *La speculazione edilizia* to suggest a number of constant stylistic tendencies in Calvino which find explicit approval in his literary testament to the next millennium.

1. VARIANTS IN THE PERIOD 1945–64

In his first novel, *The Path to the Spiders' Nests* (1947), Calvino made no fewer than three substantial sets of alterations: firstly when he modified the original typescript for the novel's first publication in 1947; secondly when it was reissued in 1954; and lastly in the definitive 1964 edition. Between the typescript and the 1947 edition, he eliminates the details about Pin's sister dancing 'with her skirt lifted up' (I, 1258), Mancino's anticlerical remarks (I, 1258) and some of Cugino's comic antifeminist ravings in Chapter VIII:

> 'It's the women, the women, I'm telling you,' Cugino insists, 'they're the cause of everything. Mussolini got the idea of the war from the Petacci sisters. The Petacci sisters live in a huge villa in Rome where no one is allowed in except Mussolini, the King and the Pope. And all three of them together decided on declaring war when they were in the Petacci sisters' villa.'
>
> The men make comments on this and tease Cugino: it is true that Mussolini has the Petacci sisters, and the King and the Pope will have their women too; but maybe all three of them decided on war without the advice of the women, because they had their own reasons for doing so. (I, 1258–9)

Even though Cugino's misogyny is laughable and indeed is mocked in this passage, Calvino felt that it was too strongly expressed here even for the first printed edition of the novel. Similarly the hint of Cugino's impotence was clearly felt to be excessive and was gradually toned down and then eliminated in the course of the three rewritings:

> They say that [Cugino] *is impotent because he* hates women and always wants to be the one who executes women who have been spies . . . *maybe he wants to kill all women, fighting in order to overcome his impotence.* We all have a secret *impotence* which we fight in order to overcome. (I, 1259)

In the 1947 edition the motif of impotence is suppressed:

> They say that he hates women and always wants to be the one who executes women who have been spies . . . We all have a secret wound which we fight in order to overcome. (I, 1256)

Finally in the 1964 edition, even Cugino's hatred is attenuated and reduced to this brief statement: 'They say he's out for revenge on a woman who betrayed him' (I, 109; *The Path*, 143). One other motive for this attenuation of the theme of impotence may have derived from the author's association with Pavese, who appears to have been impotent and was certainly something of a misogynist: the manuscript of *The Path* was read by Vittorini and Pavese, and it may well have been the latter who suggested the suppression of the impotence motif for the novel's publication in 1947. In any case, by that date Calvino was working more closely with Pavese at Einaudi – he had even been entrusted by Pavese with the task of translating *Lord Jim* – so the younger writer might have become more sensitive to this topic, and there is even a polemical exchange of letters by the two men inspired by Calvino's criticism of the unconvincing women in Pavese's *Tra donne sole* (Pavese, 1966, 408–9).

The other substantial sequence omitted in the transition from typescript to print was this description of the battle at the opening of Chapter XI:

> After an initial success due to the surprise attack in which the partisans inflicted heavy losses on the enemy, capturing weapons and eliminating both men and vehicles, the arrival of Fascist reinforcements changed the fortunes of battle and many partisans fell. (I, 1259–60)

This piece of almost journalistic reportage, portraying the partisans' momentary success in rather vague terms, becomes more specific and visual in the definitive version:

> The Germans, passing through a defile, had suddenly found the heights around them pullulating with shouting men and blazing with firearms; many of them had rolled into the ditches at the side of the road, one or two lorries began belching fire and smoke like furnaces and were soon reduced to nothing but black scrap-iron. Reinforcements then came up, but there was little they could do except wipe out a few partisans who had stayed on the road against orders or been cut off in the confusion. (I, 125; *The Path*, 161)

I will return to the broader significance of this more vivid portrayal of the battle later on.

Between 1947 and 1954, Calvino altered no fewer than seventeen passages, which appear to fall under four categories:

1. The elimination of the more explicit extremist slogans mouthed by the Trotskyite cook, Mancino: 'And I've explained everywhere to the proletariat that they have to revolt. And one day we will all get together and we will have a revolution' (I, 1251); 'The worse it gets, the better it will be! The rich will be ruined and the poor will start the revolution.' 'Fucking Trotskyite!' shout his comrades, as they round on him and thump him with their fists. (I, 1252)
2. The toning down or total excision of misogynistic sequences concerning Cugino: for instance, the original explanation for his antifeminism – 'They say he hates women because he's castrated' (I, 1251) – is made more politically respectable: 'Apparently there was some story about a woman he was in love with, this winter, who caused the death of three of our men' (I, 66; *The Path*, 98). But his more extreme antifeminist remarks are excised: 'As far as I'm concerned, these women utterly disgust me: there are millions of them at this very moment, on their back with their legs spread wide on their sweaty beds; I've been all over the world and I've seen them at it, and every time I think about it I feel sick' (I, 1252).
3. The suppression of violent elements in the narrative: 'Pin thinks about the strange rituals of graves being dug and prayers said with the pistol barrel between the prisoners' teeth' (I, 1251).
4. The elimination of passages that contain both sex and violence: 'For Pin that would be just as good as seeing a man and a woman chasing each other,

> knife in hand, through the ruins of the hut, and flinging themselves on top of each other, caressing and wounding each other' (I, 1253).

These four categories: political extremism, antifeminism, sex and violence, subtend these substantial cuts made between 1947 and 1954, and show that even by the mid 1950s Calvino had abandoned key aspects of neorealist poetics.

At least another twenty-seven passages were altered between the 1954 and 1964 editions, but they nearly all concern antifeminism. Calvino deletes once more a number of misogynistic statements made by Cugino:

> 'And in every country I've been in I saw brothels full of women with soldiers queuing . . . And women outside the brothels going with the soldiers into the fields or taking them into their bedrooms . . . That's the way it always is, with those disgusting creatures, women.' (I, 1255)

But in particular he cuts out the antifeminist sentiments shared by both Pin and Cugino, which presumably could have sounded dangerously close to a point of view shared by the narrator:

> [It seems that] Cugino hasn't understood what Pin has always known: that [women] are a disgusting lot and that it is hard to understand what pleasure there can be in mixing with them . . .; Pin understands that even up in the mountains you can't get rid of these damned women . . . The wife of the little man keeps smiling all to herself, something that her husband doesn't notice and Pin would like to say to him: 'Look, Mancino, bloody hell, if I were you I wouldn't trust that woman so much . . . Cugino understands everything: even that women are disgusting creatures. (I, 1253–4, 1257)

Also suppressed are the expressionist descriptions of Mancino: his 'clucking voice' (I, 1253); his association with his pet falcon: 'But the little man with the sailor's jerkin has an evil look and a croaking voice, just like the grim, angry falcon he carries on his shoulder' (I, 1254); and his extremist speeches which are said to be 'similar to the squawks of his chained falcon' (I, 1256).

Although Calvino made no mention of these considerable modifications at the time, he did eventually acknowledge them in 1983 in a conversation with students from Pesaro:

> I had written things that seemed to me too brutal or exaggerated [in *The Path to the Spiders' Nests*]. So I tried to attenuate some of those overstated and certainly brutal passages, even although they were attributed to the thoughts of other characters, not to me. Perhaps it was also to do with the fact that, when I wrote the book, I imagined that it would be read by just a few hundred people, as happened at that time for works of Italian literature. Instead when I realised that its readership was so much more numerous, the novel's status changed in my own eyes. I reread it and thought 'How on earth could I have written such things?' So I made some corrections. Of course there are still exaggerated elements in the novel: these are due to the almost adolescent phase I was still undergoing when I wrote the book, a phase which young people go through. It is the book of a very young man. (I, 1247)

Calvino here suggests that his success as an author meant that the novel was read by a larger public than he had intended, and he wished to tone down the 'adolescent' extremism of the book. But it is not just 'adolescent extremism' that unites the many alterations made: political extremism, misogyny, sex, violence, explicit political message, all are forms of excess in writing that Calvino eschewed in his pursuit of balance and 'leggerezza' even at this early stage.

Some of the largest cuts in this period occur in 'Avventura di un soldato (Adventure of a Soldier)', between its first appearance in *Ultimo viene il corvo* (1949) and its version in *I racconti* (1958), which then becomes the definitive redaction. Most of the excisions were made, as Calvino says, 'along anti-pornographic lines' (I, 1298), with words such as 'coscia (thigh)' (I, 1298) twice becoming 'gamba (leg)' (I, 320) and the omission of several intimate details about the soldier's hand between the woman's knees (I, 1299) and inside her bra (I, 1300). But more interesting than these is the fact that the three more substantial passages omitted are eliminated not just because of their mildly pornographic nature, but also because they reveal emotion or tenderness on the part of the characters. In the first, the movement of the train puts the soldier in physical contact with the widow, 'opening up chasms of tenderness in his blood' (I, 1299). In the second and longest omitted paragraph, again it is emotional as much as physical details that Calvino cuts out:

> He then discovered that the woman's stockings were held up, not by suspenders, which were perhaps uncomfortable for travelling, but by elastic bands which gripped her flesh halfway up her thigh, and over which the stocking tops were rolled down. Over the sheer and stretched silk which encased her thigh lay the tops of her stockings, so contrastingly empty and shapeless. This detail of the elastic bands was a secret so tenderly childish in a woman so big and proud that Tomagra was moved by it, and at that moment she really did diminish in his eyes, and he felt a sort of affectionate compassion, a frenzied pity which made him caress tenderly those strips of bare thigh, slipping his finger between her skin and the elastic as though to ease the discomfort of that tightness, a discomfort that was also derived from that modest, girlish trust which she had placed in Tomagra by revealing herself to him in this way. (I, 1299–300)

The other cuts made in the rewriting of this story prove that it was as much these expressions of emotion in the characters as the details of the woman's underwear that Calvino found disruptive of 'leggerezza'. The definitive version excises any mentions of tenderness, pity or girlish trust. In the final passage of the story, the explicitly reciprocal nature of the emotion is stressed but is entirely omitted in the definitive edition: 'and the woman's flesh seemed to respond to his constant attentions' (I, 1300). Again, Calvino's aim is clearly to produce a less emotional, more geometric tale, the soldier's desire contrasting with the repeated leitmotif of the widow's impassibility, uncluttered by sentiment or tenderness on either side. Even in the few modifications made to the *Marcovaldo* stories we find similar motives for omission: sexuality and sentiment. Thus the prostitutes of the libretto 'La panchina' (I, 1374–5) written in 1956 become merely contraband cigarette dealers in the Marcovaldo story in *I racconti*, and disappear entirely when the tale appears as 'La villeggiatura in panchina (Park-bench Vacation)' in the 1963 volume *Marcovaldo ovvero le stagioni in città* (I, 1071–8). In 'Un viaggio con le mucche' (1956), the passers-by originally seem to be talking about 'sport o ragazze', but in the 1963 edition the subjects are 'sport o quattrini' (I, 1382). The most substantial alteration occurs in 'Il bosco sull'autostrada' (1953): a long passage about Marcovaldo 'not having the heart' to cut down trees in the park or a park bench, or a school desk (I, 1379). Again, any hint of sentimentality in the character of the protagonist is excised.

Autobiographical tales naturally generate a significant level of rewriting and omission. Thus the three short stories that comprise the trilogy of memory, *L'entrata in guerra* (*The Entry into War*) (1953) undergo a proportionately very high number of alterations between their first appearance in book form in 1954 and their subsequent redaction in both *I racconti* and the single-volume edition (1974). They are mostly omissions rather than rewritings and are largely descriptions of secondary characters, family and friends, omissions therefore determined by the autobiographical nature of the stories: from 'Entrata in guerra' disappear the opening descriptions of the narrator's friend Jerry Ostero and their admiration for England (I, 1319, 1320–1), of his brother Filiberto (I, 1320), of the father's life in Yucatan (1321) and of his brother's interest in the navy (I, 1321–2). In 'Le notti dell' UNPA' the only omission is the character-sketch of Palladiani (I, 1328). The highest number of cuts occurs in 'Gli avanguardisti a Mentone' and they involve: school memories relating to Biancone, in reality Calvino's school friend Duilio Cossu (I, 1322–4), the narrator's reluctance to wear uniform getting him into trouble at school (I, 1324), his school enemy Ceretti (I, 1324) who deliberately fails exams in English and Greek for ideological reasons (I, 1327), the Southern immigrant centurione Bizantini (I, 1324–5), Starace's and Bottai's failed attempt to get to Nice and their D'Annunzio-like plan to attack Nice in a motorboat (I, 1325–6), the narrator and Biancone urinating at the French frontier (I, 1326), the portrait of the Tuscan Fascist (I, 1326–7) and the narrator's despair at the seemingly endless victories of Fascism (I, 1327).

For *The Baron in the Trees* (1957) there are some interesting rejected passages in manuscript cited by Barenghi. Calvino deletes them since they contain superfluous character details about Cosimo's parents, his sister and about the protagonist himself. This last sequence is worth reproducing here because I believe it is eliminated not just because Calvino is notoriously uninterested in psychology, but also because it is deeply autobiographical:

> You will already have realised that an element of remorse [*rimorso*] for having separated [*per aver sottratto*] his life from immediate contact with others was

> present in my brother's mind, and you will also have realised that, without ever wanting to turn back on his decision, he always tried to establish a balance between the unjustifiable [*ingiustificabile*] whim of having chosen to remain in the trees and a justification [*giustificazione*] of it that had a social dimension. (I, 1334)

That the vein of autobiography is as strong here as it is in *L'entrata in guerra* is confirmed by the author's repeated insistence elsewhere on his own remorse at abandoning the rural paradise of San Remo, in 'La strada di San Giovanni' (1962), 'La poubelle agréée' (III, 71–2), and in some autobiographical writings (*Eremita a Parigi*, 146–7). One passage in particular from a 1978 interview underlines with verbal echoes the autobiographical component in the passage about Cosimo:

> I have to justify [*giustificarlo*] what I write, even to myself, by appealing to something that is not just indvidual to me. Perhaps this is because I come from a secular family of intransigent scientists, whose image of civilization was a human-vegetable symbiosis. Separating myself from that scientific morality [*Sottrarmi a quella morale*], from the duties of the agricultural smallholder, made me feel guilty [*in colpa*]. (*Eremita a Parigi*, 210)

There is a similar pattern of autobiographically and politically motivated omissions, as we have seen (Chapter 4), in the various redactions of *La speculazione edilizia* (1957).

To sum up, then, this first section: Calvino's rewritings in the first twenty years of his literary activity (1945–64) appear to follow consistent laws. He tones down all forms of excess: from antifeminism and political extremism, to scenes of sex and violence, to character detail, psychology, emotions and sentimentalism, and in particular to overtly autobiographical material. He is already in this first phase of his literary career in pursuit of that narrative lightness and geometric writing that become his hallmark. It is worth adding that his aversion to psychological depth of character remains a constant in his writing. The seemingly trivial omission of the adjectives 'piccino e ranocchietto (small, like a little frog)' and 'coraggioso (courageous)' to describe Zeffirino in 'Pesci grossi, pesci piccoli (Big Fish, Small Fish)' (II, 1442) finds an echo in the elimination of this detail of the protagonist's cowardice when Calvino rewrites 'L'inseguimento' (1967): 'I'll never have the courage to leave the car, even if he got out of his' (II, 1357) becomes simply 'so obviously I mustn't get out of my car even if he leaves his' (II, 325; *Time and the Hunter*, 126). The omission of this psychological element is perfectly appropriate in this 'mathematical' tale, but it is also perfectly consistent with a major strand of Calvino's overall poetics. These, then, are some of the ways in which Calvino effectively carried out the claim made in the first page of the Harvard lecture on 'Lightness': 'above all I have tried to remove weight from the structure of stories and from language' (*S*, 631; *Six Memos*, 3).

2. VARIANTS IN THE PERIOD 1965–85

We can now move on to draw some general conclusions from the rest of the textual apparatus to *Romanzi e racconti*. Firstly, many more alterations were made to the works written before 1965 than to those written afterwards: whereas we know of few alterations to *Invisible Cities* (1972) or *If on a Winter's Night a Traveller* (1979), the works of the first twenty years register a large number of authorial interventions and revisions even after the work has appeared officially in print. This is partly because the mature writer was more likely to feel dissatisfied with the works of his literary apprenticeship. It is also due to the fact that many of the early stories appeared first in newspapers or journals, where editorial exigencies of space could have overruled the author's aesthetic preferences. A third reason must be that even by the time of collecting his short stories in 1958, Calvino felt uncomfortable particularly with the poetics of neorealism that had underpinned much of his work in the previous decade.

A second general conclusion is that in the pre-1965 works Calvino tends to remove rather than add material, again presumably for the above reasons (Milanini, 1998). By contrast, *Cosmicomics* (1965) and *The Castle of Crossed Destinies* (1973) contain significant additions. 'Un segno nello spazio' (1964), for instance, was substantially expanded in 1965 in the light of the new theories of the sign and semiotics, around twenty passages such as this being added: 'I had lost everything: the sign, the point, the thing that caused me – being the one who had made the sign at that point – to be me' (II, 112; *Cosmicomics*, 35). Similarly in 'Priscilla' a more scientific rewriting of the tale turns the countless allusions to 'citoplasma' and 'bastoncini' into the more accurate 'protoplasma' and 'cromosomi' (II, 1351–4). However, he was still keen to keep erotic particulars at bay, excising the following detail from the finale of 'Un segno nello spazio (A Sign in Space)' (1964): 'the point where a bit of red skin met a fold in the flesh of the upper part of the thigh of a certain Yvonne seen from behind as she lay on her front' (II, 1333). But on the whole the cosmicomic tales are expanded, and in 1984, as we have seen (Chapter 6), Calvino rearranged and even added more stories to produce *Cosmicomiche vecchie e nuove*. Similarly the 'Castle' section of *The Castle of Crossed Destinies* (1973) was expanded from five to seven chapters as the author's interest in the project grew (II, 1368–69). But in the composition of *Palomar* (1983), as we have seen (Chapter 9), Calvino returned to removing rather than adding material. In his rewriting of what had originally appeared as newspaper articles in the *Corriere della sera* or *la Repubblica*, the material is subjected more to excision than to expansion. In particular he omits all elements of 'cronaca' in rewriting the *Palomar* pieces for publication: there is now no mention of dates, nor are there any cultural allusions as he deletes references to artists, such as Hokusai (II, 1414) or to books alluded to in the original journalistic pieces. We even find an instance of an omission of autobiographical elements in this passage deleted from the original newspaper redaction of 'Il fischio del merlo' (10 August 1975):

> Like that knowledge which [Mr Palomar] could have easily picked up from a surviving source, if he had paid more attention in his childhood to birdsong and the flight of birds and the voice of his father who each time carefully told him their names. Rather than the cultivation of precise nomenclature and classification of species practised by his parents perhaps with excessive didactic insistence, the son had preferred the constant pursuit of a precision unsure in defining the modulating, the shifting, the composite: that is, in defining the indefinible. (II, 1417)

In the more generic passage in the book *Palomar*, all references to parents have been elided:

> No book can teach what can be learned only in childhood if you lend an alert ear and eye to the song and flight of birds and if you find someone who knows how to give them a specific name. Rather than the cultivation of precise nomenclature and classification, Palomar had preferred the constant pursuit of a precision unsure in defining the modulating, the shifting, the composite. (II, 892; *Mr Palomar*, 21)

As at the beginning of his literary career, so here at the end this suppression of contemporary references or personal baggage provides a kind of lightness and neutrality in Calvino's writing. Contini (1974) summed up Ariosto's technique in rewriting as being primarily 'arte del levare (the art of removing material)' (238). Similarly Calvino's corrections, as we have seen, tend to move in the direction of removing rather than adding. As he said in a famous interview with Maria Corti in 1984:

> There are works which are generated by the exclusion of material . . . The volume *Palomar* is the product of many phases of this kind of elaboration, in which 'removing' material has had much more importance than 'adding' it. (*S*, 2925)

3. FROM 'LA SPECULAZIONE EDILIZIA' TO THE 'LEZIONI AMERICANE'

As for strictly stylistic developments, it is worth starting with the two ideas articulated in the famous essay 'La sfida al labirinto (The Challenge to the Labyrinth)', written in 1962. There Calvino states that in his earliest works he had usually opted for a 'reductive style (stilizzazione riduttiva)', presumably referring to the brief, paratactic sentences in the Hemingway manner that had studded the works of the 1940s and early 1950s. However, more recently he had felt the need for a 'discourse that would be as articulated and encompassing as possible, embodying the epistemological and technological complexity of the world we live in' (*S*, 114). The writer that Calvino cites as embodying this more complex style is Joyce, and presumably he is thinking of the more elaborate, hypotactic periods of the fictions he was working on at this time, which have intellectual protagonists: 'Adventure of a Reader', *A Plunge into Real Estate*, *Smog*, *The Watcher* (Mengaldo 1989). This last work in particular contains some of Calvino's longest sentences (notably the one lasting a page and a half which tries to define the complexities of Communism), and an almost mannerist use of the parenthesis – though Calvino himself claimed that his use of the parenthesis was 'a stylistic necessity not an option (*bisogno*, non proposito stilistico)' (II, 1313), in order to convey his sense of the complexity of the world. By contrast, when the story's protagonist goes into the courtyard for a cigarette, the style also changes, as the enormous, parenthetic sentences are replaced by short staccato ones while the scrutineer relaxes:

> Era spiovuto. Anche dai cortili desolati si levava un odore di terra e primavera. Qualche rampicante fioriva un muro. (II, 40) (The rain had stopped. Even from those desolate courtyards a smell of earth rose, of spring. A few climbing plants were in flower against a wall.) (*The Watcher*, 35)

This predilection for short sentences, though largely absent in this text, will return in the descriptions of Amerigo's successor, Mr Palomar.

The textual variants cited in the three volumes of *Romanzi e racconti* permit us to say more about changes in content than about stylistic developments, so in order to deal with the latter I have used a different control, namely the manuscripts of Calvino's most heavily rewritten realistic novel, *La speculazione edilizia* (1957). In the second manuscript (B) in Pavia there are a number of alterations which concern merely *elocutio* rather than *inventio*, and which may be banded in three broad groups. The alterations in the first group represent the avoidance of the more common verbs (*essere*, *dire*, *avere*, *andare*, etc.):

1. disse → suggerí (*B*, 14); dirsi in dissenso → manifestare il suo dissenso (*B*, 18 *bis*); stava dicendo → stava ripetendo (*B*, 29); che arriva → che s'impianta (*B*, 31); e giunto a questo punto disse → ma sentí giunto il momento di reagire (*B*, 31); dava risposte → interloquiva brusco (*B*, 32 *bis*); gridava → inveiva (*B*, 65); andò a casa → saliva verso casa → saliva verso la villa (*B*, 87).

This last alteration, from the final chapter, is presumably made in order to echo one of the opening sentences of the novella: 'Quando Quinto saliva alla sua villa . . .' (I, 782). This general pursuit of less overused locutions has already been documented for the period 1945–50 (Falaschi 1988b, 123), and we can find other instances of it elsewhere: in 'Mai nessuno degli uomini seppe' (1950), '*tornò* l'eco delle fucilate' (II, 1443) becomes '*rimbalzò* l'eco delle fucilate' (II, 997), and in 'Giochi senza fine (Games without End)' (1965), 'non *aveva* fine' (II, 1340) becomes 'non *finiva* mai' (II, 136).

The second group lists the elimination of colloquialisms for more elegant expressions and register:

2. una strana sua remora → una sua confusa remora (*B*, 12); all'idea che il fratello pigliasse un po' in mano → all'idea che fosse il fratello a prendere un

po' in mano (*B*, 44); se ci stavo a firmargli → se ero disposto a firmargli (*B*, 46); la storia → la questione (*B*, 47); convenienti di costo → convenienti di salario (B, 49); alto → gigantesco (*B*, 58); cose risapute → concetti risaputi (*B*, 64); parte d'un tutto → parte d'un processo (*B*, 85); questa storia → questo suo tentativo (*B*, 7).

Again there are other instances of this process from other periods: in 'Senza colori (Without Colours)' (1964), 'grido' (II, 1336) becomes 'guaito' (II, 126), while in 'La distanza della Luna (The Distance of the Moon)' (1964) 'poppa' (II, 1325) becomes 'mammella' (II, 87), and 'l'enorme disco lunare m'apparve incredibilmente contratto, anzi, ecco che s'andava sempre piú contraendo' (II, 1326) becomes 'l'enorme disco lunare pareva non fosse piú lo stesso di prima, tanto era rimpicciolito, anzi, ecco che s'andava sempre piú contraendo' (II, 91), thus avoiding the repetition of 'contrarre'.

The most interesting group is the third, which illustrates a consistent tendency to shift towards abstract, substantive locutions:

3. trovar simpatico Caisotti → provar simpatia per Caisotti (*B*, 13); separare nettamente → segnare una separazione incolmabile (*B*, 15); progetti sulla città futura → progetti sulla società futura (*B*, 18) ; vendere il terreno → ripiegare sulla semplice vendita del terreno (*B*, 32 *bis*); versi e prose scabri ed essenziali → versi e prose di pietrosa essenzialità (*B*, 50); operai delle grandi fabbriche → operai delle grandi industrie (*B*, 51).

The penultimate example is the most interesting one here, for in this passage from Chapter XIV discussing the poets of the Ligurian Riviera, Calvino's re-writing deliberately avoids the blatant intertextual allusion to the famous *incipit* of one of the sections of Montale's 'Mediterraneo' in *Ossi di seppia*: 'Avrei voluto sentirmi scabro ed essenziale . . .' But this general tendency towards abstracts is a consistent element of Calvino's style and can be documented from other areas of his work: in 'Senza colori' (1965) 'quella tinta bituminosa' (II, 1336) is rewritten as 'quella luminosità caliginosa' (II, 127); in 'Ti con zero' (1967) 'ciò vuol dire' (II, 1355) becomes 'la conseguenza che devo trarne è' (II, 311); in 'La pantofola spaiata' (1975) the phrase 'ha riparato a una disparità' (II, 1433) becomes in the definitive version of *Palomar* 'ha messo riparo a una disparità' (II, 959); and there is even an important example from the 1980s, in 'La pancia del geco' (1982): 'Le zampe e la coda segmentate ad anelli, il capo e il ventre picchiettati di minute piastre granulose, dànno al geco . . .' (II, 1421) becomes 'La segmentazione ad anelli di zampe e coda, la picchiettatura di minute piastre granulose sul capo e sul ventre dànno al geco . . . (The segmentation of legs and tail into rings, the speckling of tiny granulous plates on his head and belly give the gecko . . .)' (II, 923; *Mr Palomar*, 54).

While the changes indicated in (1) and (2), avoiding overused verbs and seeking out more elegant formulations, are typical processes of most writers and have been commented on by other critics, the modifications under (3), the move towards more abstract expression, have not been discussed before and seem more specific to Calvino at all stages of his literary career. Of course Calvino has a predictable antipathy towards an extreme form of this tendency, an obscurely abstract Italian. His remarks at the end of his 1965 essay, 'L'italiano, una lingua tra le altre lingue (Italian, a Language amongst Other Languages)', are indicative of this: 'My linguistic ideal is an Italian which is as *concrete* and *precise* as possible. The enemy that must be defeated is the Italian tendency to use *abstract* and *generic* expressions' (*S*, 153). But in practice he exhibits a fondness for that kind of abstraction which at the same time avoids opacity, and which is one of the most obvious features of his final literary legacy to the next millennium, in the *Lezioni americane*. There the five qualities recommended are all abstracts, and one form of lightness in writing is defined as 'any kind of description that involves a high degree of abstraction' (*S*, 644; *Six Memos*, 17).

The directions in which the above rewritings and variants move illustrate how Calvino dynamically realises all five qualities in his own writing and rewriting, from his earliest literary apprenticeship to his last works. 'Lightness' is achieved, as we saw in the rewritings of his first novel, by his elimination of all forms of emotional excess, whether due to autobiography or sentiment. The incompatibility of autobiography with lightness is confirmed in this passage from the Harvard lectures describing Perseus, the symbol of lightness and conqueror of the 'petrifying' Medusa:

> Soon I became aware that between the facts of life that should have been my raw materials and the quick, light touch I wanted for my writing, there was a gulf that cost me increasing effort to cross. Maybe I was only then becoming aware of the weight, the inertia, the opacity of the world – qualities that stick to writing from the start, unless one finds some way of evading them . . . Perseus comes to my aid even at this moment, just as I too am about to be caught in a vise of stone – which happens every time I try to speak about my own past. (*S*, 632; *Six Memos*, 4)

'Quickness' is evident particularly in his more economic handling of the conclusions to stories, as we saw above (Chapter 1), an economy he learned from fairy tales, which he studied primarily because of his 'interest in style and structure, in the economy, rhythm and hard logic with which they are told' (*S*, 660; *Six Memos*, 35). 'Exactitude' we have observed in his moving beyond the common term for a more precise one, a movement he defines as his 'patient search for the *mot juste*' (*S*, 670; *Six Memos*, 48). 'Visibility' is everywhere in Calvino's work, but one early instance of it is that more visual rewriting of the partisan battle against the Germans in Chapter XI of *The Path to the Spiders' Nests*. 'Multiplicity' is evident not just in the new thematics of global complexity which emerge in the early 1960s, but also in that move we have observed from a linear to a more complex style towards the end of the 1950s in the many stories which revolve around intellectual protagonists.

Calvino's style is, then, a complex achievement, deliberately attuned to his subject matter, whether the latter is marginal and quotidian or of cosmic complexity, and even his fondness for abstraction is in the interests of lightness rather than opacity. His style, so often described as crystalline, is often the fruit of patient rewriting rather than spontaneity, the result, as we have seen, of a deliberate attempt to excise the 'heaviness' of autobiographical details or extremes of a sexual, political or violent nature. But the author himself should have the last, typically paradoxical word on the subject:

> The important thing is spontaneity as an impression which the work conveys, but this objective cannot necessarily be reached by using spontaneity as a method; in many cases it is only patient labour which allows one to arrive at the most felicitous and apparently 'spontaneous' solution. (*S*, 2924)

Conclusion

This study has been primarily concerned with the stories and novels published by Calvino in his lifetime. Since his death we have been given access to the twenty-six fictions which he wrote before 1945 (III, 767–830), and to others which he then wrote between 1945 and 1985, some published, some unpublished. A number of these latter items might have formed separate 'modular' works if the author had endowed them with the overall structure which would have turned them into a finished book. The most important of the latter projects was the book on the five senses, first conceived in the 1970s and eventually issued posthumously with the title *Sotto il sole giaguaro* (*Under the Jaguar Sun*) (1986). By the time of his death Calvino had completed three of the projected five tales: the one on smell, 'Il nome, il naso (The Name, The Nose)', written in 1972; the one on taste, 'Sotto il sole giaguaro (Under the Jaguar Sun)', composed in 1982, and originally published with the title 'Sapore sapere (Taste, Knowledge)'; and the one on hearing, 'Un re in ascolto (A King Listens)', which began as a libretto written in 1977 for the homonymous Berio opera, and was rewritten in narrative form in 1984 (III, 1214–19). Whether or not the book would have had a frame – though the author's widow provides reasons for thinking that it would (*Under the Jaguar Sun*, 85–6) – there is a sense in which the book can be virtually completed, since the other two senses not covered by the three stories written, touch and sight, are already present in Calvino's fictions: one of the earliest *Difficult Loves* tales, 'Avventura di un soldato (Adventure of a Soldier)' is a tour de force narration entirely devoted to the soldier's tactile sensations, while the whole of the rest of Calvino's oeuvre, and in particular *Palomar*, privileges above all others the sense of sight.

This journey through the forest of Calvino's works is now at an end. An overview of his entire output suggests appropriately conflicting conclusions about a writer who rejected univocal judgments. On the one hand he appears to be a 'scrittore dimezzato', his works deriving from the realist tradition in the first twenty years and then spiralling towards the experimental and postmodern in the second two decades. But even within these two broad swathes there are conflictual tensions: the works of the 1940s and 1950s hover between realism and fantasy, while those from the 1960s to the 1980s oscillate between the cosmic and the fragmentary. Atlernatively, it could be argued that his output has a chiastic pattern, beginning with the realism of the early short stories and first novel before moving to the fantasy of the trilogy; then he embraces science fiction and semiotic experimentalism before returning to a minimalist, phenomenological (hyper)realism at the end of his career.

There is a further paradox in the fact that despite Calvino's conscious cult of literary *varietas*, always writing books that are the antithesis of his previous work, there are also many constants which pervade the entire series of fictions he wrote. Each text, no matter when it is written, is generated by literary intertexts which contrast with the content of the work: the unlikely pairing of Stevenson and Hemingway lie behind the Resistance matter of *The Path to the Spiders' Nests*; Stevenson again and the atmosphere of the Cold War pervade *The Cloven Viscount*; Voltaire, Tolstoy and the Soviet suppression of the Hungarian revolt are in the background of *The Baron in the Trees*; Ariosto and the 'machine men' of the beatnik age are key ingredients in *The Non-Existent Knight*; Thomas Mann, Balzac and the Italian economic boom generate *A Plunge into Real Estate*, though it also contains within its overall denunciation of the bourgeoisie another antithetical element, an affectionate homage to the author's mother: she is portrayed hidden amidst the flora of her garden (and the foliage of Calvino's prose) in three important cameos (I, 787, 841, 889–90). Leopardi and the spaceshots of the early 1960s are the scientific backdrop to the cosmicomic tales, but literary sources and intertexts are of equal importance here; Marco Polo's fabulous voyage to the Orient is juxtaposed with the decline of the urban environment in the West in *Invisible Cities*; Ariosto again, and semiotic theory about signification and the loss of the subject, form the background to *The Castle of Crossed Destinies*; Borges, and the whole of contemporary fiction, along with speculation about writer's block, are present in *If on a Winter's Night a Traveller*; while Pasolini and Valéry's Monsieur Teste, as we have seen, are closely linked to the genesis of *Palomar*. Calvino's works stem as much from other literary texts as from 'the unwritten world'.

In terms of genre, Calvino moves from writing novels in the 1940s and 1950s to an exclusive concentration on short fictions contained within a macrotext after 1963. This abandonment of a totalising form, such as the novel, for the partial, fragmentary poetics of short narratives is paralleled by an analogous change in his theoretical writings. Until 1964 the titles of his major essays had ambitious, global dimensions: 'Natura e storia nel romanzo (Nature and History in the Novel)', 'Il mare dell'oggettività (The Sea of Objects)', 'La sfida al labirinto (The Challenge to the Labyrinth)'. But after 'L'antitesi operaia (The Working Class as Antithesis)' of 1964, he adopts a less emphatic note, beginning with a brief essay whose title reflects this change: 'Non darò piú fiato alle trombe (No More Loud Blasts)' (*S*, 143–5). Calvino discusses this major change in his essays in 'Sotto quella pietra (Underneath that Stone)' (1980), a discarded preface to *Una pietra sopra* (*S*, 399–405). In it he notes that his early writings, fiction and non-fiction, formed part of a coherent attempt to construct a literature that would mould society in a certain way, but he realised in the 1960s that instead society only responded either to huge, millennarian changes or to minute, barely detectable influences, while literature remained a self-contained world with little or no interface with the unwritten world. Consequently Calvino had to change the basic premise of his writing, and the tools that would help effect this shift were those of linguistics, structural anthropology and semiotics. He would continue to write short fictions, but his 1959 definition of the novel as 'a narrative work which can signify and be enjoyed on many different planes which intersect' (*S*, 1525) prefigures the frames that would intersect with the micro-narrations in his future works, making them signify (Badini Confalonieri, 1985).

A major transformation, then, takes place in Calvino's writing around 1963–64: though his earlier fictions had been concerned with nature and history, it now becomes impossible for him to write without keeping in mind man's place in the cosmos, so the fictional genres, plots, characters and even styles that he subsequently adopts have this cosmic dimension – even the fragmentary observations of Palomar are a response to this sense of cosmic vastness and human insignificance. The 'unwritten world' which is in a sense the old 'sea of objects' is now admitted into his narrative but is filtered into fragments through a conscious grid (Musarra, 1996). The ultimate paradox is here: as in his formal choices he abandons the traditional novel for ever in favour of short narratives, and as his essays relinquish global titles and aspirations for the pulviscular and fragmentary, at the same time his thematics move in the opposite direction, from the marginal to the cosmic. Even those last fictions about the five senses are concerned with man's place in the universe, while each unit of the planned book on everyday objects – *Gli oggetti* (*Objects*) (III, xx, 1225–8) – contains, paradoxically, a micro-history of the world: in the time it takes for the protagonist of 'La glaciazione (Glaciation)' to fetch the ice for a glass of whisky, his speculations have situated that quotidian action within the cosmic context of the past and future ice ages (III, 257–60). Similarly grandiose thematics haunt the other everyday narrations about the petrol pump, the telephone, the shower, the mirror, the television (III, 261–311). As the author himself puts it in the discarded first Harvard lecture, 'Sul cominciare e finire (On Beginnings and Endings)': 'My problem could be formulated in these terms: is it possible to tell a story in the context of the universe?' (*S*, 751).

Yet, in case this turning point seems too rigid a formulation, the germs of this later cosmic aspiration are already anticipated, as has been seen (see Chapter 1), as far back as the close of his earliest postwar story, 'La stessa cosa del sangue (In the Blood)':

> And while the two brothers, sitting on the edge of the ravine, waited for Giglio, the Communist went around wondering how the rocks, the ravines and the mountains had originally formed, and how old the earth was. And all of them discussed the layers of rocks, the age of the earth and when the war would end. (I, 227)

Similarly with style, already in his university thesis, Calvino describes Conrad's language at its best as 'leggero e lineare' (thesis, p. 22), an ideal to which even the late Calvino would subscribe. Perhaps even his early distinction in the thesis between Kipling's excellence in his treatment of children and animals and Conrad's superiority in his depiction of older men (p. 88) anticipates respectively the thematics of Calvino's early and later works. But in case this dichotomy seems too neat, we remember that the aspiration towards maturity and integration with the world which informs the young protagonists of his early fiction, from Pin and Nino Torre to Rambaldo, is analogous to the later pursuit of a wholeness of existence within the universe.

Calvino's aesthetic ideals thus both changed and remained constant. As has been noted, he consistently raised the stakes of literature, challenging it to adapt to the new age in which it is written, but at the same time he constantly confronted certain key questions about man's place in that changing world (II, xi–xiii). His aesthetics evolved as he (and others) abandoned the earlier Marxist programme of attempting to change the world through writing. But his thematics continued to be concerned with man's place in nature, history and the cosmos, and to be characterised by an 'ethical thrust' (Barenghi 1984), while his poetics remained, both before and after 1963, those of eclecticism, antithesis and paradox. As he tells us at the close of the Harvard lecture on 'Quickness', his ideal was of

> immense cosmologies, sagas, and epics all reduced to the dimensions of an epigram. In the even more congested times that await us, literature must aim at the maximum concentration of poetry and thought . . . I would like to edit a collection of tales consisting of one sentence only, or even a single line. (*S*, 673; *Six Memos*, 51)

Epics within epigrams, and a *brevitas* that opens up vistas of infinity: these are the antithetical ideals of Calvino's fiction. They are also indicative of another key strand in his writing: his modern awareness of classic texts and their literary values, from Homer, Lucretius and Ovid through Dante to modern classics such as Conrad and Borges. In the seminal essay in this area, 'Perché leggere i classici? (Why Read the Classics?)' of 1981, Calvino provides at least fourteen contrasting definitions of what constitutes a classic, of the type: 'A classic is a work which has never exhausted what it has to say to us.' A fifteenth definition might have come from his own oeuvre: 'A classic is a work which (like each of Calvino's texts) retains a consciousness of its own modernity without ceasing to be aware of other classic works of the past.' Bonsaver's formula summing up Calvino's approach also hits the mark: 'sperimentazione e classicità' (Bonsaver, 1995c, 269–70).

For a writer who eschewed sweeping superlatives and univocal statements, it would be inappropriate to end on a eulogistic or hagiographic note about Calvino's place in twentieth-century literature, but an appropriate, perhaps Calvinian, measure of his contribution to fiction this century, and of his legacy to the next millennium, can also be gained from the sense of void in Italian and world literature since his death.

Appendix

Chronology of Calvino's Fictions

The following list provides a chronological survey of all the prose fiction written by Calvino and published hitherto. It does not include any of the poetry, or prose works for theatre, cinema, music and the other arts included in *Romanzi e racconti*, Vol. III, works to which the author himself attached only minor significance (III, xvii). The first date given is the date of composition, if known; dates in brackets give date and place of first publication.

The major source for this chronology is the textual apparatus to *Romanzi e racconti*, Vols I–III, including Luca Baranelli's 'Bibliografia degli scritti di Italo Calvino' (III, 1351–516). For the cosmicomic tales the most up-to-date source is now Claudio Milanini, 'Cronologia cosmicomica', in Italo Calvino, *Tutte le cosmicomiche*, ed. Claudio Milanini (Milan: Mondadon; 1997), 393–417.
The following abbreviations are used:

C	= *Il Contemporaneo*	*R*	= *la Repubblica*
Cdp	= *Corriere dei piccoli*	*U*	= *l'Unità*
Cds	= *Corriere della sera*	UVC	= *Ultimo viene il corvo*

1943

1. Passatempi, 2.3.43 (*Roma Fascista*, 29.4.43)
2. Dieci soldi in plastilina, 2.3.43 (*Roma Fascista*, 29.4.43)
3. Invece era un'altra, 7.3.43 (*Roma Fascista*, 29.4.43)
4. L'uomo che chiamava Teresa, 12.4.43
5. Il profeta muto, 21.4.43
6. Il lampo, 25.4.43
7. Il giudice sul mulo, 15.5.43
8. Chi si contenta, 17.5.43
9. Non fidarsi è meglio, 12.6.43
10. Importanza di ognuno, 12.6.43
11. Un dio sul pero, 20.10.43
12. Disorganizzazione, 31.10.43
13. L'uomo delle palafitte, 31.10.43
14. Fiume asciutto, Oct. 1943
15. La serva, 17.11.43
16. La siepe, 30.11.43
17. Coscienza, 1.12.43

18. Solidarietà, 3.12.43
19. Giuda, 4.12.43
20. La fila, Dec. 1943

1944

21. L'autista incerto, 1944
22. Il funerale, 16.2.44
23. Tutte bugie, 19.2.44
24. La pecora nera, 30.7.44
25. La caduta di Sparta, 8.10.44
26. Come non fui Noè (Buon a nulla), 1943–44

1945

27. La stessa cosa del sangue, 1945 (UVC, 1949)
28. Attesa della morte in un albergo, 1945 (UVC, 1949)
29. Angoscia in caserma, 1945 (*Aretusa*, Dec. 1945, but not published until 1946)
30. Andato al comando, 1945 (*Il Politecnico*, 19.1.46)
31. Come un volo d'anitre, 1945 (*Il Settimanale*, 3.5.47)

1946

32. Di padre in figlio (*U*, 28.4.46)
33. Vento in una città, May 1946 (withdrawn at proof stage from UVC)
34. E il settimo si riposò (*U*, 9.6.46)
35. Uomo nei gerbidi (*U*, 23.6.46)
36. Paura sul sentiero (*Darsena nuova*, Jun./Jul. 1946)
37. Campo di mine (*U*, 18.8.46)
38. I fratelli Bagnasco (*U*, 22.9.46)
39. Ragionamento del cugino (*U*, 29.9.46)
40. Cinque dopodomani: guerra finita! (*U*, 7.11.46)
41. Ultimo viene il corvo, Dec. 1946 (*U*, 5.1.47)
42. Furto in una pasticceria, 1946 (*U*, 19.6.47)
    Il sentiero dei nidi di ragno, Autumn–Dec. 1946 (published 10.10.47)

1947

43. Amore lontano di casa, Jan. 1947 (withdrawn at proof stage from UVC)
44. Visti alla mensa (*U*, 8.1.47)
45. Alba sui rami nudi (*Agorà*, Jan. 1947)
46. L'occhio del padrone (*U*, 30.3.47)
47. La fame a Bèvera (*U*, 18.5.47)
48. Un bastimento carico di granchi (*U*, 6.7.47)
49. Va' cosí che vai bene, 1947 (*Racconti*)
50. Si dorme come cani, 1947 (*U*, 11.6.48)
51. Dollari e vecchie mondane, 1947 (*Antologia Einaudi*, 1948)
52. Uno dei tre è ancora vivo, 1947 (UVC, 1949)
53. Un pomeriggio Adamo, 1947 (UVC, 1949)
    Il bianco veliero, Dec. 1947–April 1949 (unpublished novel)

1948

54. I figli poltroni (*U*, 8.1.48)
55. Il giardino incantato (*U*, 1.2.48)

56. Impiccagione di un giudice, (*Rinascita*, Feb. 1948)
57. Il bosco degli animali (*U*, 20.4.48)
58. Com'era grande il mare (*Milano sera*, 22–3.6.48)
59. Il gatto e il poliziotto (*U*, 28.8.48)
60. Pranzo con un pastore (*U*, 15.9.48)
61. Voglia di mare (*U*, 16.10.48)
62. Isabella e Fioravanti (*U*, 31.10.48)
63. Chi ha messo la mina nel mare? (*U*, 23.11.48)

1949

64. Freddo a Napoli (*U*, 8.1.49)
65. Lasciare Anna (*U*, 2/4/49)
66. La casa degli alveari (UVC, 1949)
67. Avventura di un soldato (UVC, 1949)
68. Desiderio in novembre (UVC, 1949)
    Ultimo viene il corvo, finished 27.2.49 (published 30.7.49)
69. Un letto di passaggio (= Avventura di un bandito), end of 1949 (*Racconti*)

1950

I giovani del Po, 28.1.50–28.7.51 (*Officina*, 1957)

70. Lettera ad Amelia sui dischi volanti (*U*, 7.4.50)
71. Storia del soldato che portò il cannone a casa (*U*, 17.8.50)
72. Cimitero di biciclette (*Rinascita*, Nov.–Dec. 1950)
73. Pesci grossi, pesci piccoli (*Inventario*, Autumn 1950)
74. Mai nessuno degli uomini lo seppe (*U*, 9.11.50)

1951

75. Il reggimento smarrito (*U*, 15.7.51)
76. Avventura di una bagnante (*Paragone*, Aug. 1951)
77. Tre soldati e un generale, 1951
    Il visconte dimezzato, Jul.–Sep. 1951 (published 12.2.52)

1952

78. Un compagno venuto da lontano (*U*, 6.6.52)
79. Un bel gioco dura poco, 29.6.52 (*Racconti*)
    La collana della regina, 24.6.52–17.12.54 (unpublished novel, chapter published as 'Frammento di romanzo' in *I giorni di tutti*, Dec. 1960)
80. Funghi in città (*U*, 28.9.52)
81. Il piccione comunale (*U*, 12.10.52)
82. La pietanziera (*U*, 19.10.52)
83. La formica argentina, Aug. 1949–Apr. 1952 (*Botteghe Oscure*, 1952)
84. Gli occhi del nemico (*U*, 2.11.52)
85. La fabbrica occupata (*U*, 9.12.52)
86. La ragazza licenziata (*U*, 14.12.52)
87. Gli avanguardisti a Mentone, 25.12.52–18.1.53 (*Nuovi argomenti*, May–Jun. 1953)

1953

88. Le disgrazie di un paese (*U*, 14.1.53)
89. Il bosco sull'autostrada (*U*, 1.2.53)
90. La cura delle vespe (*U*, 15.2.53)

91. La storia di Kim–Ghi–U (*U*, 2.4.53)
92. Paese infido (*U*, 30.4.53)
93. L'aria buona (*U*, 5.7.53)
94. Avventura di un impiegato (*Paragone*, August 1953)
95. L'entrata in guerra, 14.6.53–5.7.53 (*Il Ponte*, Aug.–Sep. 1953)
96. Le notti dell'UNPA, 24.9.53 (*L'entrata in guerra*)
    L'entrata in guerra (published 25.5.54)
97. Un paese disgraziato (*U*, 14.10.53)
98. Il generale in biblioteca (*U*, 30.10.53)

1954

99. La fabbrica nella montagna (*U*, 28.2.54)
100. La bomba addormentata nel bosco (*Incontri oggi*, Jun. 1954)
101. Libertà! Libertà! (*C*, 7.8.54)
102. I mozzatori di nasi (*C*, 21.8.54)
103. Dove va l'avvoltoio? (*C*, 28.8.54)
104. Il dittatore (*C*, 4.9.54)
105. Lo *Jus Primae Noctis* (*C*, 11.9.54)
106. L'adultera (*C*, 25.9.54)
107. La lente d'ingrandimento (*C*, 9.10.54)
108. I marziani (*C*, 23.10.54)
109. La domenica delle follie (*C*, 11.12.54)
110. Il coniglio velenoso (*C*, 25.12.54)
111. Un viaggio con le mucche, 1954 (*Il Caffè*, Jan. 1956)
112. La gallina di reparto, 1954 (*Nuova corrente*, Jul.–Dec. 1958)

1955

113. La panchina (libretto), 1955 (performed 2.10.56 → La panchina, *Racconti*)
    Fiabe italiane, Apr. 1955–Nov. 1956 (published 12.11.56)
114. La follia del mirino (*C*, 30.4.55) (→Avventura di un fotografo, *Gli amori difficili*, 1970)

1956

115. Luna e gnac, 1956 (*Corriere d'informazione*, 4–5.5.57)
116. *La speculazione edilizia*, Apr. 1956–Jul. 1957 (*Botteghe Oscure*, Autumn, 1957)
    Il barone rampante, 10.12.56–26.2.57 (published 4.6.57)

1957

117. La gran bonaccia delle Antille (*Città aperta*, 25.7.57)
118. La tribù con gli occhi al cielo, Oct. 1957
119. Avventura di un viaggiatore, 1–13.11.57 (*Il Verri*, Oct. 1958)

1958

120. Dialogo sul satellite (*Città aperta*, Mar. 1958)
121. Monologo notturno di un nobile scozzese (*Espresso*, 25.5.58)
122. Avventura di un poeta, 24.7–7.8.58 (*Racconti*)
123. Una bella giornata di marzo (*Città aperta*, Jun.–Jul. 1958)
124. La notte dei numeri (*Il Mondo*, 15.7.58)
125. Avventura di un lettore (*Tempo presente*, Aug. 1958)
126. La signora Paulatim (*Il Caffè*, Sep. 1958)
127. La nuvola di smog, 23.6–18.8.58 (*Nuovi argomenti*, Sep.–Oct. 1958)

128. Avventura di un miope (*Racconti*)
129. Avventura di una moglie (*Racconti*)
130. Avventura di due sposi (*Racconti*)
I racconti (published 20.11.58)

1959

131. Avventura di uno sciatore (*Successo*, May 1959)
Il cavaliere inesistente, Mar.–Sep. 1959 (published 30.11.59)
Il barone rampante, ed. ridotta da IC (published 18.11.59)

1960

I nostri antenati, preface, Jun. 1960 (published 27.6.60)
La collana della regina, 1952–54 (chapter published as 'Frammento di romanzo' in *I giorni di tutti*, Dec. 1960)

1961

Un ottimista in America (unpublished)

1962

132. La strada di San Giovanni, Jan. 1962 (*Questo e altro*, 1962)

1963

La giornata d'uno scrutatore, 1953–20.1.1963 (published 28.2.63)
La speculazione edilizia (published 28.6.63)
133. Diario in clinica (*L'Europa letteraria*, Apr.–Jun. 1963)
134. Marcovaldo al supermarket (*Cdp*, 20.10.63)
135. La pioggia e le foglie (*Cdp*, 27.10.63)
136. La fermata sbagliata (*Cdp*, 3.11.63)
137. Fumo, vento e bolle di sapone (*Cdp*, 10.11.63)
138. Dov'è piú azzurro il fiume (*Cdp*, 24.11.63)
139. La città smarrita nella neve (*Cdp*, 8.12.63)
140. Un sabato di sole, sabbia e sonno (*Marcovaldo*)
141. La città tutta per lui (*Marcovaldo*)
142. Il giardino dei gatti ostinati (*Marcovaldo*)
143. I figli di Babbo Natale (*Marcovaldo*)
Marcovaldo ovvero le stagioni in città (published 23.11.63)
Che spavento l'estate (unfinished, unpublished novel)

1964

144. La distanza della Luna, Nov. 1963–29.6.64 (*Il Caffè*, Nov. 1964)
145. Sul far del giorno, Nov. 1963–16.4.64 (*Il Caffè*, Nov. 1964)
146. Un segno nello spazio, Nov. 1963–17/18.5.64 (*Il Caffè*, Nov. 1964)
147. Tutto in un punto, Nov. 1963–19/21.5.64 (*Il Caffè*, Nov. 1964)
Il sentiero dei nidi di ragno, Preface, Jun. 1964 (published 20.6.64)
148. Senza colori, 28–31.8.64 (*Il Giorno*, 11.4.65)
149. Giochi senza fine, 26.9–10.10.64 (*Il Giorno*, 24.10.65)
150. Lo zio acquatico, Nov. 1963–17.10.64 (*Il Giorno*, 1.5.65)
151. Quanto scommettiamo, 14.11.64 (*Le cosmicomiche*)
152. Fino a che dura il Sole, 4/7.9.64–23.11.64 (*Il Giorno*, 18.4.65)
153. La Luna come un fungo, 27.11–8.12.64 (*Il Giorno*, 16.5.65)

1965

Il barone rampante, pref. di Tonio Cavilla (published 31.3.65)
La nuvola di smog, La formica argentina (published 20.10.65)
154. I Dinosauri, Nov. 1963–14/23.9.65 (*Le cosmicomiche*)
155. La forma dello spazio, 24.7–8.8.65 (*l'Espresso, 14.11.65*)
156. Gli anni–luce, 18–20.8.65 (*Le cosmicomiche*)
157. La spirale, 22.4–27.9.65 (*Le cosmicomiche*)
158. I meteoriti, 10–12.9.65 (*Il Giorno*, 31.10.65)
159. La molle Luna, 11.9–21.11.65 (*Ti con zero*)
Le cosmicomiche (published 15.11.65)

1966

160. Il sangue, il mare, 9.4.66–10.7.66 (*Rendiconti*, Jul. 1967)
161. Priscilla: Mitosi, 22–9.7.66 (*Nuova corrente*, Feb. 1967)
162. Ti con zero, 6–10.8.66 (*Almanacco Letterario Bompiani*, Nov. 1966)
163. Le conchiglie e il tempo, 7–15.10.66 (*La memoria del mondo*)

1967

164. L'origine degli Uccelli, 1964–23/27.1.67 (*Linus*, Jul. 1967)
165. I cristalli, 4–11.2.67 (*Il Giorno*, 11.6.67)
166. L'inseguimento, 14–28.4.67 (*Il Giorno*, 28.5.67)
I fiori blu (published 27.4.67)
167. La memoria del mondo, 5–7.5.67 (*Il Giorno*, 2.7.67)
168. Il guidatore notturno, Jun. 1967 (*Il Giorno*, 30.7.67)
169. Meiosi, 26.7–15.8.67 (*Ti con zero*)
170. Il conte di Montecristo, 29.8–11.9.67 (*Ti con zero*)
171. Morte, 14–17.9.67 (*Ti con zero*)
Ti con zero (published 28.10.67)
Orlando furioso raccontato da Italo Calvino (published 31.12.67)

1968

172. Le figlie della Luna, 19–29.2.68 (*Playmen*, May 1968)
173. Tempesta solare, 28.3.68–2.4.68 (*La memoria del mondo*)
174. Il cielo di pietra, 1–3.6.68 (*La memoria del mondo*)
La memoria del mondo e altre storie cosmicomiche (published Nov. 1968)
Fiabe italiane, ed. ridotta (Nov. 1968)

1969

175. La decapitazione dei capi (*Il Caffè*, Aug. 1969)
Ultimo viene il corvo (revised edn., 15.11.69)
Il castello dei destini incrociati, ed. Franco Maria Ricci (Nov. 1969)

1970

Avventura di un fotografo (see 114 above), Mar. 1970 (*Gli amori difficili*)
Gli amori difficili (published 20.6.70)
Le città invisibili, 23.7.70–3.11.72 (published 3.11.72)

1971

176. Dall'opaco (*Adelphiana*, Jun. 1971)

177. Il nome, il naso, Dec. 1971–Jan. 1972 (*Playboy*, Nov. 1972)

1972

Le città invisibili, 23.7.70–3.11.72 (published 3.11.72)

1973

178. L'incendio della casa abominevole (*Playboy*, Feb.–Mar. 1973)
Il castello dei destini incrociati (published 27.10.73)
179. La glaciazione, 1973–74 (*Cds*, 18.11.75)

1974

180. Ricordo di una battaglia (*Cds*, 25.4.74)
181. L'uomo di Neanderthal, Spring 1974 (*Le interviste impossibili*, 1975)
182. Montezuma, Jul. 1974 (*Le interviste impossibili*, 1975)
183. Autobiografia di uno spettatore (F. Fellini, *Quattro film*, 28.9.74)
184. La pompa di benzina (*Cds*, 21.12.74)
Eremita a Parigi (published Dec. 1974)
185. La poubelle agréée, 1974–76 (*Paragone*, Feb. 1977)

1975

186. L'antipatico, early 1975 (unpublished)
187. Prima che tu dica 'Pronto' (*Cds*, 27.7.75)
188–9. La corsa delle giraffe, Del mordersi la lingua (*Cds*, 1.8.75)
190–1. Il fischio del merlo, Del prendersela coi giovani (*Cds*, 10.8.75)
192. Lettura di un'onda (*Cds*, 24.10.75)
193. La pantofola spaiata (*Cds*, 18.9.75)

1976

194. Un chilo e mezzo di grasso d'oca (*Cds*, 23.1.76)
195. Gli dei indios che parlano dalla pietra (→ Serpenti e teschi) (*Cds*, 16.7.76)

1977

196. L'ansia annullata nei giardini giapponesi (→ L'aiuola di sabbia) (*Cds*, 16.1.77)
197. Piccolo sillabario illustrato (*Il Caffè*, Mar. 1977)
198. I disegni arrabbiati (*Cdp*, 21.7.77)
199. Un uomo e un seno nudo all'orizzonte (→ Il seno nudo) (*Cds*, 2.8.77)
200. Dialogo con una tartaruga, summer 1977 (unpublished)
201. Il richiamo dell'acqua, Oct.–Nov. 1976 (V. Gobbi, S. Toresella, *Acquedotti ieri e oggi*, 1976)
La foresta–radice–labirinto, 29.11–4.12.77 (published 1981)

1978

202. Il drago e le farfalle, 1–2.9.77 (*Cds*, 4.2.78)
203. Lo specchio e il bersaglio, 23–7.9.77 (*Cds*, 24.12.78)
204. Le tre isole lontane, 8–11.10.77 (A. Porta (ed.), *L'astromostro. Racconti per bambini*, 1980)

1979

Se una notte d'inverno un viaggiatore, 1.1.77–1.1.79 (published 2.6.1979)

1980

Una pietra sopra (published 16.2.80)
205. Apologo sull'onestà nel paese dei corrotti (La coscienza a posto) (*R*, 15.3.80)
206. Visita a un gorilla albino, 11.5.80 (*R*, 16.5.80)
207. L'altra Euridice (*Gran Bazaar*, Sep.–Oct. 1980)

1981

208. Sapore, sapere (= Sotto il sole giaguaro), Jul. 1981 (*FMR*, Jun. 1982)
209. Le memorie di Casanova, Aug. 1981 (*R*, 15–16.8.82)
210. L'invasione degli storni (*R*, 3.12.81)

1982

211. Il museo dei formaggi, 16–30.3.82 (*Palomar*)
212. Giove con la sciarpa (= L'occhio e i pianeti) (*R*, 15.4.82)
213. Il mondo guarda il mondo (*Cnac Magazine*, Jul.–Aug. 1982)
214. La pancia del geco, 6.8.82 (*R*, 12.8.82)
215. Henry Ford, 26–30. 9.82 (unpublished)
216. Dal terrazzo, 21–6.11.82 (*Palomar*)
217. Gli amori delle tartarughe, 7–8.12.82 (*Palomar*)
218. Il prato infinito, 8–9.12.82 (*Palomar*)
219. Luna di pomeriggio, Dec. 1982 (*Palomar*)

1983

220. L'ordine degli squamati, 8–15.5.83 (*Palomar*)
221. Il marmo e il sangue, 18–20.7.83 (*Palomar*)
222. Nuotare nella spada (*R*, 29.7.83)
223. Dietro il retrovisore, 17–19.8.83
224. Per non sprecare le stelle (= La contemplazione delle stelle) (*R*, 2.8.83)
225. Il signor Mohole (Contro l'universo, Il sosia, L'implosione), 22–6.8.83 (unpublished)
226. Il modello dei modelli, 28.8–2.9.83 (*Palomar*)
227. L'universo in uno specchio, 3–6.9.83 (*Palomar*)
228. Come imparare ad essere morto, 6–13.9.83 (*Palomar*)
Palomar, 1.8.75–Nov. 1983 (published 19.11.83)
229. L'ultimo canale, 25–7.12.83 (*R*, 3.1.84)

1984

230. Un re in ascolto, Jul.–Aug. 1984 (*R*, 12–13.8.84)
231. Il niente e il poco, 14–21.8.84 (*R*, 2–3.9.84)
232. L'implosione, 3–4.9.84 (*R*, 13.9.84)
Collezione di sabbia (26.10.84)
Cosmicomiche vecchie e nuove (20.11.84)

Bibliography

For the most detailed bibliography of Calvino's primary works, see the 'Bibliografia degli scritti di Italo Calvino', ed. Luca Baranelli (III, 1351–516). For fuller bibliographical surveys of secondary works, see the 'Bibliografia della critica', ed. Mario Barenghi, Bruno Falcetto and Claudio Milanini (III, 1517–44), and for an overview of the period 1985–95 see McLaughlin (1996b).

This appendix provides:

1. a list of primary texts by Calvino, including (a) fiction, (b) non-fiction, (c) the collected works;
2. a list of the English translations used throughout;
3. a list of any other primary and all the secondary works referred to.

1. PRIMARY TEXTS

All works cited below were published in Turin by Einaudi except where otherwise indicated.

(a) Fiction

Il sentiero dei nidi di ragno (1947).
Ultimo viene il corvo (1949).
Il visconte dimezzato (1952).
L'entrata in guerra (1954).
Fiabe italiane (1956).
Il barone rampante (1957).
I racconti (1958).
Il cavaliere inesistente (1959).
I nostri antenati con prefazione (1960).
La giornata d'uno scrutatore (1963).
La speculazione edilizia (1963).
Marcovaldo ovvero le stagioni in città (1963).
Il sentiero dei nidi di ragno, con prefazione (1964).
Il barone rampante, Prefazione e note di Tonio Cavilla (Letture per la scuola media, 1965).
Le cosmicomiche (1965).
Ti con zero (1967).
La memoria del mondo e altre storie cosmicomiche (1968).
Gli amori difficili (1970).

Le città invisibili (1972).
Il castello dei destini incrociati (1973).
Se una notte d'inverno un viaggiatore (1979).
Palomar (1983).
Cosmicomiche vecchie e nuove (Milan: Garzanti, 1984).
Sotto il sole giaguaro (Milan: Garzanti, 1986).
La strada di San Giovanni (Milan: Mondadori, 1990).
Prima che tu dica 'Pronto' (Milan: Mondadori, 1993).
Tutte le cosmicomiche, ed. Claudio Milanini (Milan: Mondadori, 1997).

(b) Non-Fiction

(i) Essays

Una pietra sopra (1980).
Collezione di sabbia (Milan: Garzanti, 1984).
Lezioni americane (Milan: Garzanti, 1988).
Sulla fiaba, ed. M. Lavagetto (1988).
Perché leggere i classici (Milan: Mondadori, 1991).
Enciclopedia: Arte, Scienza e Letteratura (*Special Issue of 'Riga', vol. 9*), ed. Marco Belpoliti. (Milan: Marcos y Marcos, 1995).

(ii) Letters

I libri degli altri. Lettere 1947–1981, ed. Giovanni Tesio (1991).

(iii) Autobiographical Works

Eremita a Parigi. Pagine autobiografiche (Milan: Mondadori, 1994).
Album Calvino, eds. Luca Baranelli and Ernesto Ferrero (Milan: Mondadori, 1995).

(iv) Others

Joseph Conrad (tesi di laurea in Letteratura Inglese, Facoltà di Lettere, Università di Torino, Anno Accademico 1946–47).
'Lettera a Mario Boselli', *Nuova corrente*, 11.32–3 (Spring–Summer 1964), 102–10 (partly cited in I, 1355–6).

(c) The Collected Works

The following volumes were all published in Milan, by Mondadori, in the series 'I Meridiani':

Romanzi e racconti, vol. I (1991).
Romanzi e racconti, vol. II (1992).
Fiabe italiane, con prefazione di Mario Lavagetto (1993).
Romanzi e racconti, vol. III (1994).
Saggi, 2 vols (1995).

2. TRANSLATIONS IN ENGLISH

(a) Fiction

Adam One Afternoon, trans. by Archibald Colquhoun and Peggy Wright (London: Minerva, 1992).
Cosmicomics, trans. by William Weaver (London: Picador, 1993).

Difficult Loves. Smog. A Plunge into Real Estate, trans. by William Weaver (London: Picador, 1985).

If on a Winter's Night a Traveller, trans. by William Weaver (London: Minerva, 1992).

Invisible Cities, trans. by William Weaver (London: Secker & Warburg, 1974).

Italian Folktales, trans. by George Martin (Harmondsworth: Penguin, 1980).

Marcovaldo or The Seasons in the City, trans. by William Weaver (London: Minerva, 1993).

Mr Palomar, trans. by William Weaver (London: Minerva, 1992).

Numbers in the Dark and Other Stories, trans. by Tim Parks (London: Vintage, 1996).

Our Ancestors, trans. by Archibald Colquhoun, with an introduction by the author (London: Minerva, 1992).

The Castle of Crossed Destinies, trans. by William Weaver (London: Secker & Warburg, 1977).

The Path to the Spiders' Nests, trans. by Archibald Colquhoun, revised by Martin McLaughlin (London: Jonathan Cape, 1998).

The Road to San Giovanni, trans. by Tim Parks (London: Jonathan Cape, 1993).

The Watcher and Other Stories, trans. by William Weaver (San Diego–New York–London: Harcourt Brace, 1971).

Time and the Hunter, trans. by William Weaver (London: Picador, 1993).

Under the Jaguar Sun, trans. by William Weaver (London: Vintage, 1993).

(b) Non-Fiction

The Literature Machine. Essays, trans. by Patrick Creagh (London: Secker & Warburg, 1987).

Six Memos for the Next Millennium, trans. by Patrick Creagh (London: Vintage, 1996).

'The Written and Unwritten Word [*sic*]', trans. by William Weaver, *New York Review of Books*, 21 May 1983, 38–9.

3. SECONDARY WORKS

Adler, Sara M. (1979) *Calvino: The Writer as Fablemaker* (Potomac, MD: José Porrúa Turanzas).

Ajello, Nello (1979) *Intellettuali e PCI 1944/1958* (Bari: Laterza).

Alinei, Mario (ed.) (1973) *Spoglio elettronico dell'italiano letterario contemporaneo*, Vol. 2: *I. Calvino, 'Il sentiero dei nidi di ragno'* (Bologna: Il Mulino).

Almansi, Guido (1971) 'Il mondo binario di Italo Calvino', *Paragone*, 22.258, 95–110.

Andrews, Richard (1984) 'Calvino', in Michael Caesar and Peter Hainsworth (eds), *Writers and Society in Contemporary Italy* (Leamington: Berg), 259–81.

Badini Confalonieri, Luca (1985) 'Calvino e il racconto', in Giorgio Bàrberi Squarotti (ed.), *Metamorfosi della novella* (Foggia: Bastogi), 413–27.

Baranelli, Luca (1996) 'Un ricordo di Italo Calvino', *Annali della Facoltà di Lettere e Filosofia dell'Università di Siena*, 17, 355–64.

Barenghi, Mario (1984) 'Italo Calvino e i sentieri che s'interrompono', *Quaderni piacentini*, 15, 127–50.

Barenghi, Mario (1996) 'Gli oggetti e gli dèi. Appunti su una metafora calviniana', in *Sequenze novecentesche per Antonio De Lorenzi* (Modena: Mucchi), 197–218.

Baroni, Giorgio (1988) *Italo Calvino. Introduzione e guida allo studio dell'opera calviniana. Storia e antologia della critica* (Florence: Le Monnier).

Belpoliti, Marco (1990) *Storie del visibile. Lettura di Italo Calvino* (Rimini: Luisè).

Belpoliti, Marco (1992) 'Al contatto dell'occhio', *Nuova corrente*, 39.110, 357–72.

Belpoliti, Marco (1993) 'Il foglio e il mondo. Calvino, lo spazio, la scrittura (prima parte)', *Nuova corrente*, 40.112, 355–78.

Belpoliti, Marco (1994) 'Il foglio e il mondo. Calvino, lo spazio, la scrittura (seconda parte)', *Nuova corrente*, 41.114, 215–42.

Belpoliti, Marco (1996) *L'occhio di Calvino* (Turin: Einaudi, 1996).

Benedetti, Carla (1993) 'Calvino e i segni dell'autore', in Roelens and Lanslots (eds) (1993), 79–102.

Benussi, Cristina (1989) *Introduzione a Calvino* (Bari: Laterza).

Berardinelli, Alfonso (1991) 'Calvino moralista ovvero, restare sani dopo la fine del mondo', *Diario*, 7.9 (February), 37–58.

Bernardini Napoletano, Francesca (1977) *I segni nuovi di Italo Calvino. Da 'Le cosmicomiche' a 'Le città invisibili'* (Rome: Bulzoni).

Bertone, Giorgio (ed.) (1988) *Italo Calvino: la letteratura, la scienza, la città. Atti del convegno nazionale di studi di Sanremo* (Genoa: Marietti).

Bertone, Giorgio (1994) *Italo Calvino. Il castello della scrittura* (Turin: Einaudi).

Bertoni, Roberto (1993) *Int'abrigu int'ubagu. Discorso su alcuni aspetti dell'opera di Italo Calvino* (Turin: Tirrenia).

Biasin, Gian Paolo (1989) 'The surface of things, the depth of words', in Ricci (ed.) (1989a), 157–70.

Biasin, Gian Paolo (1994) 'Under Olivia's teeth: Italo Calvino, *Sotto il sole giaguaro*', in *The Flavors of Modernity. Food and the Novel* (Princeton, NJ: Princeton University Press), 97–127.

Bonsaver, G. (1994) 'Il Calvino "semiotico": dalla crisi del romanzo naturalistico all'opera come macrotesto', *The Italianist*, 14, 160–94.

Bonsaver, G. (1995a) 'Cities of the imagination: traces of Italo Calvino in Jeanette Winterson's fiction', *The Italianist*, 15, 213–30.

Bonsaver, G. (1995b) '*Il menabò*, Calvino and the *avanguardie*: some observations on the literary debate of the sixties', *Italian Studies*, 50, 86–96.

Bonsaver, G. (1995c) *Il mondo scritto: Forme e ideologia nella narrativa di Italo Calvino* (Turin: Tirrenia).

Bonura, Giuseppe (1972) *Invito alla lettura di Calvino* (Milan: Mursia).

Borges, Jorge Luis (1989) *Obras Completas*, 3 vols (Barcelona: Emecé).

Boselli, Mario (1992) 'Il complesso stile calviniano', *Nuova corrente*, 39.109, 189–98.

Botta, Anna (1997) 'Calvino and the Oulipo: an Italian ghost in the combinatory machine', *Modern Language Notes*, 112, 81–9.

Briganti, Paolo (1982) 'La vocazione combinatoria di Calvino', *Studi e problemi di critica testuale*, 24, 199–225.

Bryce, Judith (1989) 'Rousseau and Calvino: an unexplored ideological perspective in *Il barone rampante*', in Judith Bryce and Doug Thompson (eds), *Moving in Measure. Essays in Honour of Brian Moloney* (Hull: Hull University Press), 201–14.

Cadioli, Alberto (1993) 'Le "materie prime" dell'esperienza narrativa. Italo Calvino direttore di *Centopagine*', in Clerici and Falcetto (eds) (1993), 141–65.

Califano Bresciani, Mimma (1993) *Uno spazio senza miti: scienza e letteratura. Quattro saggi su Italo Calvino* (Florence: Le Lettere).

Calligaris, Contardo (1973) *Italo Calvino* (Milan: Mursia; revised edn, 1985).

Cannon, JoAnn (1981) *Italo Calvino: Writer and Critic* (Ravenna: Longo).

Cannon, JoAnn (1985) 'Calvino's latest challenge to the labyrinth: a reading of *Palomar*', *Italica*, 62, 189–200.

Cannon, JoAnn (1989) 'Italo Calvino: *Mr Palomar* and *Collezione di sabbia*', in her *Postmodern Italian Fiction: The Crisis of Reason in Calvino, Eco, Sciascia, Malerba* (London–Toronto: Associated University Presses), 95–115.

Capozzi, Rocco (1988) 'Mitopoiesi come ripetizione e differenza: *Cosmicomiche vecchie e nuove*', *Studi novecenteschi*, 15.35, 155–71.

Capozzi, Rocco (1989) '*Cosmicomiche vecchie e nuove*: keeping in tune with the times', in Ricci (ed.) (1989a), 65–84.

Carlton, Jill Margo (1984) 'The genesis of *Il barone rampante*', *Italica*, 61, 195–206.

Carter III, Albert Howard (1987) *Italo Calvino: Metamorphoses of Fantasy* (Ann Arbor, MI: UMI Research Press).

Cases, Cesare (1955) 'Un romanzo picaresco', *Il Contemporaneo*, 4 June, 8–9.

Cases, Cesare (1987) 'Calvino e "il pathos della distanza"', in idem, *Patrie lettere* (Turin: Einaudi), 160–6.

Celati, Gianni (1987) 'Palomar, nella prosa del mondo', *Nuova corrente*, 34.100, 227–42.

Centofanti, Fabrizio (1993) *Italo Calvino. Una trascendenza mancata* (Milan: Istituto Propaganda Libraria).

Cerina, Giovanna (1979) 'L'eroe, lo spazio narrativo e la costruzione del significato. Lettura di *Ultimo viene il corvo* di I. Calvino', in *Dalla novella rusticale al racconto neorealista* (Rome: Bulzoni), 115–53.

Clerici, Luca and Bruno Falcetto (eds) (1993) *Calvino e l'editoria* (Milan: Marcos y Marcos).

Clerici, Luca and Bruno Falcetto (eds) (1994) *Calvino e il comico* (Milan: Marcos y Marcos).

Coletti, Vittorio (1988) 'Calvino e l'italiano "concreto e preciso"', in Bertone (1988) 36–43.

Conrad, Joseph (1994) *Lord Jim. A Tale* (Harmondsworth: Penguin).

Conrad, Joseph (1995) *Heart of Darkness with The Congo Diary*, ed. Robert Hampson (Harmondsworth: Penguin).

Contini, Gianfranco (1974) 'Come lavorava l'Ariosto', in idem, *Esercizi di lettura sopra autori contemporanei* (Turin: Einaudi, 1974), 232–41.

Corti, Maria (1974) 'Prefazione' in Elio Vittorini, *Le opere narrative*, 2 vols, ed. Maria Corti (Milan: Mondadori), xi–lx.

Corti, Maria (1975) 'Testi o macrotesto? I racconti di Marcovaldo', in *Strumenti critici*, 9.27, 182–97 (later in Corti 1978a, 185–200).

Corti, Maria (1978a) *Il viaggio testuale* (Turin: Einaudi).

Corti, Maria (1978b) 'Neorealismo', in Corti (1978a), 21–100.

Corti, Maria (1990) 'Nel laboratorio di Calvino (da lettere inedite)', *Strumenti critici*, n.s. 5.63, 137–46.

Cottafavi, Betto and Maurizio Magri (eds) (1987) *Narratori dell'invisibile. Simposio in memoria di Italo Calvino* (Modena: Mucchi).

Daros, Philippe (1988) 'Italo Calvino et le nouveau roman', in Falaschi (1988a), 305–21.

Daros, Philippe (1993) '*I libri degli altri* ou soi-même comme un autre', *Strumenti critici*, n.s. 8.72, 171–88.

Daros, Philippe (1995) *Italo Calvino* (Paris: Hachette).

De Federicis, Lidia (1989) *'La giornata d'uno scrutatore' di Italo Calvino* (Turin: Loescher).

Deidier, Roberto (1993) 'Figure del labirinto: appunti sui boschi di Calvino', *Otto/Novecento*, 17.1, 153–62.

Deidier, Roberto (1995) *Le forme del tempo. Saggio su Italo Calvino* (Milan: Guerini Studio).

De Lauretis, Teresa (1989) 'Reading the (post)modern text: *If on a Winter's Night a Traveler*', in Ricci (ed.) (1989a), 131–45.

De Nicola, Francesco (ed.) (1994) *Italo Calvino scrittore* anche *per la scuola. Atti del seminario di studi aggiornati (Chiavari, 2 marzo 1991)* (Lavagna: Serigraf).

De Santillana, Giorgio (1962–63) 'Fato antico e fato moderno', *Le conferenze dell'Associazione Culturale Italiana*, 12, 37–62.

De Tommaso, Piero (1965) *Narratori italiani contemporanei* (Rome: Ateneo).

De Vivo, Alberto (1990) *Il tempo: ordine e durata nei 'Racconti' di Italo Calvino* (Abano Terme: Piovan).

Di Carlo, Franco (1978) *Come leggere 'I nostri antenati' di Italo Calvino* (Milan: Mursia).

Dini, Andrea (1993) 'Calvino al Premio Riccione 1947', *Paragone*, 44.524–6, 33–59.

Dolfi, Anna (1993) 'L'ultimo Calvino o il labirinto dell'identità', in her *In libertà di lettura. Note e riflessioni novecentesche* (Rome: Bulzoni), 225–62.

Dombroski, Robert S (1995) 'Italo Calvino's *Le città invisibili* and architecture: postmodern rhetoric', in idem, *Properties of Writing. Ideological Discourse in Modern Italian Fiction* (Baltimore, MD and London: Johns Hopkins University Press), 171–84.

Eversmann, Susanne (1979) *Poetik und Erzählstruktur in den Romanen Italo Calvinos: zum Verhältnis von Literarischer Theorie und narrative Praxis* (Munich: Wilhelm Fink).

Faeti, Antonio (1988) 'Con Cosimo e con Gurdulú. Note su Italo Calvino e la scuola', in Falaschi (ed.) (1988a), 53–81.

Falaschi, Giovanni (1976) *La Resistenza armata nella narrativa italiana* (Turin: Einaudi).

Falaschi, Giovanni (ed.) (1988a) *Italo Calvino. Atti del convegno internazionale (Firenze, 26–28 febbraio 1987)* (Milan: Garzanti).

Falaschi, Giovanni (1988b) 'Negli anni del neorealismo', in Falaschi (ed.) 1988a, 113–40.

Falcetto, Bruno (1988) 'Fiaba e tradizione letteraria', in Frigessi (ed.) (1988) 39–60.

Falcetto, Bruno (1992) *Storia della narrativa neorealista* (Milan: Mursia).

Falcetto, Bruno (1994) 'Sorriso, riso, smorfia', in Clerici and Falcetto (eds) (1994), 43–81.

Feinstein, Wiley (1989) 'The doctrinal core of *If on a Winter's Night a Traveler*', in Ricci (ed.) (1989a), 147–55.

Ferraro, Bruno (1987) 'Il castello dell'If e la sua struttura in *Le città invisibili*', *Letteratura italiana contemporanea*, 22, 95–113.

Ferraro, Bruno (1988) 'Italo Calvino's *Le città invisibili* and *La sfida al labirinto*', *The Italianist*, 8, 56–65.

Ferraro, Bruno (1994a)'"La collana della regina" e la città fabbrica in alcune opere di Italo Calvino degli anni Cinquanta e Sessanta', *Critica Letteraria*, 22, 703–13.

Ferraro, Bruno (1994b) 'Percorsi narrativi e tracciati temporali nelle *Città invisibili* di Italo Calvino', *Italianistica*, 23, 483–90.

Ferretti, Gian Carlo (1988a) 'Calvino e l'alterità cosmicomica', *Letteratura italiana contemporanea*, 9, 25–9.

Ferretti, Gian Carlo (1988b) 'La collaborazione ai periodici', in Falaschi (ed.) (1988a), 41–52.

Ferretti, Gian Carlo (1989) *Le capre di Bikini: Calvino giornalista e saggista* (Rome: Editori Riuniti).

Ferrua, Pietro (1991) *Italo Calvino a Sanremo* (Sanremo: Famija Sanremasca).

Finocchiaro Chimirri, Giovanna (ed.) (1987) *Italo Calvino tra realtà e favola* (Catania: CUECM).

Folena, Gianfranco (ed.) (1989) *Tre narratori: Calvino, Primo Levi, Parise* (Padua: Liviana).

Fortini, Franco (1975) 'Calvino e i giovani', *Corriere della sera*, 22 August, 2 (now in idem, *Insistenze. Cinquanta scritti 1976–1984* (Milan: Garzanti, 1985), 121–4).

Frasson-Marin, Aurore (1986) *Italo Calvino et l'imaginaire* (Geneva and Paris: Editions Slatkine).

Frasson-Marin, Aurore (1991) *Italo Calvino. Imaginaire et rationalité* (Geneva: Editions Slatkine).

Frigessi, Delia (ed.) (1988) *Inchieste sulle fate. Italo Calvino e la fiaba* (Bergamo: Lubrina).

Fusco, Mario (1988) 'Italo Calvino entre Queneau et l'Ou.li.po.', in Falaschi 1988a, 297–304.

Gabriele, Tommasina (1992) 'Literature as education and the near-perfect protagonist: narrative structure in *Il barone rampante*', *Stanford Italian Review*, 11, 91–102.

Gabriele, Tommasina (1994) *Italo Calvino: Eros and Language* (London and Toronto: Associated University Presses).

Gaetani, Marco (1994) 'Conrad, Hemingway, Defoe: una triade calviniana', *Rivista di studi italiani*, 12, 74–90.

Gardair, Jean-Michel (1988) 'Lumi e ombre del Settecento', in Falaschi (ed.) (1988a), 289–95.

Gatt-Rutter, (1978) *Writers and Politics in Modern Italy* (London: Hodder & Stoughton).

Ghidetti, Enrico (1988) 'Il fantastico ben temperato di Italo Calvino', in Falaschi (ed.) (1988a), 171–85.

Giametta, Sossio (1992) 'Palomar e dintorni', in *Palomar, Han, Candaule e altri. Scritti di critica letteraria* (Bari: Palomar Varietà), 7–43.

Gioanola, Elio (1988) 'Modalità del fantastico nell'opera di Italo Calvino', in Bertone (ed.) (1988), 20–35.

Giovannetti, Paolo (1993) 'Calvino, la scuola, l'editoria scolastica', in Clerici and Falcetto (ed.) (1993), 35–82.

Gronda, Giovanna (1983) 'Comunicazione/espressione: su un racconto semiologico di Italo Calvino', *The Italianist*, 3, 53–63.

Guj, Luisa (1987) 'The loss of the self: "la selva oscura" of Mr Palomar', *Modern Language Review*, 82, 862–8.

Guj, Luisa (1988) 'The shapeless and the well-designed: an unresolved dichotomy in Calvino's narrative?', *Forum for Modern Language Studies*, 24, 206–17.

Guthmüller, Bodo (1990) 'Calvinos Partisanenerzählungen', *Romanische Forschungen*, 102, 228–54.

Hannay, John (1988) 'Description as science and art: Calvino's narrative of observation', *Mosaic*, 21, 73–86.

Heaney, Seamus (1985) 'The sensual philosopher', *New York Times Book Review*, 19 September, 1, 60.

Hume, Kathryn (1986) 'Calvino's framed narrations: writers, readers, and reality', *Review of Contemporary Fiction*, 6.2, 71–80.

Hume, Kathryn (1989) 'Calvino's *La memoria del mondo*: the forgotten records of lost worlds', in Ricci (ed.) (1989a), 85–102.

Hume, Kathryn (1992a) *Calvino's Fictions: Cogito and Cosmos* (Oxford: Clarendon Press).

Hume, Kathryn (1992b) 'Grains of sand in a sea of objects', *Modern Language Review*, 87, 72–85.

Hume, Kathryn (1992c) 'Sensuality and the senses in Calvino's fiction', *Modern Language Notes*, 107, 160–77.

Italian Quarterly (1989) 30, 115–16 (Winter–Spring).

Jacobsen, Mara Mauri (1992) '*Palomar* e il viaggio di Calvino dall' "esattezza" alla "leggerezza"', *Italica*, 69, 489–504.

Jeannet, Angela M. (1989) 'A writer's project: cornerstones, milestones, and headstones', in Ricci (ed.) (1989a), 207–25.

Jeannet, Angela M. (1991) 'Escape from the labyrinth: Calvino's Marcovaldo', *Annali d'italianistica*, 9, 212–29.

Jeannet, Angela M. (1992) 'Requiem for the idyll: Italo Calvino's first Marcovaldo stories', *Stanford Italian Review*, 10, 177–98.

Jeannet, Angela M. (1994) 'Collodi's grandchildren: reading *Marcovaldo*', *Italica*, 71, 56–78.

Knaller, Susanne (1988) *Theorie und Dichtung im Werk Italo Calvinos: Untersuchungen zu 'Le città invisibili' und 'Se una notte d'inverno un viaggiatore'* (Munich: Wilhelm Fink).

Kurtz, Gunde (1992) *Die Literatur im Spiegel ihrer selbst . . . Italo Calvino, Antonio Tabucchi - zwei Beispiele* (Frankfurt, Bern, New York and Paris: Peter Lang).

Lessle, Christine (1992) *Weltreflexion und Weltlektüre in Italo Calvinos Erzählerischem Spätwerk* (Bonn: Romanistischer Verlag).

Longo, Nicola (1995) *Il peso dell'imponderabile: Lettura de 'Il cavaliere inesistente' di Italo Calvino* (Rome: La goliardica).

Lonsdale, Jeremy (1991) 'Calvino and "Leggerezza"', *Stanford Italian Review*, 10, 199–223.

Lucente, Gregory L. (1986) 'Self-conscious artifacts: Calvino's fictions', in idem, *Beautiful Fables. Self-consciousness in Italian Narrative from Manzoni to Calvino* (Baltimore, MD and London: Johns Hopkins University Press), 266–300.

Lucente, Gregory L. (1987) 'Un'intervista con Italo Calvino', *Nuova corrente*, 34.100, 375–86.

Lucente, Gregory L. (1991) 'Modernism and postmodernism in Italian fiction and philosophy', *Annali d'italianistica*, 9, 158–66.

McLaughlin, Martin L. (1989a) 'Calvino's library: labyrinth or laboratory?', in E. Haywood and C. O. Cuilleanáin (eds), *Italian Storytellers* (Dublin: Irish Academic Press), 263–87.

McLaughlin, Martin L. (1989b) 'Il "Fondo Italo Calvino"', *Autografo*, 17, 93–103.

McLaughlin, Martin L. (1993a) 'Calvino's visible cities', *Romance Studies*, 22, 67–82.

McLaughlin, Martin L. (1993b) 'The genesis of Calvino's *La speculazione edilizia*', *Italian Studies*, 48, 71–85.

McLaughlin, Martin L. (1996a) 'Borges e Calvino: la letteratura e l'intelletto', in *Borges, Calvino, la literatura (El coloquio en la Isla)*, 2 vols (Caracas and Madrid: Editorial Fundamentos), I, 85–103.

McLaughlin, Martin L. (1996b) 'Words and silence: Calvino criticism 1985–1995', *Romance Studies*, 28, 79–105.

Mann, Thomas (1954) *Bekenntnisse des Hochstaplers Felix Krull* (Frankfurt am Main: Fischer, 1954).

Markey, Constance (1983) 'Calvino and the existential dilemma: the paradox of choice', *Italica*, 60, 55–70.

Martignoni, Clelia (1997) 'Alcuni percorsi nelle *Città invisibili* di Italo Calvino', *Autografo*, 34, 15–27.

Mengaldo, Pier Vincenzo (1973) 'L'arco e le pietre (Calvino, *Le città invisibili*)', in *La tradizione del Novecento* (Milan: Feltrinelli), 406–26.

Mengaldo, Pier Vincenzo (1989) 'Aspetti della lingua di Calvino', in Folena (ed.) (1989), 9–55.

Milanini, Claudio (1980) *Neorealismo. Poetiche e polemiche* (Milan: Il Saggiatore).

Milanini, Claudio (1990) *L'utopia discontinua. Saggio su Italo Calvino* (Milan: Garzanti).

Milanini, Claudio (1994) 'L'umorismo cosmicomico', in Clerici and Falcetto (eds) (1994), 19–41.

Milanini, Claudio (1997) 'Calvino e la Resistenza: l'identità in gioco' in Andrea Bianchini and Francesco Lolli (eds), *Letteratura e Resistenza* (Bologna: CLUEB), 173–91.

Milanini, Claudio (1998) 'Calvino editore di se medesimo', in Giorgio Bertone (ed.), *Atti del Convegno Internazionale di Studi: Italo Calvino, a Writer for the Next Millennium* (forthcoming).

Mondello, Elisabetta (1990) *Italo Calvino* (Pordenone: Studio Tesi).

Montella, Luigi (1996) *Italo Calvino. Il percorso dei linguaggi* (Salerno: Edisud).

Motte, Warren F. (1989) 'Telling games', in Ricci (ed.) (1989a), 117–30.

Musarra Schroeder, Ulla (1986) 'Duplication and multiplication: postmodern devices in the novels of Italo Calvino', in Douwe Fokkema and Hans Bertens (eds), *Approaching Postmodernism* (Amsterdam and Philadelphia: John Benjamins), 135–55.

Musarra Schroeder, Ulla (1987) 'Italo Calvino e il pensiero del labirinto', in Finocchiaro Chimirri (ed.) (1987), 133–59.

Musarra Schroeder, Ulla (1996) *Il labirinto e la rete. Percorsi moderni e postmoderni nell'opera di Italo Calvino* (Rome: Bulzoni).

Naldini, Nico (1989) *Pasolini, una vita* (Turin: Einaudi).

Nava, Giuseppe (1987) 'La geografia di Italo Calvino', *Paragone*, 38.446, 21–39.

Nava, Giuseppe (1991) 'Calvino e il fantastico', *Paragone*, 42.502, 49–64.

Nava, Giuseppe (1994) 'Calvino interprete di Borges', *Paragone*, 45.532–4, 24–32.

Nocentini, Claudia (1987) 'Il paesaggio ricorrente nella narrativa di Italo Calvino', *Bulletin of the Society for Italian Studies*, 20, 13–22.

Nocentini, Claudia (1989) 'La San Remo invisibile di Calvino', *The Italianist*, 9, 79–88.

Nuova civiltà delle macchine, 5.1 (1987).

Nuova corrente 34.99 (1987), and 34.100 (1987).

Olken, I. T. (1984) *With Pleated Eye and Garnet Wing: Symmetries of Italo Calvino* (Ann Arbor: University of Michigan Press).

Olken, I. T. (1990) 'The written and unwritten words of Marcovaldo and Calvino', *Quaderni d'Italianistica*, 11, 72–83.

Ossola, Carlo (1987) 'L'invisibile e il suo "dove": "geografia interiore" di Italo Calvino', *Lettere italiane*, 39, 220–51.

Palmieri, Pierre (1988) 'Il sistema spaziale del *Barone rampante*', *Lingua e stile*, 32, 259–70.

Papa, Marco (1980) 'La realtà, la fotografia, la scrittura. Postille in margine a *L'avventura di un fotografo*', *Rassegna della letteratura italiana*, 84, 257–86.

Pasolini, Pier Paolo (1976) 'Lettera luterana a Italo Calvino', in *Lettere luterane* (Turin: Einaudi), 179–84.

Pasolini, Pier Paolo (1979) 'Italo Calvino, *Le città invisibili*', in *Descrizioni di descrizioni* (Turin: Einaudi), 34–9.

Patrizi, Giorgio (1989) 'Il modello della via lattea. Note su Calvino saggista', in Folena (ed.) (1989), 73–88.

Paulicelli, Eugenia (1996) 'Dalla città invisibile alla città futura. Italo Calvino: storia, impegno, linguaggio', *The Italianist*, 16, 143–60.

Pavese, Cesare (1966) *Lettere 1945–1950*, ed. Italo Calvino (Turin: Einaudi).

Pedriali, Federica (1998) '"Piú per paura che per gioco"? Three textual explorations of Calvino's *Il sentiero dei nidi di ragno*', *Modern Language Review*, 93, 59–70.

Pellizzari, Lorenzo (ed.) (1990) *L'avventura di uno spettatore. Italo Calvino e il cinema* (Bergamo: Lubrina).

Pepe, Massimo (ed.) (1992) *Conversazioni su Italo Calvino. Atti del Convegno dell'Università degli studi di Roma 'Tor Vergata'* (Rome: Edizioni Nuova Cultura).

Perrella, Silvio (1988) 'Risonanze montaliane in Italo Calvino', in Bertone (ed.) (1988), 156–63.

Perrella, Silvio (1990) 'I commiati di Calvino. Breve e divagante parabola degli anni Settanta', *Autografo*, 19, 57–73.

Perrella, Silvio (1991) 'Calvino editore', *The New York Review of Books. La Rivista dei Libri*, 1.6, September, 5–7.

Pescio Bottino, Germana (1967) *Calvino* (Florence: La Nuova Italia).

Petroni, Franco (1976) 'Italo Calvino dall' "impegno" all'Arcadia neocapitalistica', *Studi novecenteschi*, 5, 57–101.

Polacco, Marina (1992) 'Dalle *Città del mondo* alle *Città invisibili*: viaggio, dialogo, utopia', *Italianistica*, 10, 227–54.

Ponti, Annalisa (1991) *Come leggere 'Il sentiero dei nidi di ragno' di Italo Calvino* (Milan: Mursia).

Prete, Antonio (1987) 'Palomar o la vertigine della misura', *Nuova corrente*, 34.100, 243–50.

Propp, Vladimir (1968) *Morphology of the Folktale*, 2nd edn, rev. and ed. Louis A. Wagner (Austin, TX: University of Texas Press).

Puletti, Ruggero (1991) *Un millenarismo improbabile. Le 'Lezioni americane' di Italo Calvino* (Rome: Lucarini).

Pullini, Giorgio (1959) *Narratori italiani del Novecento* (Padua: Liviana).

Quaini, Massimo (1988) 'La Sanremo di Italo Calvino', in Bertone (ed.) (1988), 60–6.

Re, Lucia (1990) *Calvino and the Age of Neorealism: Fables of Estrangement* (Stanford, CA: Stanford University Press).

Regn, Gerhard (1989) 'Il ritorno al romanzesco: Calvino e i rapporti col *Gruppo Tel Quel*', in Folena (ed.) (1989), 57–71.

Review of Contemporary Fiction, 6.2 (1986).

Ricci, Franco (1984) 'Silence and the loss of self in Italo Calvino's *Gli amori difficili*', *The Italianist*, 4, 54–72.

Ricci, Franco (1986) 'Introversion and effacement in *I racconti* of Italo Calvino', *Italica*, 63, 331–45.

Ricci, Franco (ed.) (1989a) *Calvino Revisited* (Ottawa: Dovehouse, 1989).

Ricci, Franco (1989b) 'Painting with words, writing with pictures', in Ricci (ed.) (1989a), 189–206.

Ricci, Franco (1990) *Difficult Games. A Reading of 'I racconti' by Italo Calvino* (Waterloo, Ontario: Wilfrid Laurier University Press).

Ricci, Franco (1995) 'The quest for sonship in *Le città invisibili* and *La strada di San Giovanni*', *Forum Italicum*, 29, 52–75.

Ricci, Franco (1996) 'De Chirico city: Calvinian ambulations', *Modern Language Review*, 91, 78–93.

Riga, 9 (1995) – see listing in section 1(b)(i) on p. 175.

Rizzante, Massimo (1993) *Il geografo e il viaggiatore. Variazioni su Italo Calvino e Gianni Celati* (Fossombrone: Tipografia Metauro).

Roelens, Nathalie (1989) *L'odissea di uno scrittore virtuale. Strategie narrative in 'Palomar' di Italo Calvino* (Florence: Franco Cesati).

Roelens, Nathalie and Inge Lanslots (eds) (1993) *Piccole finzioni con importanza. Valori della narrativa italiana contemporanea* (Ravenna: Longo).

Rushdie, Salman (1981) 'Review of *If on a Winter's Night a Traveller, The Path to the Nest of Spiders, Our Ancestors, Cosmicomics, Invisible Cities, The Castle of Crossed Destinies*', *London Review of Books*, 17–30 September, 16–17.

Scarpa, Domenico (1993) 'Il fotografo, il cavaliere e il disegnatore. Italo Calvino nel 1964', *Belfagor*, 48, 519–32.

Schulz-Buschhaus, Ulrich (1986) 'Aspekte eines Happy-Ending - Über das XII Kapitel von Calvinos *Se una notte d'inverno un viaggiatore*', *Italienisch*, 16, 68–81.

Schulz-Buschhaus, Ulrich (1987) 'Palomars Introspektion', *Italienisch*, 19, 38–43.

Schulz-Buschhaus, Ulrich (1988) 'Italo Calvino und die Poetik des *Barone rampante*', *Italienisch*, 20, 39–55.

Schulz-Buschhaus, Ulrich (1994) 'Calvino e il "comico delle idee"', in Clerici and Falcetto (eds) (1994), 7–17.

Segre, Cesare (1979) 'Se una notte d'inverno uno scrittore sognasse un aleph di dieci colori', *Strumenti critici*, 13.39–40, 177–214.

Segre, Cesare (1991) 'Riflessioni sul punto di vista', in *Intrecci di voci. La polifonia nella letteratura del Novecento* (Turin: Einaudi), 13–26.

Serra, Francesca (1996) *Calvino e il pulviscolo di Palomar* (Florence: Le Lettere).

Sommer, Martin Paul (1979) *Die Stadt bei Italo Calvino. Versuch einer thematischen Interpretation* (Zurich: Juris Druck).

Sorice, Michele (1989) *La città ideale: Italo Calvino dal 'pessimismo dell'intelligenza' all'intelligenza dell'utopia* (Rome: Merlo).

Spinazzola, Vittorio (1987) 'L'io diviso di Italo Calvino', *Belfagor*, 42, 509–31.

Spriano, Paolo (1986) 'Un Calvino rivoluzionario', in idem, *Le passioni di un decennio 1946–1956* (Milan: Garzanti), 11–32.

Stephens, Joanna (1993) 'Calvino's *I giovani del Po*: a study in grey', *Romance Studies*, 22, 83–97.

Stephens, Joanna (1995) 'L'egotista di Grenoble: Calvino and Stendhal', *The Italianist*, 15, 175–212.

Stevenson, Robert Louis (1922) 'Father Damien', in *The Works of Robert Louis Stevenson*, vol. 15 (London: Heinemann), 479–501.

Surdich, Luigi (1988) 'Italo Calvino e il "Premio de *l'Unità*"', in Bertone (ed.) (1988), 164–72.

Usher, Jonathan (1988) 'The Grotesque as metaphor in Calvino's *Giornata d'uno scrutatore*', *Bulletin of the Society for Italian Studies*, 21, 2–14.

Usher, Jonathan (1990) 'Interruptory mechanisms in Calvino's *Se una notte d'inverno un viaggiatore*', *Italian Studies*, 45, 81–102.

Usher, Jonathan (1995) 'Calvino and the computer as writer/reader', *Modern Language Review*, 90, 41–54.

Usher, Jonathan (1996) 'From "super-albero" to "iper-romanzo": lexical continuity and constraint in Calvino's *Se una notte d'inverno un viaggiatore*', *Italian Studies*, 51, 181–203.

Valéry, Paul (1946) *Monsieur Teste*, Nouvelle édition augmentée de fragments inédits (Paris: Gallimard).

Waage Petersen, Lina (1989) 'Il fantastico e l'utopia: percorsi e strategie del fantastico in Italo Calvino con speciale riguardo a *Le città invisibili*', *Revue Romane*, 24, 88–105.

Waage Petersen, Lina (1991) 'Calvino lettore dell'Ariosto', *Revue Romane*, 26, 230–46.

Watson, David S. (1988) 'Calvino and the problem of textual referentiality', *The Italianist*, 8, 66–78.

Watson, David S. (1996) 'The representation of reality in Italo Calvino's *racconti partigiani*', *Canadian Journal of Italian Studies*, 19, 1–18.

Weiss, Beno (1992) 'Cottolengo: Calvino's living Hell. The speculating intellectual at the crossroads', *Italian Culture*, 10, 145–58.

Weiss, Beno (1993) *Understanding Italo Calvino* (Columbia, SC: University of South Carolina Press).

Wimbledon, 2 (June 1990), 2–3.

Wood, S. (1991–92) 'Mr Palomar goes shopping: eros and morphology in Italo Calvino', *Spunti e ricerche*, 7–8, 23–26.

Wood, S. (1994) 'The reflections of Mr Palomar and Mr Cogito: Italo Calvino and Zbigniew Herbert', *Modern Language Notes*, 109, 128–41.

Woodhouse, John R. (1968) *Italo Calvino: A Reappraisal and an Appreciation of the Trilogy* (Hull: Hull University Press).

Woodhouse, John R. (1970) 'Fantasy, alienation and the *Racconti* of Italo Calvino', *Forum for Modern Language Studies*, 6, 399–412.

Woodhouse, John R. (1989) 'From Italo Calvino to Tonio Cavilla: the first twenty years', in Ricci (ed.) (1989a), 33–50.

Index